Priscilla and Conrad Reining

Minneapolis, 1957.

THE NGONI OF NYASALAND

The publication of this study was made possible by funds granted by the Carnegie Corporation of New York. That Corporation is not, however, responsible for any of the statements made or views expressed therein.

THE NGONI
OF NYASALAND

by

MARGARET READ

Ph.D. London, M.A. Cambridge, C.B.E.

Published for the
INTERNATIONAL AFRICAN INSTITUTE
by the
OXFORD UNIVERSITY PRESS
LONDON   NEW YORK   TORONTO
1956

Oxford University Press, Amen House, London E.C.4

GLASGOW   NEW YORK   TORONTO   MELBOURNE   WELLINGTON
BOMBAY   CALCUTTA   MADRAS   KARACHI   CAPE TOWN   IBADAN

Geoffrey Cumberlege, Publisher to the University

Printed in Great Britain by
Butler & Tanner Ltd., Frome and London

PREFACE

THE material on which this book is based was collected during three periods in Nyasaland as a Research Fellow of the International African Institute: May–December 1935; April 1936–June 1937; July 1938–August 1939.

The choice had to be made whether to concentrate on one Ngoni area and omit the other, and also whether to present Ngoni culture as a common element in both areas or to regard them as separate cultural areas. I decided to gather material from northern and central Ngoniland, and accordingly spent about one-third of the time in north Nyasaland and about two-thirds in central Nyasaland. I used the Nyanja language all the time in central Ngoniland, and found that many people understood it in the north. I learned some Zulu, enough to read and hear Ngoni when spoken, but it was dying out as a language except for certain ceremonial and legal terms and expressions. Very few people spoke it in central Ngoniland; most of the older people knew it in the north and in one area it was still the language of the home in 1936.

The decision to present Ngoni culture as a common constituent of Ngoni life in all parts of Nyasaland was made after the material had been analysed. I decided also to attempt a reconstruction of Ngoni life at the time of the first European contacts, when the kingdoms were at the height of their power. Men and women were still alive, when I was in Ngoni villages, who had fought as warriors, who had organized large households, who had been present at the accession and death of the Paramounts. Their experiences were part of Ngoni culture and inseparable from much of what was regarded as essentially 'Ngoni' in the 1930's.

In both areas the informants were of two kinds: those who welcomed an anthropologist who would collect and record Ngoni history, patterns of social organization, and cultural behaviour of which they were intensely proud; and those who were reluctant at first to give information, either because they were Christians and had been at school and said they had 'forgotten'; or because they were suspicious of all Europeans, and did not want to speak of what to them was a treasured and hidden heritage.

Working in more than one language medium and bringing into the open Ngoni terms not as a rule used in the presence of Europeans presented a number of problems both of terminology and orthography. I have included a glossary of Ngoni terms used frequently in the book. There were several variations of the prefixes in common use with Ngoni words, as for example *abalumuzana*, *alumuzana*, *malumuzana*, all three of which were used in northern and central Ngoniland. The clicks, *c, x, q,* had disappeared in central Ngoniland, and were only pronounced correctly by the older Ngoni in the north. The honorific prefixes before clan names in addressing people, and before first names in reference, also varied according to area, age group and clan ranking. Apparent inconsistencies in spelling which occur in the book reflect these variations.

I have adopted English translations of certain Ngoni expressions and have used them throughout without quotation marks. An obvious example is Paramount for *inkosi*; and the use of 'house' for the Ngoni institution, and 'hut' for the dwelling place.

I acknowledge with gratitude the Fellowship given by the International African Institute which made possible the visits to Nyasaland; the grant from the London School of Economics for the research assistants, Miss Ruth Jones and Mr. G. P. Hall, who helped me collate material; the officials and missionaries in Nyasaland who gave hospitality and assisted me in every possible way; and the African people of the Ngoni kingdoms who, as my hosts in the villages and my helpers at all times, welcomed me into their midst and gave me an insight into their Ngoni culture.

London, 1955   MARGARET READ

CONTENTS

PART I

INTRODUCTION

CHAPTER I

THE NGONI PEOPLE

IN the census of Nyasaland of 1945, there were 193,482 people enumerated as Ngoni. Their distribution extended from the extreme north in Karonga district through every other district to the extreme south in Port Herald district. There were concentrations of Ngoni people, however, as Table I shows, in the Mzimba district in the north, in the Dowa, Lilongwe, Dedza and Ncheu districts of the central province, and in the Blantyre district in the south. The Ngoni in the Mzimba district were known as Mbelwa's Ngoni [1] and will be called in this book

Table I

Distribution of Ngoni in Nyasaland by Provinces and Districts from 1945 Census

Northern Province	. . . .	*Total 45,539*
Mzimba district	. . . .	44,948
Karonga ,,	. . . .	295
Chinteche ,,	. . . .	296
Central Province* .	. . . .	*Total 80,943*
Kasungu district	. . .	2,539
Dowa ,,	. . .	20,329
Lilongwe ,,	. . .	17,707
Dedza ,,	. . .	14,757
Ncheu ,,	. . .	15,242
Kotakota ,,	. . .	4,838
Fort Manning ,,	. . .	5,531
Southern Province	. . . .	*Total 67,000*
Blantyre district .	. . .	25,224
Zomba ,,	. . .	6,972
Liwonde ,,	. . .	7,572
Neno ,,	. . .	10,211
Cholo ,,	. . .	9,185
Fort Johnston ,,	. . .	1,343
Chikwawa ,,	. . .	1,029
Chiradzulu ,,	. . .	4,655
Mlanje ,,	. . .	751
Port Herald ,,	. . .	58
Total	. . . .	*193,482*

* In 1931 this was included in the Northern Province.

---

[1] Tew, M. *Peoples of the Lake Nyasa Region.* O.U.P., 1950, p. 91.

the northern Ngoni kingdom. Other groups of these Ngoni were found in three separate states in the Dowa and Kotakota districts. The Ngoni in the Ncheu district were known as Gomani's Ngoni and will be called in this book the central Ngoni kingdom. Four states which separated from this kingdom were found in the Dedza, Lilongwe and Cholo districts. The Ngoni in Fort Manning district belonged to Mpeseni's kingdom in the Fort Jameson district of Northern Rhodesia.

According to these census figures, the northern Ngoni kingdom with the three separated states accounted for 69,706; the central kingdom with the four separated states accounted for 46,891. Leaving out the Fort Manning Ngoni, there were 71,354 Ngoni in the rest of Nyasaland who had at one time formed part of the northern and central kingdoms and their offshoots, but who had dispersed in search of work and had made large settlements in the towns and on the estates of the southern province where employment was to be found. A similar dispersion from the main Ngoni concentrations in Nyasaland to Southern and Northern Rhodesia and the Union of South Africa had taken place which formed part of the extensive emigration from Nyasaland in search of better employment than that available in the territory.

The existence of two Ngoni kingdoms, several smaller Ngoni states, and a still larger number of people enumerated as Ngoni but dispersed in every district of Nyasaland, poses a number of problems for the anthropologist. In this book I have concentrated on the two Ngoni kingdoms and on the Ngoni culture found in them in the 1930's. It was my intention, by focusing on the two kingdoms, to show that there was an Ngoni culture which had common elements in both areas and hence was shared to some extent by all the Ngoni living in Nyasaland. We shall be asking the questions in Part I—Who can be called Ngoni? What is Ngoni culture? Why do people in every district of Nyasaland enumerate themselves as Ngoni though a large number no longer live in the Ngoni kingdoms or in the Ngoni states? Are we discussing a people whose cultural affiliation survives political dispersal? The chief problem in the relation between the Ngoni kingdoms as political states and Ngoni culture will be stated in Part I and illustrated and analysed in the rest of the book. In this chapter, we shall examine the ethnic composition of the inhabitants of the two Ngoni kingdoms.

ETHNIC ELEMENTS IN THE NGONI KINGDOMS

There were four main groups of people in the Ngoni kingdoms, distinguished by the areas from which their ancestors came and designated by the Ngoni as 'those from the south', 'those from south of the Zambesi', 'those from the march' and 'those from this country'. The Ngoni said that the clan descent name of a person showed to which group he or she belonged.

(a) 'Those from the south'

These were the descendants of the leaders of the two main Ngoni groups represented by the two Ngoni kingdoms, with their followers, who left Natal during the wars of Shaka. They were South-eastern Bantu of Nguni stock, and when they were first encountered by Europeans in Nyasaland, the Europeans called them Zulus and spoke of their language as Zulu. Ngoni informants in the 1930's who were regarded as most reliable repudiated their relationship with the Zulu, and always referred to their ethnic origin as a people of Swazi stock. Y. M. Cibambo whose knowledge of Ngoni traditions was unrivalled, said in his book *My Ngoni of Nyasaland*—'Very many of them [the Ngoni] came from Swaziland, which is north of Zululand'.[1] A nostalgic refrain occurred in more than one of their traditional songs:

> Come let us go to Swaziland
> Where the people die fat.[2]

Cultural affinities between the Ngoni in Nyasaland and the people now living in Swaziland and, to a lesser degree, with the Zulu, will be examined in several chapters of this book. In the chapter on clan descent names in Part III, we shall compare the clan names called Swazi by the Ngoni with the lists of clan names given by Bryant in *Olden Times in Zululand and Natal* [3] and with the list given by Kuper, in *An African Aristocracy*,[4] of the Swazi and pre-Swazi clans. The military organization of the Ngoni, the age-set system which formed part of it, and other cultural features which will be discussed in Chapter III of this section, all show a general cultural affinity with the peoples of the northern Nguni group of the South-eastern Bantu.

The separation of the Ngoni group from the parent stock, which took place at about the same time as the Ndebele and the Shangaan groups fought their way north, occurred before the Swazi and Zulu kingdoms took final form. It is more correct, therefore, to say that Ngoni cultural affinities were with the northern Nguni group as a whole than to say they were off-shoots of either the Zulu or the Swazi. The Ngoni themselves used the designation 'Swazi' for the people with clan descent names whose ancestors left the south with the original party. Some of the older men remembered their fathers and grandfathers speaking of their clan as having belonged to the Ntungwa group, the Mtetwa group, the Msane group, before the departure of the Ngoni took place. This differentiation into pre-Swazi tribal and clan groupings was not in the 1930's one to which the Ngoni gave much attention. In talking about their southern origin it was the Swazi connexion which they emphasized.

[1] Cibambo, Y. M. *My Ngoni of Nyasaland.* Lutterworth Press, 1942, p. 8.
[2] Read, M. 'Songs of the Ngoni People.' *Bantu Studies*, March 1937, p. 10.
[3] Bryant, A. T. *Olden Times in Zululand and Natal.* Longmans, 1929, pp. 681–97.
[4] Kuper, H. *An African Aristocracy.* O.U.P., 1947, p. 233.

Ngoni tradition placed the departure of the two main groups under the leadership of Zwangendaba Jere and Ngwana Maseko during Shaka's wars, according to some traditions just before, and to others just after, the death of Zwide, ruler of the Ndwandwe people. The separate departure of the two Ngoni groups which later formed the two kingdoms was determined partly by their separate leadership under the Jere and Maseko clans, partly by their march by different routes to the Zambesi and after crossing it; and partly by the clan descent names of the Swazi element in the two kingdoms, which with few exceptions were different.

Two traditional songs, sung at marriages, at dances at the Paramounts' villages, and the first in the church of the Scottish mission at Ekwendeni in north Nyasaland, reminded the Ngoni of their departure from Natal, of their separation from the Ndwandwe people under Zwide, and of the hazards of a small military band fighting its way northwards.

> All the nations
> Are gathered together against us.
> How shall we fight?
> They are called together against us.
> Whence shall we summon help?
> The big husky ones, ho!
> They are called together against us.
> We are reinforced by whom?
>
> It is because of Zwide, chief of the Ndwandwe people
> That though I lie down I cannot sleep.
> O Zwide, chief of the Ndwandwe people!
> Though I lie down I cannot sleep.
> Shaka scatters us among the forests of Soshangane land.

There were several informants in both Ngoni kingdoms who had preserved the story of the departure of the Ngoni from the south. Y. M. Cibambo in his book gathered together the traditions and gave what he considered the most authentic version of the departure. One text from the northern kingdom is given here, partly because it was typical of the kind of material Cibambo had to work on, and also because the author, Mlonyeni Jere, had heard it from his mother who, as a young girl, had lived at the court of Zwangendaba. The text gives the genealogy of Zwangendaba, and the connexion of his line with Zwide, ruler of the Ndwandwe people. It emphasizes the immediate cause of Zwangendaba's departure—namely the fear of meeting Shaka and his warriors in open battle, and the fact that he was not called a chief until he had made a breach with Zwide. The summons to the mourning for his uncle Mafu, which he ignored, was considered by the Ngoni to be the final act by which Zwangendaba cut himself off from his kinsfolk who remained in the south. This breach with his former kin and the assumption of chieftainship marked out Zwangendaba as a leader and his followers as a separate group.

THE DEPARTURE OF THE NGONI
by Mlonyeni Jere

⟨ Zwangendaba was the son of Hlacwayo, the son of Magangata, the son of Magalela, the son of Cenge of Enhlekisweni.

Magangata had three sons, they were borne by one mother. The first-born was Gumede, the second was Hlacwayo, and the third was Mafu. Gumede did not marry, he hated them badly, he did not eat the food that was cooked by the women, and the same Gumede was the chief of all Magangata's sons. He did not love his brother Hlacwayo. He said that Hlacwayo was black and also he was dwarf, but he said Mafu will be the one to take his chieftainship. Mafu was refusing to take that possession while his brother was still alive and he said that though the people say that Hlacwayo is black, he is not black to me but he is red. And also though they say he is dwarf he is not dwarf to me, but he is tall. When Gumede died the chieftainship was taken by Hlacwayo and Mafu was his second since they were all born from one mother.

Magalela was at Ndwandwe the village of Langa. Langa was the father of Zwide and Zwide was a very bad chief. Zwide did not treat Zwangendaba well. When Hlacwayo died his chieftainship was taken by Zwangendaba his son. Zwide was called Nxumalo, and these people of Nxumalo were strong men there in Natal and some were afraid of them.

Dingiswayo, the son of Jobe of Elangeni, went to Zwide for a visit at Ndwandwe. As soon as he appeared Zwide caught him and killed him. When Shaka heard that Zwide had killed Dingiswayo, he grew angry for Shaka had grown up there at Dingiswayo's. He said ' Zwide has killed the chief who taught me how to fight better.' At the same time he ordered warriors to go and fight against Zwide at Ndwandwe.

Zwangendaba refused to fight with Shaka because he heard the story of Shaka, that he was a great warrior. Then he told his father Mafu that he must go away from Zwide. Zwide was troubling the Jere people. When they cooked beer he was snatching it, and when a man married a good girl he was snatching her, and when they killed a cow he was snatching the meat and taking it to Ndwandwe. When Zwide quarrelled with Shaka, Zwangendaba was glad that he had found a way of going away from Zwide. Zwide fought against Shaka and Zwangendaba ran away. The leaving of Zwangendaba nobody knew and nobody followed him. Also there was no one to follow him for Zwide was busy with war against Shaka.

They sent a message to Zwangendaba that Mafu had died:—'Come to the mourning.' Zwangendaba did not go back to the mourning. All the people who were in Mafu's villages did not follow Zwangendaba. They also went on their own way, and we do not know where they went. Zwangendaba came with only two sons of Mafu, Cenge and Mgayi. Thus many children of Mafu stayed in Natal.

Zwangendaba was with his brother Ntabeni when leaving Natal.

Ntabeni had his own village named Engwenyameni, and the big village of Zwangendaba was called Elangeni, and there were others.

When Zwangendaba left with his brother Ntabeni, they built their village near a path. That was the time that he departed from Zwide and he was at this time called a chief and had his own people. When Zwide was running away, Zwangendaba was on the way, and he was building his villages and spent a year at one place, and sometimes more than a year.

The following text on the departure of the central Ngoni from the south was written by Ishmael Mwale, the treasurer of Paramount Gomani II of the central Ngoni kingdom. As Cibambo had done in the north, he had collected and put together the oral traditions of the old men. This story also began with a flight from Shaka's army by two leaders, Nqaba (spelt by Bryant, Nxaba) of the Msane people and Ngwana of the Maseko people. They fought the Ngoni group led by the Jere clan, and the group under Gaza which were later called the Shangaan people, and were defeated by both. The tradition of crossing the Zambesi by dividing the waters with a stick was common to the northern and central Ngoni. After crossing the Zambesi, the central Ngoni went west of the Shire river to the Kirk Range on the eastern slopes of which they found the people called Ntumba.

THE DEPARTURE OF NGWANA FROM SWAZILAND
by Ishmael Mwale

❡ Nqaba, son of Mbekani, made war on Shaka, but was defeated and retreated to Swaziland. Then Ngwana said 'If you run away from Shaka, he will trouble us, so I am going to leave.' Chief Nyathi told Shaka that Ngwana was leaving, and Shaka said: 'Prevent him from leaving.' So Nyathi fought Ngwana and Ngwana knew that he was waiting for Shaka's army. So he performed a rite, and caused rain to come and darkness. In the middle of the darkness Ngwana left together with Nqaba. They came to the country of Nancekwani at Mauwa, and fought with the people. They defeated the four chiefs there and conquered the country. Ngwana went straight to Ulozi to the village of Mamba, father of Lewanika. He destroyed the country of the Lozi and died there. Magadlela his brother entered the chieftainship. When Magadlela left Ulozi he went to the country of Ndunduwali, and from there to the Nyika. He arrived at Cidima Mbirasweswe, and there Zwangendaba found them. There was fighting between Magadlela and Zwangendaba, and many people were killed and they did not know who they were because it was night. When Magadlela ran away he made for Golongozi where Nqaba was, and explained to him about the war. They mobilized the army to follow Zwangendaba. When they found him they destroyed many of his men. Somfuya and other brothers of Zwangendaba were killed. When they returned from the war with Zwangendaba they went to Cikwanda. There they found Gaza and fought him and were defeated. Magadlela and Nqaba ran away. Nqaba took a friendly farewell of Magadlela because there was hunger and there were many people without food. Magadlela allowed him to leave and went straight to the country of the Makombe. They conquered it and came to the Nyungwi and conquered them too.

When they wanted to cross the Zambesi they made medicine and beat the water with a stick and separated it. All the army crossed and reached Kalumbi. They fought there, and there Magadlela died and Mgoola took care of the chieftainship. Mgoola came with all the army to Ntumba and caught many Ntumba people. In the Ntumba country Mputa entered the chieftainship.

(b) 'Those from south of the Zambesi'

In the northern kingdom two main groups were included in this category: those whose clan names showed Tsonga origin and those who showed Karanga origin. Bryant [1] wrote of the army under Zwangendaba hacking its way through Tsongaland almost by the same route as the army under Soshangane, who fought and defeated him on the headwaters of the Sabi river. To his Tsonga adherents Zwangendaba added a number from the Karanga country, many of whom, trained to fight by the Ngoni, became famous warriors in the Ngoni campaigns farther north.

The Ngoni under Ngwana with Nqaba and his army kept nearer to the coast, and fought their battle with Soshangane (whom they called Gaza in the text quoted) on the Busi river near Sofala. The two main groups of adherents whom they forced to join them were from the Ndau and Venda peoples, called collectively the Venda group by the Ngoni. Bryant [1] spoke of Nqaba's conquest of the Ndau people on the Busi river, which would indicate that the Venda leaders and their families were already part of the Ngoni army when the Ndau were added. Although, according to central Ngoni tradition, Ngwana's army with its followers zigzagged across the country between the Sabi river and the Zambesi, they do not appear to have collected adherents in any large numbers from the tribal areas through which they passed. This supposition is only based on internal evidence, that of the clan names recognized by the Ngoni as having come from south of the Zambesi.

(c) 'Those from the march'

After crossing the Zambesi, the central Ngoni went by the Kirk Range into the western part of what is now the Ncheu district. Then they turned east, crossed the Shire river near Fort Johnston and went up the east side of the lake to the Livingstone mountains in the Songea district of Tanganyika where they fought with the northern Ngoni under the Gama clan. The clan descent names of followers acquired on this route included those from the Ntumba people on the Kirk Range whom they conquered on their first arrival in Nyasaland, and the Tengo people from Songea, some of whom were incorporated with

[1] op. cit. p. 461

these Ngoni before they were defeated and driven out of Songea by the
Gama group of Ngoni.

The northern Ngoni, who travelled east of the Luangwa valley into
Tanganyika, acquired followers with clan descent names from the
Nsenga in Northern Rhodesia and the Safwa and Sukuma in Tangan-
yika.

(d) 'Those from this country'

Under this category were included all the local peoples in Nyasaland
who either were conquered by the Ngoni or surrendered to them, and
who were brought within the rule of the Ngoni kingdoms. These in the
northern kingdom were chiefly of Tumbuka and Henga clans, with
others from Cewa and Bemba stock. In the central kingdom the local
clan names were of Cewa and Yao origin.

Two conclusions emerge from this review of the ethnic composition
of the Ngoni kingdoms. The first is that the use of Ngoni as a tribal
designation causes confusion. In this study the term Ngoni will be used
when referring to persons whose clan descent names show that their
ancestors were of Swazi or trans-Zambesi stock—that is categories
(a) and (b) in this chapter. This criterion of who were Ngoni would
probably not correspond with the criteria used in the 1945 census
enumeration. The enumerators may have asked a direct question, 'Are
you Ngoni?'; they may have asked the person's clan descent name; they
may have asked to which kingdom or chiefdom he belonged; or they
may have asked all four questions or any two. Since the Ngoni were
found in every district in the country it was likely that there was little
uniformity in the form of the questions asked by the enumerators or in
the criteria admitted by those being questioned for declaring themselves
to be Ngoni.

The second conclusion is that even if the criterion is accepted that
the Ngoni were those whose ancestors crossed the Zambesi, the Ngoni
kingdoms as political states included all the four elements (a), (b), (c)
and (d). The status of the ethnically distinct groups in the kingdoms
varied according to their clan names which indicated whether they came
from the south or had been incorporated at a later stage. Ngoni forms
of culture were found not only in groups (a) and (b), as would be expected, but often among families in group (c) who, through fighting in
the Ngoni armies and marrying into Ngoni families, had adopted their
social and ritual pattern.[1]

[1] Since the first draft of this book was written, Dr. Barnes's study of the Fort Jameson
Ngoni, *Politics in a Changing Society* (O.U.P., 1954), has appeared. The early history of
the Ngoni in the northern kingdom is the same as that of the Fort Jameson Ngoni, up
to the final separation of the kingdoms under Mpeseni and Mbelwa. Dr. Barnes's
excellent bibliography gives the sources for the historical documentation of their travels.
A brief sketch of the history of the two groups under the leadership of the Jere and
Maseko Paramounts is given in Mary Tew's *Peoples of the Lake Nyasa Region.*

CHAPTER II

THE NGONI KINGDOMS

IN 1933, by the Native Authorities Ordinance and the Native Courts Ordinance, Mbelwa was recognized as Paramount of the northern Ngoni kingdom with six Subordinate Native Authorities under him, and his court was constituted the appeal court for their six courts. The same procedure was followed in the central kingdom for Paramount Gomani with six Subordinate Native Authorities, and his court as the appeal court for their courts. They were the only rulers in Nyasaland with S.N.A.[1] under them. Two other chiefs, Cikulamayembe of the Henga in Mzimba district and Kyungu of the Ngonde in North Nyasa district, had respectively four and five courts subordinate to them, but the chiefs owning these courts were not recognized as their subordinates. The Ngoni comment on these ordinances was 'Ha! Now they see what big chiefs we have. Only our chiefs are called *inkosi*.'

The northern kingdom was in Mzimba district, and Paramount Mbelwa's royal village was at the southern end of his kingdom. The central kingdom included the whole of Ncheu district with Paramount Gomani's royal village at the northern end. This kingdom had Portuguese territory on its western frontier, close to the royal village. When the Portuguese boundary was fixed in 1891, the Ngoni kingdom under the Maseko Paramount was cut in two and a section under a Maseko ruler became a separate kingdom under the Portuguese. There was constant trouble in the 1930's over this Portuguese frontier, for Gomani's Ngoni visited their relatives, grazed their cattle and hoed gardens on the Portuguese side; and from time to time claims by the Portuguese for rent for gardens and grazing lands and disputes about taxation, needed judicious handling in the District Commissioner's court.

The figures in Table II for Mzimba and Ncheu districts in 1926, 1931, and 1945 show the changes in the ethnic composition of the districts, some of which are difficult to account for. In Mzimba district the Henga under Cikulamayembe were included in the figures for the Tumbuka and hence the northern Ngoni kingdom did not include all the 156,208 in the district. In Ncheu, the total district population of 87,690 were all included in the central Ngoni kingdom, showing the mixed ethnic elements, among which the Ngoni, or those who were enumerated as Ngoni, had declined from 64,023 in 1926 to 15,242 in 1945. Between 1931 and 1945 the decrease in the number of Ngoni (31,066) was almost balanced by the increase in the number of Nyanja

---

[1] This abbreviation will be used henceforward in referring to Subordinate Native Authorities.

(35,107). It is difficult not to assume that many Nyanja had formerly called themselves Ngoni.

Table II

	1926	1931	1945
Mzimba district			
Ngoni	25,484	24,627	44,948
Tumbuka	46,029	78,483	89,135
Cewa	14,041	2,411	21,891
Yao	20	—	—
Tonga	3,052	605	32
Nkonde	141	—	—
Others	334	156	202
Total	89,101	106,282	156,208
Ncheu district			
Ngoni	64,023	46,308	15,242
Cewa	11	4,372	2,815
Nyanja	334	25,393	60,400
Cikunda	360	940	1,336
Yao	203	1,064	3,267
Nguru, etc. . . .	—	—	4,448
Others	13	278	182
Total	64,944	78,355	87,690

Since the two Ngoni kingdoms are the subject of this book and not the secession states, the position of the rulers of those states as Native Authorities and the circumstances of their secession from the two main groups will not be examined here. The three secession states in the north were under Chiefs Ciwere and Msakambewa in Dowa district and Jere in Kotakota district. The four connected formerly with the central Ngoni were under Chiefs Kacere and Kacindamoto in Dedza, Masula in Lilongwe and Vumbwe in Cholo.

In the 1930's, when I was living sometimes in the northern kingdom, sometimes in the central, and for a time in the Ngoni state under Chief Jere, I was aware that the existence of the two kingdoms and of the seven secession states did not preclude a great deal of contact between the Ngoni of the different areas. The stream of travel in Nyasaland from south to north and from north to south along the one trunk road, brought Ngoni as visitors from one kingdom to the other, from the smaller states to both kingdoms, and from 'the Ngoni of the dispersion' living in towns to visit their relatives and friends in the Ngoni kingdoms and states. These visits might be social, to see parents or to marry a wife; they might be for economic purposes, to invest in or sell cattle, to supervise cotton or tobacco marketing; or they might be for ritual purposes such as mourning. When I travelled in the central Ngoni kingdom in 1936 with Y. M. Cibambo, the historian of the northern

Ngoni, he was welcomed everywhere as one who could speak with authority about the culture and customs of his people, and the central Ngoni, when talking about their history and customs, wanted him to realize that they too were 'real Ngoni' (*Ngoni eni eni*). The general relationships before 1939 were that the political separation between the kingdoms and their secession states was accepted as final. On the social and cultural level, the Ngoni from one state sought contacts with the Ngoni from another state or kingdom in preference to contacts with other ethnic groups. In using the term Ngoni in this context, as throughout this book, I am referring to people with Swazi and trans-Zambesi clan descent names.

THE MAIN POLITICAL ELEMENTS IN THE NGONI KINGDOMS

The District Commissioner of Ncheu in his report for 1935, after the Native Administration Ordinance had been in operation for over a year, wrote of the central Ngoni kingdom: 'The tribal system is, comparatively speaking, intact under a chief who commands universal respect.' [1] The political system of the Ngoni in both kingdoms was based on a ruling aristocracy in which the Paramount of the royal clan was the head, supported by influential members of his own clan and of other leading clans. There were three main elements in this ruling aristocracy: the Paramount, with whose office was linked provision for a regency at the death of the incumbent and during the minority of his successor; the subordinate chiefs who ruled under him in recognized areas; and the heads of Swazi clans called *alumuzana*. I shall use these terms, chiefs and *alumuzana*, when speaking of the Ngoni kingdoms. In the northern kingdom all six chiefs was of the royal clan. In the central kingdom none of the six chiefs were of the royal clan but, with one exception, all were recognized as *alumuzana*. This distribution of authority among the six chiefs under the Paramount in the northern kingdom meant that several of the leading *alumuzana* felt excluded from political control of the villages and area which they were said to 'own', because they had no recognized court. This led at times to friction between them and the chiefs of the royal clan. In the central kingdom the position was different, for though some *alumuzana* were recognized as chiefs, others were not, and friction occurred at times between the chiefs and other *alumuzana*, and also between the chiefs and members of the royal clan. In both areas allegiance to the Paramount was, however, a strong unifying element.

The ruling aristocracy was in its turn supported by a hierarchy of officials, some traditional, some appointed to meet modern requirements

[1] *Annual Report of the Provincial Commissioner for the Nyasaland Protectorate.* 1935, p. 54.

in the political organization. Some of these officials were also members of Swazi and trans-Zambesi clans, but many were not. The officials served the Paramount in his court and his administration, and also the chiefs, and formed the lines of communication between them. This created a network of relationships between the Paramount and the chiefs at the top level, and between the chiefs and the village headmen under them at the lower level. From this network were excluded, in the northern kingdom, all the *alumuzana* and, in the central kingdom, all those *alumuzana* who were not chiefs. In the two kingdoms the *alumuzana* exercised unofficial control over a varying number of villages, and were inclined to assert their social superiority because they were excluded from official recognition.

The foundations of the political structure within which the ruling aristocracy operated were a series of related institutions which will be described and analysed later in the book, but which must be referred to here, partly in order to explain the terminology used. The South-eastern Bantu, whose culture the Ngoni brought with them, had an institution in all important villages known as 'houses', which was a grouping of huts and of the wives owning them round the hut of one or more of the leading women. This institution, with its variations among the southern and northern Nguni people, was described by Mrs. Hoernlé in the chapter on 'Social Organization' in *The Bantu-speaking Tribes of South Africa*.[1] The Ngoni institution of houses had developed from the basic pattern among the South-eastern Bantu into an independent form. In the first place it was only found in relation to the Paramount, the chiefs and leading men of the royal clan, and the *alumuzana*. It did not, as in South Africa, form the basic pattern of all villages in the Ngoni kingdoms. Where, as in most villages owned by *alumuzana*, mixed ethnic groups lived together, the house system existed only for the head of the clan, his brothers and his successor. It was specifically an Ngoni institution in the cultural and social sense. In the second place, the terms 'right-hand' and 'left-hand' house, common among the South-eastern Bantu, were not used by the Ngoni in the 1930's. The two terms they used were the 'big house' and the '*gogo* house', and I propose to use these terms here. The principle behind the use of these terms was that the big house was the one from which the heir should come to succeed the Paramount, the chief, or the *mulumuzana*. The *gogo* house was the one which was responsible for maintaining tradition and performing ritual.

Another institution, closely related to that of the houses, was the *lusungulu* and *gogo* villages. The Paramounts, the chiefs, and the leading *alumuzana*, when they succeeded their father after his death, moved out of his village and made their own new village, or took their households

---

[1] Schapera, I. (ed.). *The Bantu-speaking Tribes of South Africa*. Routledge, 1937, chap. IV.

and settled where another village already existed.[1] In both forms, this
new settlement was called the *lusungulu* village, 'the one which goes in
front'; and the village which was left was known as the *gogo* village.
This use of the term *gogo* (literally 'grandparent') for house and village
had a common basic connotation. It expressed the concept of being left
behind to look after something, the *gogo* house being passed over for
the heir to the Paramountcy or chieftainship but charged with ritual
and ceremonial duties; and the *gogo* village being left behind to take
care of the traditions and generally also of most of the widows of the
deceased Paramount or chief. Each *lusungulu* village eventually divided
on the death of its owner, part 'going forward' with the new successor,
part remaining behind. The main groups in the village which went
ahead or which remained were the houses connected with the new
Paramount or chief or *mulumuzana* and those connected with his dead
father. In the chapter on houses (Chapter III, Part III) this process will
be examined in greater detail.

The third related institution was the provision for guarding the spirit
of a dead Paramount or chief and those of some leading *alumuzana*. A
senior woman was always guardian of such a spirit and in her hut were
kept the ritual objects: spear, wooden dish, baskets, fire-stick, which
were used in sacrifices to the ancestors. The guardianship of the spirit
of a dead Paramount was always associated with the village which had
been his *lusungulu*. His corpse was buried on the edge of the kraal containing the cattle of the house where he had grown up, and this village
became the *gogo* village associated with him, where his spirit was
guarded in a hut, probably though not necessarily belonging to one of
his widows. The recognition of such a woman guardian was a matter
for selection and appointment, and was the responsibility of the senior
men of the *gogo* house in that village in consultation with the senior
men of the *gogo* house in the dead man's father's village. The concept
of guarding the spirits of important men, and the means by which such
guardianship was practised, will be more fully discussed in Part IV in
connexion with the ancestor cult.

THE NGONI KINGDOMS AND AFRICAN POLITICAL SYSTEMS

In the final section of this chapter we shall look at the Ngoni kingdoms in their relationship to other African kingdoms and states such
as those described in *African Political Systems*.[2] A methodological
problem arises here. In this study a number of references are made to
the Ngoni kingdoms in pre-European times, especially in connexion

---

[1] This form of the institution was found in densely populated areas and the incoming
households dominated the original ones.

[2] Fortes, M., & Evans-Pritchard, E. E. (ed.). *African Political Systems*. O.U.P., 1940
pp. 9–23.

with the military organization and the Paramountcy. The main emphasis
in the study is, however, on the Ngoni kingdoms in the 1930's, when
the Paramount and the administrative organization under him were
recognized by the Nyasaland government. Though certain elements in
the kingdoms, as for example the position and authority of the *alumuzana*, were not recognized by the ordinance, the supreme authority
of the Paramounts and the position of their appeal courts received
additional support from the colonial officials, from the financial basis
of the administration, and from the many new responsibilities of the
Paramount for his people illustrated by the bye-laws made and the
welfare measures carried out.

It is the Ngoni kingdoms as they functioned in the 1930's which will
be compared with other African political systems, bearing in mind all
the time that behind the Ngoni kingdoms lay the authority and power
of the colonial government. The comparison will be made with the
general characteristics of what were called by the editors of *African
Political Systems*, in their introductory essay, 'Group A systems', and
the references will be to the criteria and concepts in that introduction.

The main characteristics cited of the Group A systems were all to be
found in the Ngoni kingdoms: centralized authority, administrative
machinery and judicial institutions. These will be the chief material in
Part II of this book on the Ngoni political system. In *African Political
Systems* the editors stated that all the societies described in the book
which were in the category of Group A systems were 'an amalgam of
different peoples, each aware of its unique origin and history, and all
except the Zulu and Bemba are still today culturally heterogenous'.
Such a definition was appropriate for the Ngoni kingdoms, where
political authority was wielded over several different peoples, as the
ethnic grouping in the 1945 census showed, and where there was
cultural heterogeneity among the different peoples. This second characteristic will be examined more fully in Chapter III of this section,
dealing with Ngoni culture. To the factor of diversity within the Ngoni
kingdoms should be added two other points made by the editors
towards the end of their introduction where they said: 'Community of
language and culture does not necessarily give rise to political unity,
any more than linguistic and cultural dissimilarity prevents political
unity.' In the next chapter we shall be discussing the relation of
language and culture among the Ngoni, and between them and other
Nyasaland peoples. The second point in the essay which is also applic-
able to the Ngoni kingdoms and their neighbours was stated in these
terms: 'The overlapping and interlocking of societies is due to the fact
that where political relations end is not the point at which all social
relations cease.' The relevance of this statement to the Ngoni in Nyasaland has already been mentioned in connexion with the visiting which
goes on between individuals from the Ngoni kingdoms and states. It

was still more clearly demonstrated by the attitude of the Ngoni 'of the dispersion', who returned for visits, some frequently and others at varying intervals, to their former homes though they were no longer in a political sense subjects of the Ngoni Paramount.

In the Group A systems, not only is the Paramount the political head of a culturally and ethnically heterogeneous state, but he is also a territorial ruler, and everyone living within the boundaries of his state is his subject. This was peculiarly a characteristic of the so-called conquest states, when effective administrative control was established within recognized boundaries after the conquest or surrender of neighbouring peoples. In the chapter on the military organization of the Ngoni, it will be seen how the nature of the military tenure of *alumuzana*, and the relation of groups of conquered villages known as *amilaga* to the central villages of the Paramount and *alumuzana*, emphasized the limits within which Ngoni authority was effective. One of the often repeated grievances of the older Ngoni was that the Europeans 'arrived too soon', before the Ngoni were able to establish effective authority over the whole country.

Two further points emerge in the introductory essay to *African Political Systems* which relate to the balance of forces within the Group A type of state and to the position of the Paramount. Both these points will be illustrated in Part II. The first concerns the relationship of the subordinate chiefs (called 'local chiefs' in the essay) to the central authority. They represented the central authority in the areas where they ruled, and they represented the people under them and their needs to the central authority. When the older Ngoni were talking about the Paramount in pre-European days, much emphasis was laid on his control of the chiefs and *alumuzana*, and on the obligation they felt to visit the Paramount in his village frequently, in order that they might appear to be carrying out his orders and not usurping undue authority. The older Ngoni also laid stress on the accessibility of the Paramount to all his people, provided—and it was an important proviso—that a man came to him with an intermediary, either his headman or his *mulumuzana*.

The final point of comparison between Group A systems and the Ngoni kingdoms is the mystical values bound up with kingship. This will be discussed in the chapter on the Paramount (Chapter II, Part II) and it is related also to the ancestor cult. The Ngoni Paramounts were more than ruling monarchs; they were the symbol of the unity of their state; in pre-European days the Paramount was the head of the army; and the ritual at the accession and at the death of a Paramount was related to the fertility of the land and the prosperity of the people.

CHAPTER III

NGONI CULTURE

AMONG the mixed ethnic elements in the Ngoni kingdoms the ruling aristocracy were those whose ancestors were of Swazi and trans-Zambesi origin, and whose clan descent names established them as belonging to the true Ngoni group. The families with these clan names formed also a social aristocracy in the villages where they lived, in the areas of the chiefs and *alumuzana*, and in the Ngoni kingdoms. This social status, established primarily by the clan name, was visible in the position of the huts in the village, arranged at the head of the kraal; in the leading role played by the senior members of these families on all ceremonial occasions; and in the practice of a number of customs which were defined as Ngoni. Ngoni culture, as seen in social and ritual life, was a series of interwoven patterns of social organization and social behaviour. We shall outline these patterns here in order to bring together many of the forms and practices described in the rest of the book. In a more homogeneous society it would have been possible to find in these patterns a consistent and clearly defined culture. Yet one of the main problems in studying Ngoni culture in the 1930's was that there were many variations of each pattern and the anthropologist was all the time trying to find out what degree of cultural conformity existed among the Ngoni aristocracy. Of the different aspects of culture reviewed in this chapter, the ritual pattern was the one most consistently followed, and it was the one in which the Ngoni social aristocracy most clearly demonstrated that they had a distinctive common culture which was found in both kingdoms and in the secession states.

(a) Kinship pattern

Like the South-eastern Bantu from whom they came the Ngoni were patrilineal in descent and inheritance. Marriage was negotiated by go-betweens and concluded through the handing over of cattle, and the term *lobola* was used for the cattle exchanged in this form of marriage. An Ngoni woman married by this form was known as *mlobokazi*. A strict interpretation in the courts was given to this form of marriage as it affected the ownership and custody of the children. The children of a *lobola* marriage contract belonged to their father and could be claimed by him if the marriage broke up, or on the death of their mother. Traditionally, virilocal residence was an Ngoni custom, and it was supported by the house system whereby the male members of each house formed a group with economic interests in common through the joint ownership of the cattle in the name of the house. A widespread variant on virilocal residence will be discussed later and illustrated in Chapter IV of Part III.

(b) Village pattern

There was a traditional pattern of Ngoni village organization, which consisted in the siting of the huts in the village and the corresponding social groups formed in the different sections. Informants made it clear that when the Ngoni first settled in the areas where the two kingdoms now exist, the royal villages and the chiefs' villages were very large. Segmentation of these large villages, not only by the *lusungulu* 'going out' as already described, but also by sections of the village breaking off, began before the Europeans came and continued after their arrival. In the 1930's the traditional pattern was sometimes altered by a desire to build a 'model village' laid out in lines instead of in a horse-shoe curve round the kraal. Even in some of these model villages the grouping of huts, though no longer in a series of circles, indicated the house affiliation of their owners and their relationship to the head of the village.

The traditional ground-plan of an Ngoni village was based on the main kraal which occupied the centre. The gate of the kraal was on the open end of the horse-shoe formation, and the most important hut, the *indlunkulu*, was at the top of the kraal. On either side of the *indlunkulu* were grouped the huts belonging to the houses associated with the wives of the owner of the village. Behind the *indlunkulu* were the huts of his married sons and those of his brothers who chose to live with him, and this group of huts, known as *cigodlo*, spread round behind the main huts of the owners of houses. Behind each house-group of huts were the huts of the *induna* associated with the house; in large villages he often had a kraal and reproduced a similar small village plan in his own circle of huts. On the wings of the village, curving towards the gate of the kraal and called by the Ngoni 'the horns of the village', were the less important families in the village. The general principle of the village plan in terms of social status and the siting of huts was that the nearer huts were to the *indlunkulu* the higher was the prestige of their owner. The following very much simplified plan of an Ngoni village illustrates the principle of siting the huts in relation to social grouping, as it was when a new *lusungulu* village was set up. In this plan the *indlunkulu* hut was owned by the mother of the owner of the village, one of his father's widows who moved out with him. When she died the big wife on her right might move into the actual *indlunkulu* hut, or stay in her own hut while another widow of her father-in-law entered the *indlunkulu*. There was no invariable rule for this type of succession, but there were only these two possible alternatives. Reference should be made here to one other hut site—that of the *laweni* or boys' dormitory. It was usually sited behind either the big house or the *gogo* house, far enough behind the main circle round the kraal to emphasize its connexion with the *cigodlo* group.

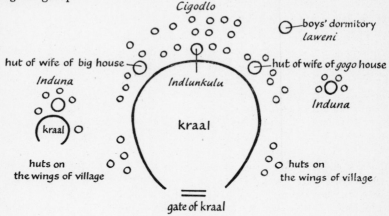

The group referred to as 'a house' has already been defined in its relation to the Paramount and his *lusungulu* village, and it will be illustrated and examined further in Chapter III of Part III. As an Ngoni institution the big house was an integral factor in the succession to high office, and the *gogo* house played an essential role in ceremonial and ritual life. Houses were also one of the most important components in village grouping. Men, women and children regarded themselves as associated with a house in one of three ways. They were related to it by descent or by marriage; or they were members of the family of the *induna* who looked after its affairs; or they served the house as servants or labourers, and were possibly the descendants of captives caught in war and assigned to that house. Thus it often happened that the people living on the wings of the village had some relationship to the house on the side of the kraal where their huts were sited. There were many Ngoni villages where all the inhabitants were said to belong to one of the two or three or more houses, even though the majority of the inhabitants had no kinship or official relationship with a house.

The term 'clan' or 'clan descent group' has been used already many times and some explanation and definition is needed as a guide to its use in Part II before it is discussed further in Chapter II of Part III. The Ngoni considered that the clan of a person was of great importance for several reasons. The use of the clan descent name was the normal mode of address between all adults. The Ngoni said they could not speak to any stranger until they knew his clan name, and they used it in all social intercourse, except when addressing the Paramount. Exogamy was strict for people with the same clan name, and sexual relations between such individuals was regarded as incest.

In the 1930's, in the villages of the *alumuzana*, individuals with the same clan name formed patrilineal groups of an extended family type. The original *alumuzana* were the leaders of groups of persons bearing their clan descent name, who crossed the Zambesi under Zwangendaba or Mputa. In Part II we shall see how these *alumuzana* were settled in the Ngoni kingdoms round the royal villages, with the result that a group of villages of mixed ethnic origin came to be associated with the village regarded as the head village of a clan. Reference is made from time to time in this study to clan heads, and to the head villages of certain clans. There was no head of a Swazi or trans-Zambesi clan who was not regarded as a *mulumuzana*. On the ground that his ancestor crossed the Zambesi with his wives and followers, the head of such a clan was always given that title. In addition to the head village of a *mulumuzana* there were a number of other villages connected with the clan, created partly by the working of the *lusungulu* system of village segmentation, and partly by other sections of the larger villages moving off to make new gardens. The association of a number of villages owned by individuals with the same descent name was due to the original settlement of the *alumuzana* who were given land at varying distances from the royal village. When the Ngoni spoke of 'clan areas' this was the connotation they gave to the term. Village censuses showed that small family groups bearing the same descent name were scattered widely over a number of villages in several of the chiefs' areas. There was, however, in connexion with each clan an area of concentration round the head village where a number of families and individuals with that descent name were living. These were sometimes referred to as clan areas, using the name of the clan with the prefix *ma*, meaning the people of that clan, in central Ngoniland, and with the prefix *u*, meaning the land of the clan, in the northern kingdom.

(c) The ritual pattern

In the rest of this study there will be descriptions and analyses of Ngoni marriage and funeral rites, of the puberty rites carried out for each boy and girl, but not in groups in initiation schools, and of the rituals associated with the ownership of cattle and with the ancestor cult. The marriage and funeral rites have South-eastern Bantu affinities, and so has the ritual associated with cattle-keeping and the ancestor cult. The northern Ngoni had a tradition that circumcision was practised among them when they left Natal, and that it was given up while they were in Tanganyika. Giving the head-ring (*cidlodlo*) to the men who were allowed to leave the regiments and settle as married men in civilian life was another ritual of southern origin which the Ngoni gave up soon after the kingdoms were established in Nyasaland.[1] The

---

[1] The early Europeans in Nyasaland reported that head-rings were worn by all the senior Ngoni men.

national ritual of the first-fruits ceremony (*incwala*), which brought all the people to the royal village, was also abandoned before the Ngoni kingdoms were finally established, for no old person alive in the 1930's had seen the *incwala* ceremony.

(d) The ceremonial pattern

Ngoni songs and dances were performed without the accompaniment of drums and the words of the songs sung in the 1930's were in the Ngoni language. The war-dance, *ligubo*, was still danced at the royal village and at the funerals of Paramounts and Royal Sisters. The *ngoma* dance, performed after the harvest by young men and girls, was encouraged by the two Ngoni Paramounts, who endeavoured to prohibit other dances which were not of Ngoni origin.

Ceremonial dress, especially the war-dress of the men, was well preserved by heads of clans in the 1930's in the central Ngoni kingdom. In both kingdoms the Ngoni leading women wore their traditional bead ornaments on the head and neck and arms, and tied their cloths on festive occasions in the way in which their ancestors wore the long lengths of soft dressed leather.

Only in Ngoni families were to be found the making of milk curds (*amasi*), the cooked blood (*ulubende*), and the stamped maize (*izinkobe*), all of which were traditional foods brought by them from the south.

(e) The linguistic pattern

In the 1930's the Ngoni language had almost disappeared as a home language, except in Chief Mperembe's area in the northern kingdom. The majority of the older men could still speak and understand Ngoni, and nearly all the men who had been away to work in Southern Rhodesia or the Transvaal had renewed their knowledge of Ngoni or learnt to understand it from working with men who spoke Ndebele, Zulu or Swazi. The texts in this book from the northern kingdom were given in the Ngoni language and translated for me by Y. M. Cibambo. His own texts were written for me in English. The texts from the central kingdom were given in Nyanja and translated by me. The vernacular terms used in this book illustrate the continued use of Ngoni terms for traditional offices and objects, though in the central kingdom many of these were being replaced by Nyanja terms. Words of traditional songs, some ritual formulae, some forms of address, some titles of senior persons or groups —all these were in Ngoni. The younger generation, however, especially if they had not been south and heard Zulu or Ndebele, were not able to make any of the clicks, or to pronounce such double consonants as *dl* and *hl*.

The Ngoni were punctilious about etiquette, and especially about the linguistic terms required by good manners for greeting persons of different rank and seniority, thanking for gifts or for an audience, taking leave after meeting, withdrawing after a case in court, and initiating or concluding many other formal or less formal occasions. Children were taught to use the correct expressions and rebuked if they made a mistake, and it was one of the requirements in Ngoni families that a uniform standard of verbal politeness should accompany correct behaviour in posture.

CULTURAL AFFINITIES AND DIFFERENCES

The anthropologist working in Nyasaland is aware of the problems inherent in any attempt to isolate cultural features within any of the larger ethnic groups found there. There were no ethnographic field studies published of any of the other ethnic groups when I was working among the Ngoni. Mary Tew, in *Peoples of the Lake Nyasa Region*,[1] referred to scattered sources published before 1939, to which I had access; and from time to time Cewa informants wrote accounts of particular social institutions or ritual, from which I was able to make certain comparisons with Ngoni ritual and institutions. Some of the earlier accounts, such as that by Hodgson on the Cewa and Ngoni in the Dowa district,[2] assumed that all the cultural changes and 'borrowings' had been by the Ngoni from their Cewa neighbours, whereas I found in that area in 1939 Cewa villages where Ngoni cultural elements had been adopted.

Ngoni cultural affinities with South-eastern Bantu	*Local tribal differences*	
Paramount and subordinate chiefs	Chiefs; no central authority except in Henga and Ngonde	
Patrilineal descent Virilocal residence Marriage by *lobola*	Cewa and southern Tumbuka	⎧ Matrilineal descent, ⎨ uxorilocal residence, ⎩ marriage witnesses
	Henga	⎰ Patrilineal descent and ⎱ virilocal residence
Clan exogamy ,, hierarchy Houses Age sets	Cewa	⎧ No clan exogamy ⎨ ,, ,, hierarchy ⎪ *Mbumba* group ⎩ Girls' initiation schools
Cattle complex Ancestor cult associated with cattle	Tumbuka Cewa in Dedza district	⎧ Formerly cattle-owners but ⎨ no terminology left and no ⎪ association with ancestor ⎩ cult
Burial customs: in skin near kraal	Cewa and Tumbuka	⎰ Graves outside village; ⎱ buried in a mat

[1] Tew, M., op. cit.

[2] Hodgson, A. G. O. 'Notes on the Achewa and Angoni of Dowa District, Nyasaland.' *J. Royal Anthropological Institute*, 1933, pp. 126–64.

The distinctiveness of Ngoni institutions, so often emphasized by the older men and by the early travellers in Nyasaland, was due to cultural affinities with the South-eastern Bantu. The attached table sets out those social and cultural elements in the Ngoni kingdoms which were most distinct from parallel features among the neighbouring peoples, and which had obvious affinity with South-eastern Bantu cultures. The main Ngoni cultural elements have already been referred to in this chapter and will be further discussed in the rest of this study. The corresponding elements among the local peoples are based partly on the earlier sources quoted by Tew and partly on local informants and my own observations. In collecting information about clans, the *mbumba* group consisting of a man with his sisters' children, and the girls' initiation schools, I had no direct contacts with any except Cewa sources.

Variations in cultural conformity among the Ngoni

In the Ngoni kingdoms among families with Swazi and trans-Zambesi clan descent names there was considerable variation in the degree to which they maintained Ngoni institutions and practised Ngoni cultural forms. The anthropologist was constantly aware that the time element was an important factor in the consolidation of Ngoni practices and in the attitudes developed towards Ngoni culture among the individuals in the different generations. The Ngoni in both kingdoms spoke of the 'older generations' (*mibadwo wa kale*), 'the middle generations' (*mibadwo wa mpkati*), and 'the present generation' (*mibadwo wa tsopano*). The first had grown to adulthood before the Europeans came, and were the older senior men and women in the 1930's; the second had been affected by European missionaries, traders, and officials while they were young men and women; the third had never known anything but European contacts and many had grown up in European schools. The senior Ngoni of the older generation often expressed the sentiment: *zatha zonse tsopano* (everything is finished now). They included in that saying the regrets of the older Ngoni for their former independence, and their resentment at the domination of European rule and European culture. It is idle to speculate what cultural changes might have taken place in the Ngoni kingdoms if European influence had been postponed another twenty to thirty years. Nevertheless it is a vital factor in assessing Ngoni culture that the kingdoms had barely twenty years of independent existence before the Europeans began to penetrate Nyasaland. The older Ngoni looked back on their former independent existence as a golden age in which they were spreading Ngoni customs and culture as well as exercising political supremacy. It is difficult to believe that this was wholly true, in view of the extensive cultural interchange going on in the country as a whole. It is, however, possible that wider acceptance of Ngoni cultural elements was prevented by the advent of the Europeans, in so far as cultural institutions and political dominance were closely associated. When warfare ceased the Ngoni could no longer force sub-ject peoples to accept their rule and their cultural institutions, and they had to acquiesce in considerable cultural heterogeneity within their kingdoms, which, according to Ngoni informants, would not have been allowed in pre-European days. The illustrations they gave were in terms of the families living 'on the horns of the village', in many cases the families of captives taken in war. Formerly, they said, those families would have been made to marry with *lobola*, to have their ears pierced in Ngoni fashion, to serve in the army, to be associated with one of the house-groups and serve them in the huts or in the gardens. When Ngoni political power declined, and when large villages broke up, some of these groups formed their own villages and reverted to their former practices of matrilineal descent and uxorilocal residence, and of girls' initiation ceremonies.

In the northern kingdom one section of the peoples under Henga leadership had adopted a patrilineal system before the Ngoni came. The effect of the Ngoni conquest was to strengthen these practices in this northern section, adding marriage by *lobola*, and to extend them to the southern Tumbuka whose kinship and marriage practices were like those of the Cewa who were their neighbours.[1] In the central kingdom, patrilineal descent, marriage by *lobola* and virilocal residence were only practised by families of Swazi and trans-Zambesi clans, and they had introduced variations in virilocal residence which will be discussed in Chapter IV, Part III. Within the true Ngoni families in both kingdoms the senior men and women in the 1930's were aware that cultural con-formity with Ngoni practices was not as strict as it had been in their parents' days. They spoke of those Ngoni families who were non-con-forming as 'people who spoil the land'.

On the other hand, the adoption of Ngoni customs by non-Ngoni in the Ngoni kingdoms, that is by families with descent names from cis-Zambesi and local clans, continued to take place after European rule began. I found several instances of this adoption in the central kingdom, and many of them were related to the acquisition of cattle by former non-Ngoni families. It was chiefly the virilocal form of residence and patrilineal descent which were taken over with *lobola* marriage. When describing the adoption of such Ngoni practices, informants always said it was *monga cingoni* (like the Ngoni). Those who belonged to the Ngoni kingdoms and had largely adopted Ngoni culture expressed strong sentiments of attachment to it; this was particularly true of town-dwellers who had come from the Ngoni kingdoms but were not mem-bers of Swazi or trans-Zambesi clans. Though they adopted many external forms of European culture in dress, houses and food, the con-sciousness of their association with Ngoni culture and the Ngoni king-doms was expressed in strongly emotional terms.

[1] Tew, M. op. cit. pp. 107, 109.

PART II
THE NGONI POLITICAL SYSTEM

CHAPTER I

THE MILITARY FOUNDATIONS OF THE NGONI KINGDOMS

AFTER the Ngoni settled in Nyasaland their political system went through three main periods of change and development up to 1939. The first was that of pre-European days, characterized by the military kingdoms. The second was the period of direct British administration, when the chief features of the Ngoni kingdoms were latent and unrecognized. The third was the period from 1933 onwards when the passing of the Native Authority and Native Courts Ordinances gave recognition to certain traditional forms of the Ngoni political system. Since, in their early forms, from the middle of the nineteenth century onward, the Ngoni kingdoms were founded on conquest, the maintenance of military power both for defence and aggression was an essential condition of their survival. We shall therefore begin the examination of the Ngoni political system with a chapter on their military organization. Men of the Swazi and of trans-Zambesi clans were proud of the part their fathers and grandfathers had played in Ngoni wars. These wars were recalled to the people in the recitals of oral tradition and in the songs and dances which were part of Ngoni culture. Cibambo, who has already been mentioned as the historian of his people, wrote for me in English the following account of Ngoni warfare in the old days, part of which, written in Tumbuka, was used as a reader for the schools in the Livingstonia Mission area. Cibambo had, as a young boy, seen the preparations for war, and had gone more than once as a carrier for his elder brothers who belonged to one of the last formed regiments.

NGONI WARFARE IN OLD DAYS

❦ To the Ngoni war was like work and his heart rejoiced to think of it. When the old men sat in the kraal the talk that roused discussion was of war and their journeyings. All the heroes of the tribe had received their praise-greetings through service in war. In this, ordinary people and slaves came together, for though they might have been unknown to begin with, if they were heroes in one or two wars the whole country knew them. The slaves who showed their courage and strength in war quickly received their freedom and many also had villages of their own because of the people they had captured in war; others obtained the standing of men in authority. Those who were cowards were humiliated and laughed at, and those who had not entered the enemy stockade or killed a man were not allowed to dance in triumph in the kraal but only to join in the *ligubo* dance along with others.

Herding as preparation for war

Preparation for war began in youth. When boys were about ten or twelve they were sent to herd goats or calves; when they were older they herded the cattle. At this time the boys were in the bush with their elders who were often haughty and fierce. The older herders taught the boys how to fight and how to defend themselves. They taught them to fight with twigs and sticks; the older herders fought with *izinduku* (knobkerries) and *izinkhonjo* (wooden swords). They were not allowed to fight with real spears though some had them. The older herders stirred up the hearts of the younger to fight and taught them to strike each other with knob-kerries and to use little shields. If the herders of one village met the herders of another, the bulls were teased till they fought, and the little herders also. The small herders were not allowed to say anything about the herding to their parents. The older herders also loved to fight as in war with those of other villages. At such times the older men and even the elders came out from the village to see the battle and to stir up the hearts of the boys. If the herders of one village ran away they were laughed at, but the winners were greatly praised.

At the time when the cattle ate the refuse in the maize-gardens, after harvest, fighting most often broke out. Some of the boys provoked their neighbours to go and drive the cattle into the maize-fields of another village deliberately. The custom was that cattle might eat in the maize-gardens of their own village and the boys ought to ask if they may go into the fields of others. The herders did this to annoy the other herders and to start a fight. Often a great struggle was the result and the young men of the village who had outgrown herding joined in the fight to help the youngsters of their village. But they did it sensibly, none caused a wound with a spear, for anyone who did that was punished by law.

So the boys grew accustomed to the first steps in fighting which would help them later in war. Those who knew how to protect themselves with a knobkerry and small shield had no scars on their heads, but there were many long ago who had scars from fighting in the herding time. Children of the chief were in the same predicament—if they could not defend themselves they were beaten by their herding companions and possibly got their heads broken. The flowing of blood was not considered very serious, only if one did it in a stealthy way then he had to pay compensation. In this way the boys grew up with stout hearts and loved fighting.

Another thing which excited the boys was the custom of whistling. The boys were very expert and quick in expressing changes of mood in whistling. This was done so that the cattle would go carefully or quickly, but also when they were fighting the herders loved to whistle and even the older men in war did so also. The whistling stirred up the hearts of those who were thinking of running away. There were many ways of whistling and some were very good at it.

Enlistment

When the young men reached the age of 21–26 they left off herding. Sometimes it was their fathers who stopped them, sometimes they themselves wished to stay at home. They took their shields (*amahawu*) and their spears and gathered together; they went to the kraal and began to dance the *ligubo* war dance. Sometimes they set themselves in order as though they were out on a raid; they came out at the right middle of the kraal and went *pa lisango*, toward the gate, singing, marching, and shaking their shields and spears. Sometimes they retreated as though running from the enemy, then turned about as though running to meet the enemy again. This was done to show how they could fight and defend themselves from the enemy. It showed that the boys were now young men and of the warrior class, and they were asking to be admitted to the status of grown men. If the old men agreed that their prayer should be granted they were formed into a new regiment (*libandla*) and were given a senior to lead and govern them.

The Army

All the war companies were under the Paramount. He had the power to call the whole army to go out against enemies. But all big villages and villages of men of reputation had their own companies, like Zulu Gama, Njerenjere Sibande and many others. These companies were under the war *induna* of the Paramount and when they were called they came quickly to the village of the Paramount which was the central meeting place. A *libandla* (company) was divided into *mabuto* (sections) sometimes of 100 or more. For each section there was an *induna* who led it in war, judged all disputes, and spoke for it to the war *induna*. The war *induna* was the eye of the Paramount in all that pertained to war.

The army was divided into companies corresponding to the districts or chiefs' villages and all the company leaders were under the war *induna*. All the parts of the army were divided in lesser parts in accordance with the generation of the young men, *amajaha*, and the older men, *amadoda*.

Mobilization

If desired the Paramount had power to send a summons through the whole country that his army should mobilize in his village in order that he might see it. The lesser chiefs had the same power for their districts. The man who delivered the summons went into the kraal and shouted that the Paramount wished the army to gather at the central meeting place. The message was spread everywhere. Then all the sections in the villages and in the districts of the lesser chiefs and clan heads hastened to come at the appointed time. The Paramount prepared cattle to be killed for the army. As the sections were marching in they sang the songs called *imihubo*. Section by section they chose their *muhubo* for arriving and entering the kraal and each section drew up by itself. An open space was left between the sections so that they might be known.

When they had all gathered in their places the herald rose and shouted '*Uyezwa na*', 'Do you hear?' '*Utsho njalo yenkosi, uti, Ayigube*', 'Thus saith the Paramount, let them dance.' This was to tell the sections to begin the war-dance. Each section got up with one heart and made a wide circle and began to dance. One of them began a song which he remembered on the spur of the moment from the *ligubo* and led off, the whole section took it up waving their shields and thrusting with their spears now right now left according to their step and each foot stamping the ground.

At the dance the warriors wore their full war-dress. Those who had the head-ring wore a little bunch of black feathers sewn together and attached to a skin and looking like a lion's mane, which came out from under the head-ring on the neck, and they tied a strip of other skin over their eyes. Those who had not the head-ring had their heads completely covered and at the side of their face they put rosettes of feather ends so that the head-dress should not hide their sight. The head-dress was of birds' black feathers, especially ravens; they took out the quills so that they were soft and they sewed them together on cowhide, the man's head resting on the skin. On the body and arms they wore a white skin of goat-hair, or a white belt with long hair, and twisted straps of skin reaching to the knee at the loins. The belts were made from the skins of white goats which had long hair and they stitched them. Round the loins they had whole skins of kids both front and back. Some tied *izinkondo*, hides made to look like a tail, at the back. In their ears they had *izicazo*, earrings of ivory, or sometimes of bone or wood. Truly they looked as terrifying as wild beasts when they stood up. So they ornamented themselves. The oldest of the men stuck a tail feather of a crane in the skin strip above the eyes.

When the dance had begun the women rose to help the men. The Paramount's wives and wives of the men of standing wore the claws of lion and leopard on the top of their hair combed up on the crown and ound the neck along with other beads. Ordinary women also wore beads on their heads and necks. All looked very well. Both men and women sang the dance songs and danced. The men spread out in a circle round the edge of the space; the women faced the men at a distance or perhaps they put them in the middle of the ring. All sang, the women commencing, the men joining in or responding. The women had little sticks or reeds in their hands shooting high up. Others came forward and went into the middle of the circle or half circle, and went singing and dancing and shaking their sticks and thrusting out their necks.

When the dance was over the herald told the army to scatter to their villages until the provisions and snuff had been prepared, and on such and such a day they were to gather again in the Paramount's village. On the day of the gathering of the army they brought their dress and food, the sections dressing as they were in the kraal. The herald called again, '*Uyezwa na*', 'Do you hear?' '*Utsho njalo yenkosi, uti, Ayikete*', 'Thus saith the Paramount, fall in.' Then all the sections stood up, each by itself but now joined together in close order, shields and spears raised above them. Then the chief *induna* or someone else who had been chosen told them the enemy stockade which it was proposed to attack, and the plan of campaign. When the sections had heard, they began to march out of the kraal one by one.

The whole day the sections had been kept in the kraal, no one was allowed to go to a house and say good-bye. Those outside were not allowed to greet the warriors inside. Children were kept out of the way, lest they should greet their fathers as they went out to war. If a man was greeted as he went out to war, the fear was that he would not come back but would die there.

When the army went out in the evening near sunset it slept near the village in grass-shelters opposite the kraal gate, and no one was allowed to go to a house or to be with his wife. They said that if a man broke this law the army would be unlucky. Even the Paramount if he still went with the army slept there outside. If the Paramount left for the war, his oldest *induna* left his own village and went to the Paramount's and stayed there till the army came back. In the royal village there was continence and all the people were ordered to control themselves in the villages, until the army left.

When the army went out the old men accompanied it, but after they had spoken words of warning they came back to the village. The chief point in it all was that the young men should have courage, and should help each other if one is wounded or there is any other difficulty, and should obey the leaders. They warned the leaders too to begin the fighting wisely and not on a bad or treacherous place. If a leader did that sort of thing and many were killed a case was brought against him. When the army went out two sections were detached to guard the village. These stayed at home along with the companies of old men. They 'kept the tribe', the Paramount and the old people and the stock.

The approach and attack

When the army went out it marched very slowly, and halts for the night were at short intervals. All the sections kept together as ordered by the war *induna*. In all the sections there were scouts to show the way for the army. In each section one or perhaps two were chosen and were put together to walk ahead and look carefully, and come and report any news, especially when they were in enemy country. When the army rested, the scouts went forward to see if there was any danger near. When the army slept in grass-shelters, one or two sections were sent to guard against danger both in front and rear. The army had provision carriers, that is, those who carried food and the coverings of the old men. These were boys and girls, sometimes women from their houses. These were not sent by the Paramount but each household chose its young people to carry the food. The section of the food carriers had another section to protect them when the enemy were attacked or when they went to meet enemies.

When the army was near the enemy stockade the leader ordered them to sit down and rest before they attacked. At such a time the warriors snuffed or smoked hemp. This hemp-smoking was preferred because it maddened the warriors and gave them hearts without fear in facing the enemy. In the enemy stockade the drums would be beating to show that their enemies were angry, but the army of the Ngoni sat and rested as though there were no enemy.

When the army had rested, the war *induna* and the other *izinduna*, or the leader of this army (for all the armies that went out were put under one man of whom they said, the owner of this army is so and so) scouted to see the difficulties of the stockade and to choose a good place for attack.

When it had been carefully chosen and the *izinduna* had agreed together how the attack should begin, then the leader roused the army and began to dance his own praise-dance. The army responded to him. After he had danced before all the sections he began to call '*Uyezwa, uti, Aiyime ncgito*', 'Do you hear? Stand to arms.' Immediately section by section got up and rushed forward with noise and whistling deafening the ears. The warriors stood in crowds near the stockade and almost surrounding it. When the army was small, they stood in the shape of a young crescent moon. While they did so, they were blowing their horns and whistling to drown the noise in the stockade.

Very soon the message was heard: '*Utsho njalo yena, uti, Aziqwebane*', 'Thus it is said, let the bulls fight.' On these words the warriors ran at the stockade with one heart and a noise like wind and the country was filled with the tread of their feet. For a short time there would sometimes be silence, then a shout would be heard from a section: '*Nginga pakati: kuti loko*', 'I am inside: I of such and such a village.' The man who was first in the stockade would name his village. Then there would be heard, '*Nginawe, mnakwetu*', 'I am with you, comrade.' All the *izinduna* and warriors fought in their own sections but once the army was inside they began to ask for the name of the first man in and those who had been near gave the name of the heroes. So each *induna* knew all about what had happened in his own section before he met the war *induna*, and when the latter reported to the Paramount at home he could tell everything.

Return from war

Long ago all that was found in the village or stockade (goats, sheep and cattle) belonged of right to the man who had entered first. That was easy when they sent only one company to the attack. All the other things belonged to the finder. Afterwards when all the warriors went to the attack together, it was difficult to distinguish who had got in first and so the spoils went to the man who reached them first. The Paramount had his portion of everything taken. Outside the stockade those who had taken cattle put aside two or three which they said were *amahloma ankosi*, the first taste to the Paramount.

On the return all who had dipped their spears in the blood of their enemies carried what the killed had been wearing and their weapons or bows. If a man had killed a woman he wore her things (that is her ornaments, bark-cloth, etc.). These things were done to fulfil a taboo. When the end of the time of purification came, all those things that were worthless were thrown away or burned, but the beautiful things were kept. Only the very old people wore the clothes of the killed.

When the army was on the way home it looked for bones of animals and burned them and ground them fine like flour, and also made charcoal dust. On the day of arrival some flour was kneaded and bone dust and the charcoal dust each by itself. They painted themselves on the face and on the body. This custom was to show those who had speared an enemy in the fight.

When the army was near their own country the war *induna* chose some messengers to go and give the news of the fighting and the names of those who had been killed. These messengers went to the important *izinduna*, and from them the news went quickly to the Paramount, headmen, and elders. The women were not told quietly; even if a man knew that his son had been killed it was not permitted to show his grief before the army had returned and mobilized in the kraal.

When the sections marched back to the village the first sections to go out to war came last and the one that had been last now led the way. The army never entered the Paramount's village in the afternoon but in the morning or before midday. They did this because it took a long time to tell all the news of the war, so if the army arrived near the village in the afternoon they slept in grass-shelters outside.

When the army was ready to enter, the sections were set in order, each one told off to follow another and each one chose its own song for the entry. When they sang the warriors covered their heads with their shields, with their spears in the middle of the shields. While they were singing one warrior of the section would jump out in front and dance his own praise-dance and the others let him; when he had fallen into the ranks again, they took up the section-song. The songs sung at the entry to the kraal were called *imihubo*. These were different from *ligubo* for they were sung by mouth only, whereas a *ligubo* was sung with stamping of the feet.

When the warriors marched on the cattle track there was heard a confused noise of singing and shouting praises. All the warriors marched very slowly as they sang, section by section but crowding together. When they came close to the gateway they stood and waited to let those who had not blooded their spears have their dance out, because once inside only the 'killers' might dance before the Paramount and the headmen. When they stood they were as though the kraal were built of men but they left a space in the middle for the Paramount and headmen to sit and watch. For a little time the warriors danced their own praise-dances and these were chiefly those whose bravery was well known.

After these had danced a little there was a shout for silence, and all kept silent waiting for the words of the war *induna*. He came out from the throng and began to dance while all the warriors responded to his war-cry or praise-names. After he had finished he began to tell the story. He began by saying that in such and such a section, so and so had been first to enter the stockade, or to throw a spear first which killed a man inside. In all the sections he went over those whose names had been taken by the *izinduna*; if he forgot anything or the name of a 'killer' he went and asked the *induna* of the section to help him. Whenever he mentioned a name, the warrior jumped forward and danced so as to be known to the Paramount and all the men. Then the Paramount and the headmen chose one of themselves to reply and thank the army; sometimes it was the chief *induna*. Before he began he also danced a little, then spoke praising or blaming. After he had finished he danced again and sat down among his peers. This the Ngoni called *ukudumisela impi*, thanking in respect for the army.

Demobilization and purification

When all was finished in the kraal the warriors scattered and went to their villages to take off all their war equipment and to put their shields on the *mpalane*, the resting place or bedstead of shields. Then they sat down by their big house and were greeted by their wives, parents, children and friends. The custom was the same as that on the birth of a child, the salutation being '*Amehlo amhlope*', 'Eyes are white', or '*Buyani*', 'Return', along with the clan name. The answer was '*Yebo*' also with the clan name. This was the custom in the houses where there had been no death. The warriors of a village where there had been a death, either in the village or killed in war, took off their equipment on leaving the kraal and went to the house of mourning.

The warriors' sections went to the head villages of their districts to tell the news and show themselves. Those of Ekwendeni there; of Echigodhl-weni there; of Elangeni there; of Emcisweni there; but the sections from the villages of the *amakanda* went together first of all to show themselves to the head villages and then went to their own villages. After the army had broken up, those who had killed a man or had helped to kill a man began a purification of four or five days for they were considered to be unclean. After the time of greetings in the village, the elders came with the bark of certain trees which had been ground or crushed and put it in a frying pan. The frying pan was put on three hearth-stones by the fire, and water poured on. When the water began to boil the men came and began to 'lick the medicine', first one hand and then the other. The first lick they spat out, then they swallowed some, and struck their palms on their knees and on their elbows. They jumped from side to side of the frying pan and as they did so, they said '*Po*'. This was said to drive away the spirits of the enemies whom they had killed because they were afraid that they might come to trouble them in sleep at night.

Very early in the morning they went to the river to wash off the paint, but they still wore the clothes of the men killed. This showed they were still being purified. They did not live with their wives or touch their children. When they returned from the river they tried to repeat the words they had heard their enemies say. Back in the village they took more of their medicine from the frying pan saying '*Po*'. After that they rubbed themselves all over with lime wash.

On the last day they went to the river again but when they had bathed they burned all they were wearing, or hung them in trees. Only the good things were left: cloth, ivory bracelets, bows and spears. The clothes of the killed they gave to the old people to wear. If water did not take off the paint on their bodies they rubbed on fat from cattle. Then the days of taboo were completed, they were considered to be clean, and could live with their wives and hold their children.

The decoration of heroes

After the warriors had been sent to the villages a short time passed, then they were called again together to dance the *ligubo*. On that day bulls were chosen to be killed for the army. Each section received a bull and it was killed by the hero of the section. While it was being skinned and cooked all the companies were dancing. When the meat was cooked and taken off the fire all the army was busied with eating it, each company by itself. When they had eaten the warriors began to get up one by one to dance and leap before their Paramount. Then the heroes of the sections were presented with the horns of the bull killed for the section. The horns had had holes bored so that bark-rope could be drawn through and they were worn by hanging on the shoulder or neck. The bulls which were killed were called *izinkunzi za impi*, bulls of the army. The man who wore the horns and danced with them was known as a man of valour.

Often the Paramount called the men who had shown valour on many occasions to come to him. When he did so he first of all searched for a fine skin and called a man who was good at cutting out a shield. When the shield was ready it was given to the famous warrior. When he received it he began to dance with the shield while the Paramount and the people there saluted him with praises for his valour. The people in the kraal were told to greet the Paramount's hero and beat on their shields. That dancing was a dance of thanks to the Paramount.

ORGANIZATION OF WARFARE

Cibambo's text brings out a number of points which emphasize that the organization for war was integral to the whole structure of the Ngoni kingdoms and to the peoples living within the kingdoms. We shall concentrate in this chapter on the political implications of the organization of warfare, and chiefly on the part played by the Paramount and his officers of state. The entire war organization was centred in the person and office of the Paramount. He was the commander-in-chief of the army, though most informants agreed he did not himself go out to fight. He claimed the sole right to make war and to declare war, but it is clear from early Europeans sources that private wars and raids did take place, and this effort to centralize and control all warfare appears to have been not wholly successful. The Paramount claimed the right to distribute all booty taken in wars, whether they were waged on behalf of the whole state or of a section of it. Through the exercise of this right he sought to suppress private warfare for private gain, but, according to Cibambo, he did not get all the booty taken, for the text mentions setting aside cattle for the Paramount.

If war was declared by the Paramount his village was the mobilization centre for the whole army. The sections of the army from the districts of the chiefs and the *amakanda* of the *alumuzana* assembled in the Paramount's village; there they danced *ligubo*, the war-dance; they went out from there to fight, and they returned there after fighting for the acclaiming of heroes and the distribution of the booty.

The Paramount worked through two leading office-bearers of the army. One was the big war *induna* whom he appointed and on whom lay the responsibility for planning the campaign and selecting the regiments for different tasks. It was he who bore the onus of ultimate success or failure. The other office-bearer whose activities the Paramount controlled closely was the chief 'doctor' of the army, the man who sometimes combined the role of diviner with that of administering 'medicines' to the army.

Finally the Paramount had the sole right of granting the head-ring to the men of a regiment who had served their time as warriors and were

allowed to marry and settle down in their villages.[1] Since he also had the
sole right of forming a new regiment of young men and giving it a name,
he controlled the intake to the army as well as the discharge of seasoned
warriors.

The big war *induna* served directly under the Paramount. Associated
with him were other subordinate war leaders or *izinduna*, one of whom
was always at the head of each regiment. Considerable emphasis was
laid by Cibambo and other Ngoni informants on the essentially military
character, in pre-European days, of the office and function of the
izinduna, who were officials serving the whole kingdom. We shall see in
Chapters III, IV and V how the term *induna* was also used for civil
officials at the royal village and in the courts, as well as for the men in
charge of sections of a village and of houses.

The account of the mobilization of the army shows that the Ngoni
had changed the system of military barracks concentrated about the
capital, described by Gluckman as typical of the Zulu military organization and by Kuper for the Swazi. Gluckman said that the chiefs
assembled their people in territorial, not age, divisions, and that the age
regiments belonged to the king alone and lived in or near his capital.[2]
In pre-European days the Ngoni, according to Cibambo and to other
informants, had in their armies territorial divisions as well as age
regiments, and there was no concentration of young warriors by age
regiments round the Paramount's village.[3]

When a summons to war went forth, the warriors in the territory of
each chief or *mulumuzana* assembled at his head village as a *libandla*.
This included the warriors from the outlying villages and from the head
village. Cibambo's use of the term *libandla* emphasized that it was a
territorial unit, divided into *mabuto* (which he called sections) on the
basis of age.

When each *libandla* arrived at the Paramount's village ready for warfare, the different age groups within it joined up with their parallel age
groups from other *mabandla* to form regiments. The Ngoni term for
these national regiments was *mabuto*, the same term as that used for the
age divisions of the *mabandla*. Old men who had been warriors in their
youth expressed to me many times their immense pride in their own
libuto, and it had for them something of the tradition and prestige of a
famous school. They would recite the names of other *mabuto*, beginning
with their own as the most recent, and going backwards through ten or
more regimental names to those who had crossed the Zambesi with

[1] Cibambo in the text spoke of warriors wearing the head-ring. The usual practice,
according to informants, was to give the head-ring at the end of service in the army.
Cibambo may have been referring to former warriors with a head-ring putting on
war-dress for a ceremony.

[2] Gluckman, M. 'The Kingdom of the Zulu', in *African Political Systems*, 1940, p. 31.

[3] One example of a concentration of young men was reported at the village of the
Queen Mother in the central kingdom in 1898 in *The Central African Times*, see
Memorandum XVI, International African Institute, 1938, p. 18.

Zwangendaba or Mputa. Some informants showed that there was not always agreement about the use of the terms *mabandla* and *mabuto* when relating stories of the past, and the connotation of age regiment was sometimes given to *mabandla*. Cibambo and the other Ngoni historians who used the Ngoni language habitually were, however, quite clear about the differentiation between the two terms, one being territorial and the other denoting an age group. This use of the term *libuto* was confirmed by Dr. Kuper in her account of Swazi military organization.[1]

The organization of Ngoni warfare included the use of divining and of medicines to ensure success in war, and the summoning of the men charged to carry out these functions. In both Ngoni kingdoms there were men alive at the time of my visits who knew the medicines for war and had performed the functions of a 'war-medicine doctor'. According to these informants there was no sharp division between the functions of the diviner and the 'doctor' in relation to their services to the kingdom and to the army. There were individuals who had acted in both capacities. The diviner's task was to prophesy about probable success in war and about attacks from the enemy. He might, and sometimes did, combine this with 'doctoring' the army.

The preparation and administering of medicines to strengthen the army were discussed by informants in terms of two main types of medicine and a third which was less often referred to. The two main types were *intonga* and *intelezi* and the third one *inhlenza*. In the northern kingdom Mopo Jere, who had been a 'war doctor' and was the son of a former famous 'war doctor', insisted that the term *intonga* could be used in several different ways: for medicines made of roots; for a rod or stick (*nduku*) which was medicated; and occasionally for the 'doctor' who used these objects. He also emphasized that each chief or *mulumuzana* had his own *intonga* and performed ceremonies for his own warriors before they left his kraal for that of the Paramount, where they went through another ceremony of having medicines administered to them before going on the campaign.

Formerly the *intonga*, that is, the stick or rod, was treated with the root of a shrub ground up and mixed with water. A beast was then killed, the Paramount ate the meat in the kraal with his senior men, and the skin was made into a bag in which the medicated *intonga* was placed. This skin bag containing the *intonga* was carried in front of the army when it was on the march. It could only be carried and handled when with the army by boys who had not yet reached puberty. The *intonga* in its bag was pointed at the enemy, as the army drew near, to make his warriors tremble and feel powerless and take to their heels. Its potency to make men powerless was so strong that no man from the Ngoni army dared walk in front of it, lest he too should lose all his strength.

[1] Kuper, H. 'The Development of the Military Organization in Swaziland.' *Africa*, Vol. X, No. 2, p. 176.

The *intelezi* was made from the roots of a creeper and a bush which grew on the banks of rivers. These roots were burned over the fire, pounded and mixed with water. The warriors were given some to lick on the tips of their fingers, some was smeared inside their shields, and the rest was beaten in a gourd till it foamed. The 'war doctor' took the tail of a gnu or of a zebra and dipped it in the foam and sprinkled the warriors as they finally passed out of the gateway of the kraal on the campaign. This medicine was for strengthening them and also for making them 'slippery', so that the enemy spears would glide by them and not pierce them, and they could slip between the posts of the enemy stockade. After being sprinkled with the *intelezi* no one could sleep with his wife or any other woman, as he would risk spoiling the effect of the medicine and therefore would be more liable to be killed.

The *inhlenza* was a spear with a barbed hook. The Paramount threw it in front of the army as they stood in the kraal until all the warriors had left. It was then put back in the *indlunkulu* where it was kept in the care of the owner of that hut.

There were thus three functions to be performed, each by one of the war medicines. The *intelezi* was to strengthen and protect individual warriors. The *intonga* was the symbol of their Paramount and their kingdom leading them to war and weakening the enemy. The *inhlenza* was the symbol of invincibility, administered by the Paramount.

There were two stages of assembling in the Paramount's village before a campaign. The first followed the initial summons to mobilize, when the local companies (*mabandla*) marched into the kraal, sorted themselves into age regiments (*mabuto*) and sang their regimental songs. Then followed the *ligubo*, the war-dance, when the warriors wore their full war-dress, and the women joined in. There was no individual dancing but a working up of corporate feeling through the dancing and songs. The Ngoni used no drums in their music, relying on achieving rhythm and unison by the stamping of their feet and their singing. After this dance the warriors left for their villages, while at the Paramount's village preparation was made for food and snuff for the campaign. Hard cakes of roasted bullrush millet, kaffir-corn and groundnuts pounded together, and dried meat, were the main supplies carried. At the second summons the warriors returned in their companies with their carriers. These carriers, who were usually young boys, carried the war-dresses and ornaments wrapped in a mat, and the food supplies.

Since on this final meeting depended much of the ultimate success of the campaign, only the warriors and the senior men were present, and all women and young children were excluded from the kraal. After the objectives of the fighting had been explained the warriors were addressed by the old men and exhorted to be brave and to help their comrades, and then the final medication by the 'war doctor' took place. The separation of the army from the civil population was complete until their return from the campaign and the purification of those who had killed any of the enemy.

Cibambo and other Ngoni informants had no idea of the size of the Ngoni armies beyond emphasizing that they were 'very big and very strong'. Evidence was forthcoming, however, from early European sources on the size of the armies which, though it can only have been based on guess-work, nevertheless gave an indication of the numbers involved. Dr. Elmslie referred in 1878 to having seen in the previous year an army of 10,000 of the northern Ngoni which went out in June and returned in September.[1] In the *B.C.A. Gazette* of December 1894, reference was made to the armies of the central Ngoni which were said to be, at the time of their last raids, 50,000 strong. In the *Blantyre District Note Book* there was an entry of 1884, giving no numbers for the army but reporting on the raid on Blantyre in that year when the 'vanguard of the army was composed entirely of young men in their first vigour of manhood, who were said to have marched 50 miles in half a day'. From such scanty references by Europeans, it is clear that the Ngoni armies in the field consisted of large numbers, were highly organized, and trained to feats of endurance as well as in fighting skill. The Blantyre reference also brought out the authority of the big war *induna*, who was presented with cloth by the Moir brothers of the African Lakes Corporation as a bribe not to attack the Blantyre area again, and kept his promise.

Objectives in warfare

Dr. Kuper wrote of the Swazi military kingdom that wars were waged 'to extend the boundaries, to retain tribal independence and to secure internal solidarity'.[2] After the Ngoni kingdoms were set up in Nyasaland, warfare had the same objectives with the additional one of bringing back captives and cattle. In north Nyasaland Dr. Elmslie, in the reference already cited, wrote that, after the four months' campaigning the Ngoni armies returned 'laden with spoil in slaves, cattle and ivory'. Up to the coming of the Europeans many of the raids and wars took place in the hope of annexing additional territory. Dr. Elmslie wrote in 1878 of the Ngoni dominating an area of 30,000 square miles in north Nyasaland from the lake-shore to the Luangwa river. In central Nyasaland the *B.C.A. Gazette* of 1894 reported that the Ngoni Paramount ruled from the Lintippe river near Lilongwe to the Luvubwe river south of the Kirk Range. The chief challenge to Ngoni security in the northern kingdom came from the Bemba, and in the central kingdom from a combination of Yao and Arabs. Dr. Laws recorded in 1886 that the Ngoni, in their final victorious campaign against the Bemba, had

---

[1] Elmslie, W. A. *Among the Wild Ngoni*. Oliphant Anderson & Ferrier, 1899, p. 79.
[2] Kuper, H. 'The Development of the Military Organisation in Swaziland.' *Africa*, Vol. X, No. 2, p. 176.

defeated an alliance between the Arabs and the Bemba in which the allies intended to dominate all the territory between the Luangwa river and the lake-shore, driving the Ngoni from their highlands and opening all the country to the slave-trade. In the central kingdom, during the interregnum after Cikusi's death in 1891, a powerful Yao chief raided the kingdom, destroyed six villages and took many captives. In both kingdoms it was necessary for the Ngoni to defend their independence by constant vigilance and preparedness, especially against a combination of Arab slave-raiders and local tribes. Since large numbers of warriors were mobilized every year, these trained armies demanded an outlet, and the policy of aggression served the dual purpose of raiding enemy territory and maintaining a defence force.

There was a difference of opinion among informants about the results of raids in terms of spoils of war. In both kingdoms captives were taken in war, especially young men of military age and women. From tsetse-free areas where cattle were to be found, live beasts were brought to add to the herds in the Paramount's village and in those of the chiefs and *alumuzana*. Ivory for trading and cloth for wearing were two of the most valued forms of booty, and Cibambo mentioned the looting of clothes and weapons from those who had been killed. From accounts by the first Europeans, it is clear that the Ngoni burned the villages and killed the inhabitants in the majority of their later raids.

If defensive and aggressive military action and the acquisition of valued forms of wealth were two of the main objectives in war, a third was undoubtedly the need to build up a national sentiment within the military kingdoms by success in warfare in the first place, and by intensive training of all young men in the second, thus integrating the youth from conquered units with those who belonged to the trans-Zambesi clans. Again and again, in talking about their past, Ngoni informants from the Paramounts downwards emphasized the discipline and training of the young men in the days of warfare, and expressed their opinion that no other training could take its place. It was not only the common military training which contributed to this national sentiment and held the Ngoni together in a common purpose of preparedness for warfare. The *libuto* or age set within the *libandla* or territorial unit, and the *impi* or national army in which the territorial units were merged, provided a military organization which was adaptable and balanced, and which, through the control of the Paramount, gave the main impetus to centralization, while encouraging pride and initiative among local and age-set groups.

The relics of a military tradition

In north Nyasaland the Ngoni never fought against the Europeans, and were not coerced into giving up warfare, but, as a result of their contacts with the Livingstonia Mission, they finally agreed to give it up voluntarily. When Dr. Laws met the Commissioner near Mponda's at the south end of the lake in 1891, he pleaded with him not to use force against the northern Ngoni. 'Don't fight them,' he urged, 'enlist them.' The military commander, Captain Macguire, who was present at the interview, showed interest in the idea of a new recruiting ground for the regular forces in Nyasaland, but his ideas were not pursued as it proved to be easier to continue recruiting the Yao and Tonga who had already shown themselves good military material.

In the central kingdom the first reactions of the Administration towards the Ngoni were favourable. Paramount Cikusi was visited by administrators in 1882 and 1886, and in 1890 concluded a treaty placing himself under British protection. On his death in 1891 his successor Gomani I sent messengers to inform the Administration of his father's death, to declare his allegiance to the British, and to present a bull and a cow, four tusks of ivory and twenty-five men to help in the war against the slave-raiders. In the following year 100 Ngoni warriors were drafted into the regular forces and Mr. H. H. Johnston reported: 'The Ngoni are altogether a splendid people and may be regarded as the backbone of British Central Africa.'[1] But this co-operative relationship did not last. In 1896 it was reported that 'Gomani and a number of his turbulent young headmen were opposed to our influence.'[2] Ngoni armies raided a mission station, an expeditionary force under British officers was sent, the Paramount's village was attacked and his army defeated. He was taken prisoner and, refusing to walk to Zomba, was shot near Dombole in his former kingdom.

In the 1930's the Ngoni of the central kingdom referred repeatedly to the expedition sent against them, the defeat of their army, the death of their Paramount and the seizure of some of their cattle. They nursed a grudge against their conqueror which coloured much of their sentiments towards Europeans. They sometimes referred to the long period of contact of the northern Ngoni kingdom with the Livingstonia Mission, and contrasted it with their contacts with several missions who appeared to them to be in league with the Administration against them and not to take their side in relations with the Government as Dr. Laws had done in the north.

When Cibambo visited the central Ngoni kingdom with me in 1936 he was interested in making comparisons with his own Ngoni of the north. He found that in central Ngoniland there were very few men who knew Ngoni songs well, and that in general the knowledge of the Ngoni language had almost died out. The big shields were not, he thought, as well cut as those in the north. Yet the war-dances were performed correctly, and the war-dress which the dancers wore was more striking than anything which had been preserved in the north.

---

[1] Johnston, H. H. *Report of the First Three Years' Administration of the Eastern Portion of B.C.A.* 1894, p. 24.

[2] Johnston, H. H. *Report on Trade and General Conditions in Nyasaland, 1896-7*, p. 7.

He was present with me in November 1936 at a big *ligubo* dance in the royal village of Maganga. It took place on the open space in front of the court-house. The Provincial Commissioner brought a party of Europeans to see it, and some members of a South African mission a few miles away were persuaded to come. Some of the missionaries before coming had been afraid that the dances and songs would be obscene, but when they saw the translations of the Ngoni songs which with Cibambo's help I had prepared, and watched the rhythm and dignity of the dances they were so favourably impressed that they asked the Paramount to send senior men to teach the songs and dances to the boys in the mission school.

At this *ligubo* dance contingents came from all over the central kingdom. The men came in groups based on the head villages of the chiefs and *alumuzana*, with young carriers bringing their war-dress fastened up in rolls of mats. They put on this war-dress in the neighbouring village of Lizulu, the *gogo* village from which Magonga had 'gone out', using the compounds of the huts belonging to the houses of the senior women for their robing. They climbed the steep path up to Maganga in companies, and near the Paramount's house they advanced in close formation with their shields held over their heads, while an official 'praiser' called out the *izibongo*, the praise names of the Paramount and his ancestors. On the open space in front of the court-house, the different detachments came together and formed a crescent facing the Paramount and his guests. The dance was chiefly a rhythmic stamping of the feet, with from time to time a slow movement of a few steps to the right and then to the left. A number of women of the Swazi and trans-Zambesi clans, including the Paramount's wife, danced in front of the warriors, facing them, carrying small sticks and small shields, and co-ordinating their steps with a rhythmic jerking of the right arm and neck, described by Cibambo as the women's dance in his account of warfare in old days. Every now and then one of the men leaped out in front, jumping high in the air, brandishing his spear and shield, and singing his own war song, the *ligiya*, the dance of the individual warrior. At intervals one of the official praisers came forward and sang the praise-songs of the Maseko line of Paramounts.

The *ligubo*, as a war-dance, could only be danced at the Paramount's village, or at the funeral of the Paramount or of his older sister by the same mother. In 1937 the older sister of the former Paramount Cikusi died, and the *ligubo* was danced during the mourning ceremonies which took place in the village of Mcakhatha.

During these funeral ceremonies the *ligubo* was danced continually from the moment when the corpse was wrapped in skins after death, until it was lowered into the grave three days later. *Ligubo*, the individual *ligiya*, and the songs of the army going out to war, went on all day and much of the night, and broke out with renewed vigour every time a fresh detachment came into the village from another part of the country. The corpse was finally carried in a cow-skin from the hut to the grave between a double line of warriors singing *ligubo* songs and thundering with their shields knocking against their knees.

The only relics, therefore, of the military tradition which could be observed in the Ngoni kingdoms in the 1930's were related either to the national gatherings at the Paramount's village, or to the mourning ritual for the royal line. The knowledge of the songs and the war-dresses was preserved by the senior leading men and women of the trans-Zambesi clans. The songs which follow were sung, except for the last one, in both Ngoni kingdoms, and not only when *ligubo* dances took place. Some were sung at marriage ceremonies, and some formerly as *umsindo* songs at the pre-marriage rite for girls. In northern Ngoniland the last two songs were sung in the churches, and tunes of other well-known war songs were used in the churches of the Scottish mission with different words written for them. Most of the songs when translated sound very brief. They were less brief when sung in the Ngoni language since there was repetition of certain lines, with repeated refrains, and with a series of 'sounds' such as *inyo ho, zi, ye ye* which accompanied the stamping of feet and the clash of shields. These untranslatable 'sounds' were sometimes the only part of the song which was known by the younger men who had never used the Ngoni language, and they chanted them in the right places as a chorus.

The first four songs were all intended to encourage the warriors at the time of mobilization before going out on a campaign. They reminded the singers that in the use of the short stabbing spear the Ngoni armies were stronger than their enemies; that they brought their fighting skill from the south-east; that, though the fight might be long, rest would come in the evening; and that the army belonged to the Paramount, the head of the kingdom. The fifth song suggested the kind of warning given to warriors by the old men—that they should not give in after a fight, but pursue the enemy and capture their cattle. The sixth song, though the reference to Longiyeka was obscure, was said to be a warning against treachery and revolt in the army. The seventh song had three themes: that death was the lot of every man, and the earth where the grave would be dug was never satisfied (*ukunona* means 'to be satisfied'); that no one would escape the universal fate of death, from the senior men wearing the head-plumes to the common people and the cattle; and that the ancestors already buried in the land would be joined by those then alive. The terms used in this song to describe the social groups among the Ngoni people were those which will occur throughout this book.

1. No Paramount can be poor because of the spear.
   Then why are you running away?

2. Do you hear?
   The Ngoni come from the south-east.

3. What are we contending for?
   In this way in the sky
   The sun is setting.

4. O alas! the Paramount!
   We fight for our Paramount only that.

5. The cattle run away, you cowards.
   Those yonder; they run, you cowards.
   The cattle, see, do they run? They run, you cowards.
   Is your young manhood over? They run.
   You are left with the carriers. They run.
   Look at the cattle, they run, they run;
   You have eyes only for the food-stuffs. They run.

6. They are talking, they are talking
   Throughout the land.
   Listen, keep silent, be still.
   They are talking.
   It will be spoken, it will be spoken
   Throughout the land.
   Longiyeka, you keep silent, you be still.
   People are being talked about.

7. The earth does not get fat. It makes an end of those who wear the
   head-plumes.
   We shall die on the earth.
   The earth does not get fat. It makes an end of those who die as
   heroes.
   Shall we all die on the earth?
   Listen, O earth! We shall mourn because of you.
   Listen, O earth! Shall we all die on the earth?

   The earth does not get fat. It makes an end of the chiefs.
   Shall we die on the earth?
   The earth does not get fat. It makes an end of the women chiefs.
   Shall we die on the earth?
   Listen, O earth! We shall mourn because of you.
   Listen, O earth! Shall we all die on the earth?

   The earth does not get fat. It makes an end of nobles.
   Shall we die on the earth?
   The earth does not get fat. It makes an end of the royal women.
   Shall we die on the earth?
   Listen, O earth! We shall mourn because of you.
   Listen, O earth! Shall we all die on the earth?

The earth does not get fat. It makes an end of the common people.
Shall we die on the earth?
The earth does not get fat. It makes an end of all beasts.
Shall we die on the earth?
Listen, you who are asleep, who are left tightly closed in the land!
   Shall we all sink into the earth?
   Listen, O earth! The sun is setting tightly.
We shall all enter into the earth.

CHAPTER II

THE PARAMOUNT

Introduction

THE Cewa term for chief (*mfumu*) was widely used in Nyasaland for chiefs of all ranks, as well as for village headmen and, occasionally, as an honorific form of address to an important individual. Among the Cewa a man could 'become a chief' by acquiring, through marriage or purchase, the right to own a site, known as a *mzinda*, on which female initiation rites were carried out. This concept of the office of chieftainship among the Cewa and other local tribes was in sharp contrast to the centralized and unified concept inherent in the Ngoni term *inkosi*. I have translated *inkosi* here as Paramount because the term Paramount Chief was adopted by the Administration to denote a ruler who had recognized subordinate chiefs under him and whose court was an appeal court for their courts. It is necessary to emphasize here how distinctive the office of Paramount was among the various types of chiefs in Nyasaland, both in official recognition, and still more in the Ngoni ideas about their Paramount. We saw in Chapter II of Part I that no Nyasaland chiefs, except the Ngoni Paramounts, had Subordinate Native Authorities under them.

When the Ngoni left the south, a number of small chiefdoms there were gradually being overcome by Shaka and, based on his armies, he had set up a new and unique type of *inkosi*. The leaders of military bands who left him—Mzilikazi, Soshangane, Zwangendaba and Ngwana—had little recognition before they left, except as military and clan leaders. Yet after the Ngoni left, Zwangendaba and Ngwana received from their followers recognition of their political leadership as *inkosi*, and this was expressed by giving to the Paramount the salute of *Bayete*. Throughout their recitals of traditions and in their accounts of their political system, Ngoni informants in both kingdoms emphasized that for each kingdom there was one *inkosi* to whom alone the *Bayete* was given. We assume, therefore, that the later Ngoni concept of the Paramount and his function and authority was largely evolved and built up during the Ngoni migration across the Zambesi and the early settlement in Nyasaland.

The office of the Paramount was supported by three typical Ngoni institutions. The first was the regency exercised by the man who was held responsible for the care of the office of the Paramount. He was called 'the one who takes care of the country', 'the one who has to put the new *inkosi* in his place', 'the one who takes care of the young *inkosi* until he enters his father's place'. We shall see later how this principle of regency operated in particular cases in the succession to the Paramountcy. It proved to be an effective provision both in the case of a minor who was recognized as his father's heir, and during an interregnum while the succession was being discussed. The Ngoni showed a clear understanding of what functions the regent ought to perform, and when he exceeded these functions and usurped, or tried to usurp, the Paramount's position they condemned his action as wrong.

The second institution which supported the Paramountcy was the 'big house' from which the heir to the Paramount had to come. We shall see later that it was not always considered essential that the heir should be the actual child of the wife in the big house. A boy could be adopted into the house and, by Ngoni kinship rules, he was then a child of that house and of the woman in it.

The third institution, which made the Paramount immortal at death after having been supreme in his life-time, was the Ngoni practice of 'guarding his spirit' in a hut, usually in the village where he had lived. The guardianship of a spirit was not practised exclusively for the Paramount. All the chiefs and the heads of the Swazi clans had this provision made for their spirits when they died, but in national crises prayers addressed to the spirits of former Paramounts were of supreme importance.

The royal clan and the big house

Among the Swazi and trans-Zambesi clans which formed the Ngoni aristocracy the royal clan had a unique position. Not only was it the clan of the Paramount, but its members had social rank and prestige because they belonged to his clan. In the northern kingdom informants showed awareness of the fact that their royal clan of Jere was not one of the well-known clans in the south. Other clan names found among them, such as Ngomezulu, Thole, Nzima, Nqumayo, and many more, were known to be clan names among the South-eastern Bantu. The following explanation was given by Cibambo about the name Jere and was the one most widely accepted:

❡ The Ngoni themselves say that the clan name of Jere was given during the journey, and that it arose out of the number of people who were with Zwangendaba. When the Ngoni want to speak of a large number of people they use two well-known words which are: '*Ngu Shaka*' (it is Shaka);

'*Ngu Jere*' (it is Jere). Perhaps Zwangendaba and others took their clan name from this, seeing that they had become a great number. It is certain that the clan name of Jere is not known in Zululand or Swaziland.

In the northern kingdom all the chiefs recognized as Subordinate Native Authorities were of the royal clan, and hence its political authority was widespread. It was noticed by the early missionaries in northern Ngoniland that the sons of Zwangendaba who were chiefs under their brother, the Paramount, showed some degree of independence in that they wanted to rule their own areas with the minimum of centralized control. The pre-eminence of the Paramount among the other Jere rulers was strengthened as time went on by the remoter kinship relationship of the other Jere chiefs to the Paramount. After Zwangendaba's death they were his brothers of the same father and different mothers. Two generations later they were farther removed from his kinship circle since each of their posts was inherited on a direct father to son principle. The political and social importance of membership of the royal clan tended to go in the direct line of relationship to the Paramount rather than to the collateral branches. Later, in Part III, we shall examine the social prestige of the *amakosana* (lit. children of the *inkosi*). It was the closeness of their relationship to the reigning Paramount which was the basis for their social prestige, though evidence showed that a sister or brother or child from a big house of a former Paramount was also given social recognition as an important personage.

The royal clan of Maseko in the central kingdom was also known in Swaziland. Dr. Kuper refers to it in connexion with the Swazi custom of cremating the body of the Maseko chief at his death on a rock by a river.[1] This custom was brought from the south by the Ngoni under Maseko leadership and carried out for each successive Paràmount up to 1891. Among these Ngoni the royal clan had special relationships with other leading clans, but the Paramount did not share his political authority with any others of his clan. His chiefs were all of other clans, and Ngoni informants said that it was a deliberate act of the Paramount Mputa to exclude his brothers from political authority and from disputing with him the control of the kingdom. In the isolated position thus established for the royal clan, two other clans had a ritual relationship with the Paramount. One was the Phungwako clan which was custodian of the Paramount's 'medicines', known as the *tonga*. The other was the Ngozo clan which provided the companion for the Paramount whom I have called the 'royal shadow' (see below, pp. 61-3). Yet another special relationship with the royal clan was that of the Nzunga clan which had *cibale*, or brotherly relations, with the Maseko clan, that involved sharing the same avoidances and excluded inter-marriage.

The relationship of the Paramount to other leaders of the royal clan

[1] Kuper, H. *An African Aristocracy*, p. 86.

was thus different in the two kingdoms. In the north he was one ruler, though a supreme one, among several ruling kinsmen of the same clan. His position in the past had been strengthened by the prestige shared by his clansmen, but also challenged by his near kinsmen in positions of authority. In the central kingdom the Paramount shared no authority with his fellow clansmen. He was unique among them as a ruler, while sharing special ritual relationships with the two other clans which supported his position without challenging it.

A new Paramount, in order to be installed in his father's place, had to be of the big house as well as of the royal clan. Dr. Kuper described the Swazi practice whereby cattle were contributed by the nation for the mother of the king, so that she was called the 'mother of the people of the country'. She also described the ritual marriage of the first wife of a ruler, who was called *sisulamsiti*, and who was never the mother of the heir.[1] The Ngoni Paramount-elect in the northern kingdom married his first wife when he was a young man and she was called *msulamsizi*, 'the one who takes the darkness off him'. The big wife, who would bear the heir, was married with a large gift of cattle taken from the herd of the big wife of the reigning Paramount and, after marriage, was attached to her big house. We shall discuss in greater detail in the next chapter the relationships of the royal women to the Paramount and to each other. Here it is important to note that the big house owned by the big wife was the place where the future chief was brought up. In the central kingdom the first marriage of the Paramount was traditionally with a woman of the Magagula clan who was said not to bear children. She held an honoured place in the social hierarchy and was married with cattle taken from the herd of the *gogo* house of the reigning Paramount. It was regarded as a ritual marriage, for if she did bear children they were not acknowledged. Informants were uncertain whether methods to prevent conception were used, or whether abortion was practised, or whether children, if born, died young or were disposed of or placed out in other households. The last alternatives were unlikely, and one of the first two expedients was in line with the phrase always used of this wife: 'she did not bear children'. The wife who bore the heir was married next and was always of another leading clan, and the cattle for her came from the herd of the big house of the reigning Paramount.

The reasons were obvious why the remembered genealogies of the Ngoni Paramounts of the royal clans were short compared with the genealogies of some other African royal houses. The remote ancestors of Jere chiefs and Maseko chiefs, who were, as we have seen, not Paramounts before they left the south, were forgotten once the departure had taken place. Only a few names had been handed down and were repeated by the official praisers, whose task it was to call out the names of the direct ancestors of the Paramount before declaiming his *izibongo* or

[1] Kuper, H. op. cit. pp. 54 & 91.

praise-songs. The northern Ngoni remembered the names of five direct ancestors of Zwangendaba, ancestors who had died before they left the south, and the central Ngoni remembered the names of three direct ancestors of Mputa who had died before crossing the Zambesi.[1]

The genealogy of the Jere Paramounts which was recited in the northern kingdom varied in different localities. Of three versions which I found two agreed, except in the name given for the earliest ancestor.

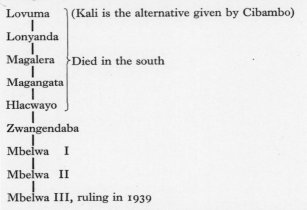

Lovuma   (Kali is the alternative given by Cibambo)
|
Lonyanda
|
Magalera   ⎫
| Died in the south
Magangata
|
Hlacwayo   ⎭
|
Zwangendaba
|
Mbelwa   I
|
Mbelwa   II
|
Mbelwa III, ruling in 1939

The list above was given by Cibambo of Ekwendeni and Simon Nhlane of Hoho, the leading member of the Nhlane clan.

Third Version:

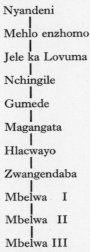

Nyandeni
|
Mehlo enzhomo
|
Jele ka Lovuma
|
Nchingile
|
Gumede
|
Magangata
|
Hlacwayo
|
Zwangendaba
|
Mbelwa   I
|
Mbelwa   II
|
Mbelwa III

[1] In 'Traditions and Prestige among the Ngoni' (*Africa*, 1936) I said (p. 466) that nine generations of ancestors were remembered in the north and seven in the centre. These referred to the Paramounts after crossing the Zambesi as well as to their ancestors who died in the south.

The third version was given by Chinombo Jere, a grandson of Zwangendaba, who came from Emcisweni. This section of the Ngoni, under Chief Mperembe, had for a time associated with Paramount Mpeseni, and not with Mbelwa. This separation gave them a slightly different set of traditions, and they were, perhaps owing to their geographical isolation, the last group to give up the old language and dress.

An attempt to check the Emcisweni version of the Jere genealogy with that of Ekwendeni showed one piece of evidence in favour of the latter. This was the tradition preserved by the Nhlane clan that the Swazi chiefs of the Nqumayo clan had as their chief *izinduna* men of the Jere clan who were of the same age regiment. The names remembered were as follows:

Swazi chiefs	*Ngoni izinduna*
Ndwandwe	Magalela
Langa	Magangata
Zwide	Hlacwayo
Sikunyane	Zwangendaba

In the central Ngoni kingdom the following was the generally accepted version of the genealogy of the Maseko Paramounts:

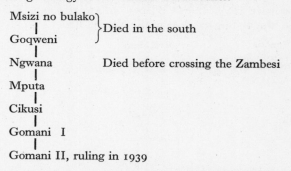

Msizi no bulako ⎤
Goqweni ⎦ Died in the south

Ngwana Died before crossing the Zambesi

Mputa

Cikusi

Gomani I

Gomani II, ruling in 1939

After the death of Ngwana before the crossing of the Zambesi, two of his brothers in turn acted as regents. Also, on the death of Mputa, his brother Cidyawonga acted as regent. In the recital of the Paramount's genealogies, however, the names of the regents were not included.

The succession to the Paramountcy and the role of the regent

It might appear that among a strictly patrilineal people like the Ngoni, where marriage was formalized by exchange of cattle, and where each wife had a recognized position and rank, it would have been easy to formulate rules for the succession to the Paramountcy, and that they would have been followed without deviation. Such had obviously not been the case. It could be argued that the unsettled conditions on the northward journey made it necessary to modify rules of succession in favour of the 'strong man'. Europeans have tried to detect an element of popular choice in the appointment of the *inkosi*, or at least of a popular verdict in favour of or against a proposed candidate. Another element suggested by Ngoni informants was nomination of his heir by the dying Paramount.

There were, however, certain principles which were clear in the accounts given by informants. One was that immediately on the death of a Paramount a regent took charge of the country, of the office of the Paramount, and of the person of the heir elect, and also of the funeral rites of the dead Paramount. The provision for a regency allowed for a period of delay before announcing the successor. There was no 'The king is dead. Long live the king.' The office of the Paramount was clearly in suspense during this interregnum which had been known to last a few days, a few months, or even years—the last in the case of a successor who was a minor. During this period the regent was responsible for carrying on the work of the Paramount, and for consultation with heads of leading clans about the successor. In the past the regent was usually a brother of the dead Paramount. The traditions of the central Ngoni were, as we have seen, that after Ngwana had led them out of the south, he died before crossing the Zambesi. Two of his brothers, Magadlera who died before the Zambesi crossing and Mgoola who died near Domwe, successively acted as regents until Mputa was old enough to enter his father's place. When the time came for the end of the interregnum, it was the regent's responsibility to summon the people and present the heir to them as the new Paramount.

The assumption of authority by a regent and the provision for an interregnum make it clear that the identity of the successor was seldom a foregone conclusion even though the heir-apparent stood with a spear at his father's grave. Among the principles of succession which determined the choice of the new Paramount, one was that he should come from the big house. This could be 'arranged' by adopting him into it if there was no likely heir who had been born there. Another principle was a less easily defined qualification, that of suitability. This was discussed by the regent with the leading clan heads, who took into account the wishes of the late Paramount and the character and personality already displayed by the proposed successor, who had stood by his father's grave. Informants made it clear that responsibility for this selection weighed heavily on the regent and the leading men, for the choice once made was final, the power of the Paramount was very great, the 'medicines' used at his accession set him aside as a person of potential supernatural power, and the prosperity of the country and of everyone in it depended on this decision.

Two famous cases of disputed succession in the past had led to major

divisions of the Ngoni kingdoms. The first occurred in the north on the
death of Zwangendaba, when his brother Ntabeni became regent, and
this dispute revolved round the principle that the heir should come from
the big house. It led to the final split between Mpeseni and Mbelwa, the
setting up of two kingdoms, and the giving of the *'Bayete'* to two Paramounts of the Jere clan. The following account was given by Chief
Mtwalo Jere, son of the Mtwalo mentioned, and he told it to me in his
own village of Ezondweni. It brings out the function and position of the
regent; the relation of 'house' to 'village'; the influence of the popular
verdict on the choice of a successor; the magnanimous attitude of other
possible rivals for the Paramountcy; and the effect of personal quarrels
on a national matter.

¶ Ntabeni went to the house of Munene, the mother of Mbelwa. She
insulted him and would not give him beer. Zwangendaba went to bathe
and when he returned Ntabeni said to him 'I have been insulted by your
wife. She called me "Sutu".' This is a great insult among the Ngoni.[1]
Zwangendaba was very angry, and he took a pan and fried groundnuts,
and said to his wife 'You must take the groundnuts in your hand.' Her
hands were very burnt because the groundnuts were too hot. 'You are
burnt because you must not abuse this your brother-in-law. You are
punished.' Zwangendaba died. Ntabeni was taking care of the country.
He was the right man to put the *inkosi*. He said to Mbelwa: 'You are not
a chief because your mother abused me.' So Mpeseni was *inkosi*, and the
second was Mtwalo. They chased away Mbelwa. When Mpeseni was
elected to be *inkosi* all the people were complaining because they said the
chieftainship should be for the village of Elangeni. The people of Elangeni
and of Ekwendeni did not want Mpeseni as *inkosi*.

Ntabeni died. The people of Elangeni and of Ekwendeni wanted to
fight Ntabeni's people because they were not told of his death, and when
he was buried they were not there. The Ntabeni people went away to
Tanganyika. All the rest left Ufipa and came to Cidlodlo. Mpeseni and
Mperembe stayed there and the rest came to Coma. Then Mperembe
returned from Mpeseni.

Mtwalo said to Mbelwa 'You are the right man to be *inkosi*. I am not the
right man because through jealousy Ntabeni gave the *inkosi* to Mpeseni.'
Then they gave *'Bayete'* to Mbelwa.

Cibambo, whose father was *mlomo wenkosi* (mouthpiece of the chief)
in Ekwendeni for old Mtwalo mentioned above, confirmed this part of
the story of the succession and the role played by Ntabeni as regent. He
also gave in his book [2] the most coherent account of an earlier dispute
about which wife of Zwangendaba was the big wife—a dispute which
illustrated the significance of the house in the succession.

---

[1] Bryant, in *Olden Times in Zululand and Natal*, said (p. 134) that 'Sutu' was an insult
because it meant 'barbarian'—one who had not had his ears pierced according to the
custom of the Zulu.

[2] Cibambo, Y. M. *My Ngoni of Nyasaland*. London, 1942, chaps. V & VI.

A disputed succession in the central kingdom arose over a struggle between Cikusi, the son of the Paramount Mputa, and Cifisi, the son of the regent Cidyawonga who took care of the kingdom after Mputa's death. When the regent died, his son Cifisi claimed the succession and war broke out between the followers of the two claimants. After fighting had continued through two generations of claimants the state under Cifisi seceded and became independent, though the *'Bayete'* was only given to Cikusi and his descendants of Mputa's main line. The following account was given in the royal village of the central kingdom by a former regent assisted by an official reciter of tradition. It related to the succession to Mputa, who died in the Songea district of Tanganyika, and to the defeat of these Ngoni by the followers of Zulu Gama. After this defeat the Ngoni under Cidyawonga returned to the west side of the lake and built on Domwe mountain.

❡ When they burned the body of Mputa, Cidyawonga stood with Cikusi, and that was the sign that Cikusi was still young but was *inkosi*. Cidyawonga was the brother of Mputa. The people told Cidyawonga 'We are in war. You must help us.' They took Cikusi and put him in the big house, because there were no children there.

Cidyawonga was the regent when they built on Domwe. When he was about to die he said to the people 'Now I leave this country in the hands of the owner, because I was only appointed to keep it for him. This is your leader.' He sent for Cikusi and gave him his father's spear, saying to him 'This country is yours.' He said to Cifisi, his own son, 'You my son do not struggle with Cikusi. He is the only Paramount here.' Cidyawonga we did not burn because he had cared for the Paramountcy. And when Cidyawonga died we put Cikusi in his place.

The relation between the regent and the Paramount emerged again from the confusion following the death of Paramount Gomani I in 1896 at the hands of the British. The record in the *Ncheu District Note Book* said that authority was divided between the dead Paramount's brother, Mandala, and NaMlangeni, the mother of Cikusi the former Paramount. After the Portuguese-Nyasaland boundary was fixed dividing the Ngoni territory, the Portuguese entered their section to administer it. NaMlangeni and Mandala resisted their entry and were taken prisoners and died. Meantime a big *mulumuzana* of Paramount Gomani I had acted as regent for his heir who had been placed in the big house. The following account by the treasurer of Gomani II described the situation during the early years of the minority of the Paramount.

❡ Chief Gomani II was born in 1893. The country was destroyed by the Europeans when this child was three years old, and he was taken care of by the big *mulumuzana* of his father, Cakumbira Mpalale Ndau. When the war of the Europeans had finished, they built the village of Lizulu, near Mlanda mountain, where the Dutch mission is today. The child was with them in that village.

When the European Mr. Walker asked the big people whether Gomani I left any children, those big people refused to tell and said 'He did not leave children, they died when they were small.' They feared lest perhaps the Europeans wanted to kill the children too. Mr. Walker (they called him Cipyoza, 'the thing that goes on boring a hole') did not stop asking because he said 'Gomani was my friend and I want to help his children.' On his second journey they revealed to him that there were two children in the village here, and they named the heir Philip Gomani and his younger brother William Gomani who died in 1919. Then Mr. Walker rejoiced. When they brought the children out before his eyes, he gave them gifts which he brought for them, clothes and other things.

The accession of the Paramount and the royal medicines

When the succession of the new Paramount had been decided according to the principles just discussed, the regent had the further responsibility of presenting the new Paramount to the people. This presentation was the act of accession and, as we have seen, it might take place a short time or a longer time after the death of the former Paramount. In describing the accession and the ritual accompanying it, I shall use illustrations from the central kingdom, partly because the material there was more co-ordinated and more complete, especially that relating to the religious and magical significance of the ritual, and also because the unique feature of the 'royal shadow' in relation to the Paramount was, so far as I could tell, peculiar to that area.

The actual accession of the new Paramount had four main elements in it. The first was the decision as to the individual who was to succeed, which was taken by the regent and the senior men. The second was the 'placing' (*kuimika*) of the chosen successor, which was the announcement to the people that he was the Paramount. The third was the instruction by the senior men, and the fourth was the administering of 'medicines' to strengthen the Paramount.

The two following accounts relate to the accession of Gomani I. The first is by Captain Rattray and was included in his collection of Nyanja texts.[1] It was dictated to him by a man who was present at the death and cremation of Cikusi. At the end of this text there is a brief reference to the acknowledgment of the new Paramount:

⁋ They allow three days to pass [after the funeral], and on the fourth every one assembles and the new chief stands at the village court on one leg. One old man steps out and says, 'Do you hear? Your new chief is so and so' (naming him by his clan-animal name). Then everyone shouts '*Bayete*', and the thunder of their shields is heard, and all around is a mass of waving plumes. Then the elders take the 'child', going with him to a hut to give him instruction, saying 'Today you stand alone. Look after

[1] Rattray, R. S. *Some Folklore Stories and Songs in Chinyanja.* London, S.P.C.K. 1907.

your people as did your father before you. If a man be at fault, forgive him; but the sin of adultery cannot be pardoned.'

Habuya Dube, the official 'praiser' of Paramount Gomani II, had been present at the funeral of Cikusi, and he confirmed that the ceremony of accession was as described above and added these further details :

⁋ At the time of the burning of the body of Cikusi, Gomani stood up in the smoke, standing on one leg with a shield in his hand. When all had been consumed by the fire, they began to open the waters and the gravedigger swept the ashes. And they picked up Gomani and went with him to the mound so that he should wash. When these things were over, we left the water to go to the house. We were dancing *ligubo* in the open place and Gomani had a headdress of *luve* [1] feathers on his head. And they followed him into the house, but all the people were dancing *ligubo* in the *bwalo* for a whole month. When the mourning was over, Bvumbwe Maseko said 'Now let us establish (*tiimike*) our chief.' So he was established.

The 'standing on one leg' referred to in both texts is the position adopted by other East and South-east African people when resting supported by the spear, with one foot flat against the other knee and the shield in front of the body. Other men inheriting their father's position stood at the grave holding a spear, but only those of the Maseko clan, succeeding the Paramount in the direct line, adopted the position of standing on one leg. 'Placing' or establishing the Paramount was done before a large gathering of people with the warriors in full war-dress, described graphically in terms of the waving head-plumes and the thunder of the shields. It was evident that all discussion of who would or would not be a suitable Paramount went on within the closed circle of the regent and the senior men, and the people were presented with the chosen Paramount whom they acclaimed.

The instruction by the senior men was a reminder to the new Paramount that, though his new powers were extensive and unique in their authority, he should not act like a cruel despot. There are references in the *Ncheu District Note Book* [2] to the passing-over of an elder brother of Gomani I on the grounds that he was of a fierce and cruel disposition, though, according to Ngoni informants, this man Mandala was a younger brother of Cikusi and an uncle of Gomani, and thus was not eligible to be Paramount. In discussing the type of man who was considered suitable to be Paramount, Ngoni informants always laid stress on the need for him not to be fierce and cruel. This pointed to an ideal type of Paramount and did not agree with European accounts of large-scale poison ordeals at Cikusi's court. The instruction to the new Paramount

[1] Feathers worn only by the Paramount. [2] *Ncheu District Note Book.* 1891.

N.N.—E

so briefly referred to was in the nature of a warning that the kingdom
must be held together and certain Ngoni customs and institutions preserved. This general mandate to a new Paramount was in keeping with
the Ngoni policy of maintaining order and justice within the kingdom,
while showing all the aggressive qualities of warfare against external
enemies.

In the story of their northward trek, the division of authority among
the central Ngoni between the Maseko and the Phungwako clans was
referred to as the Maseko taking the '*Bayete*' and the Phungwako taking
the *tonga*.[1] In central Ngoniland the *tonga* was a collective name given
to royal medicines used at different times for different purposes and was
not reserved for the medicine used in the army as in the northern kingdom. It was said to have been 'from the beginning in the south'; 'it is
very old, ever since people were born'. The following description was
given by a member of the Phungwako clan in the head village of Chief
Kacere:

❡ The Ngoni had protection for all their people of the most powerful
kind. This was the *tonga*. This was specially to protect the Paramount at
his accession. When the Ngoni were thus accustomed to being protected
by the *tonga*, there was one thing which gave them protection above all
others. If the Paramount died, in arranging matters, the *tonga* was
essential in establishing the new Paramount. And if war had to be made,
the *tonga* also gave protection so that they had strength to overcome their
enemies.

Also when the Ngoni were travelling in wild places and did not find
somewhere to stay, they began to listen to the *tonga*. The diviner, who
went ahead with the *tonga*, looked to see if there were bad omens. When
they found a place to stay and stayed there with their cattle, they were
protected by the *tonga*, so that they were not afraid of anything. They
just conquered the country and took the cattle and made the people
surrender.

When getting ready the *tonga*, they could only do it with a sheep. They
killed it, and took its blood and its fat and smeared the *tonga*. And the
big people who were set aside for the work of the *tonga*, it was they who
were doing these things. The meat of the sheep which was killed for the
tonga, they did not eat it just anyhow, no. They were eating it in a
special way, not in the house, no; nor with the women, no; but in a very
different way from the meat of every day. They ate it without being
greedy when it was divided, and they took care not to put some aside,
for they feared lest someone should eat the *tonga*. They just ate to finish
it quickly, and when they had finished they did not sleep in their houses
with their wives, but they went apart and slept in the place where this
was done for the *tonga*. Their sleeping was different from other days, for
they did not sleep on good mats, no. When they had eaten meat for the
tonga they changed their ways, to act differently from usual. Instead of

---

[1] The head of the Phungwako clan, Chief Kacere, ruled one of the Ngoni states in the
Dedza district which, in the 1930's, was separate from the central Ngoni kingdom.

sleeping on mats they slept on grass until the required days were finished, and they scattered to their homes.

This account brings out certain elements in the ritual surrounding the *tonga*. The word *tonga* in the Ngoni language means 'rod', and was used in the very ancient folk tale *Intonga yetusi*, 'The Brass Rod'. There was no rod, however, nor anything representing one, among the medicines or ingredients which together made up the *tonga*. A descendant of one of the early 'guardians' of the *tonga* said about it:

❦ The *tonga* is the horn of a sheep, and the horn by itself has no real power, but there are other things which give it power like the rib of a lion.

It is clear that in the past the *tonga* was regarded as giving protection to the Ngoni people, particularly by providing medicine at the accession of a new Paramount when he needed medicine for strengthening.

Other informants from the Phungwako clan said that the *tonga* provided the medicine with which the Paramount washed at the time of *incwala*, the feast of the first-fruits. No one alive in the 1930's had seen that ceremony and the special songs had been forgotten. A tradition remained that the Paramount had to undergo seclusion and ritual washing with medicines before the first green crops could be eaten.

Throughout the references to the *tonga* there was no hint that it was ever worshipped or addressed in any way similar to the invocations to the ancestor spirits. It was clearly a 'medicine' possessing great power and guarded as a national treasure. The ingredients of the medicine were kept in a particular way, in a particular place, in the guardianship of a particular person. I have seen the ingredients, the place and the guardian, but I gave a promise not to reveal them. I was allowed to handle the objects and, after doing so, I had to perform the ritual act of washing my hands with cowdung. This was the form of ritual cleansing practised by the Paramount after using the medicines.

There were two ways in which these medicines were used by the Paramount to strengthen him on his accession. He washed in the kraal with the medicines whipped into a foam. The old men said that in ancient times the water for making the medicines had to be fetched from the sea. In addition to washing he had to eat meat in which the medicines were mixed. The majority of informants said that beef was used for this ritual eating, while others said that, as in the ritual for preparing the *tonga*, the meat taken was sheep. This ritual was said to have taken place for the last time at the death of Cikusi and the accession of Gomani I, though it was hinted that it had been performed at the accession of the Ngoni chief of the Maseko clan now living in Portuguese territory.

It was clear that the Maseko Paramounts made use of the *tonga* as a royal medicine both at their accession and in time of war. The reference to its use at the *incwala* ceremony and dance was a reminder of the former belief in the close connexion between the health and strength of the Paramount and the fertility of the land and its crops, a belief which had its counterpart in the cremation of the Paramount and the sweeping of the ashes into the river to fertilize the land.

The *incwala*, or ceremony of the first-fruits, was of great importance among the Swazi, and the Ngoni 'took it with them' when they left the south. Among the northern and central Ngoni the tradition of the ceremony remained, but the practice was given up before the kingdoms were finally established. Cibambo collected from the old men in the northern kingdom the following account of what took place at the *incwala*:

❲ Among the dances of the Ngoni, *ngoma, umsindo, ligubo, incwala* was the best and most important. They say it lasted about two weeks, or if it began when the moon was full until it became new again. When they said '*incwala* is closed', no one sings or dances it again; when it begins everyone sings the songs of *incwala* and no others. This dance belonged to the Paramount of the whole country. A description of *incwala* is difficult because it was given up long ago. Even the old people of today have never seen it.

It began in the middle of the month of *Intokoni* (January). Young men were sent to look for ripe food in the gardens by streams. The owners had not picked any nor was much of the crop nearly ready. They took some juicy stalks of maize, and pumpkins with their roots. They also looked for a wild fruit like a gourd, very bitter, which some people use to stir up their dogs to make them fierce in hunting and quick in scent. This fruit the Ngoni call *igumuzo*. These they mix with medicines and the *inkosi* eats it without the people knowing. The belief was that if the Paramount ate the first-fruits carelessly, or if the people were the first to taste the first-fruits of the year, there would be disaster for the *inkosi* and the country. After a month, when the crops were ripening, the *incwala* began, the crops not being completely ripe and no one having yet tasted the new crops.

In the month of February the *inkosi* announced that everywhere the *incwala ye'nkosi* should begin on such-and-such a day. Quickly much beer was cooked in all the villages by everyone. On the day the beer-making began, the dance began also. The word was sent round everywhere: *incwala seigwabuliwe*, '*incwala* is now opened'. All the people went to the central village of Elangeni, the village of Hlacwayo. They took crops which had been planted in December, *impala*, and added the first *igumuzo* fruit to them. Great crowds of people gathered at Elangeni and danced. Many were in the kraal but many more were dancing outside. All were dressed carefully. They danced with reeds in their hands or with the sticks of their shields. It seemed as though the song everywhere was the same. Women going for wood and water, and children and youths, wherever they went, the song was on their lips. In dancing the women were by themselves, and the men by themselves. They faced each other in the dance. They were bending their bodies backwards and forwards, and moving their necks and shoulders.

The *inkosi* was all this time as if he were mourning and fasting. He was in the house. His body was painted with medicines, black, red and white; and round his loins was painted with black medicine. He was kept naked except for the cover of his foreskin. They fed him with the first-fruits mixed with medicines. They said that both the Paramount and all the people were fasting and under discipline at that time.

When the time for closing the *incwala* came, they again took the fruit *igumuzo* and threw it in among the dancers and called out '*incwala seimbonyiwe*', 'the *incwala* is closed'. Then the people began to separate and to go home, still with the songs on their lips, and on the way cutting juicy stalks of new maize and picking leaves of pumpkins, which meant that the new crops were set free.

These two fragments of the old *incwala* songs, which, like the war songs, were full of 'sounds' like *zi zi*, *ozi ya*, were the only ones preserved. They were known only by one or two old men among the northern and central Ngoni.

> 1. He comes the one who hates the chief.
>   Did you not see him?
>   You have seen him.

> 2. You who are rejected
>   They are carrying him lightly
>   To thrash him
>   He, the stiff-necked one.

The Royal Shadow

The special relationship between a new *inkosi* of the Maseko clan and a member of the Ngozo clan was personal and individual. I have translated it as 'royal shadow', since in discussing the relationship with leading members of the Ngozo, Nzunga and Phungwako clans the word *mtunzi* was the one most frequently used. *Mtunzi* is the term used for the shadow of a person or object cast by the sun; also for shade from the sun; also in modern phraseology for a photograph, when it is generally used in its double form, *mtunzitunzi*. In the descriptions of this relationship there seemed almost a reluctance to use a definite term. The informants kept on saying that the Ngozo boy was *monga mtunzi*, like a shadow. While they enumerated the many things he did *with* the Paramount, they avoided giving him or his relationship any specific name.

This relationship began at the accession of a new Paramount and lasted until his death when the Ngozo man leaped on to the funeral pyre, and it was marked by certain special features. On the death of the old Paramount, and before the new Paramount was given the medicine for strengthening him, a boy of the Ngozo clan was sent 'to enter the chieftainship' with the Paramount. Many cattle from the herd belonging to the big house were given to the Ngozo family from whom the boy came, 'to quieten them'. Thereafter this Ngozo boy did everything with the Paramount. He began by washing with the royal medicine at the time of the accession. He drank beer with him, he ate with him, he 'stood with him' (*amaima naye*) on all important occasions, such as sending out the army and judging cases. He slept in his own hut which was in the *cigodlo*, where the Paramount's sons built, and when he married he built huts for his wives in that same section of the royal village. At the death of the Paramount, he danced the war-dance in full war-dress and leaped on to the pyre to perish with the dead Paramount in the flames.

Informants sometimes said of this Ngozo boy that he was 'of one blood' with the Maseko clan. They described the relationship between the two clans as that of *cibale*, brotherhood, which excluded all possibility of inter-marriage. Between the Paramount and the Ngozo boy was established a joking relationship, so that the Ngozo boy could say 'good and bad things to the Paramount'.

It was clear that the ritual and social aspects of this relationship complemented and supported each other. The recurrent emphasis on the taking of medicine at the accession, on the participation in the war medicines, and most of all on the death on the Paramount's funeral pyre, were all evidence of this ritual relationship. Informants repudiated any idea of a scapegoat which involved protecting the Paramount from poison by eating before him. They reiterated several times that the Ngozo boy did not eat *before* the Paramount; in fact he ate after him though sharing his food dishes. Surrounding the Paramount were other boys called *micetho*, who performed the duties of pages or personal servants. The Ngozo boy was always distinct from them, and the distinction lay in the combined ritual and social relationship.

The concept of a 'shadow' was of something very close to a person, almost indistinguishable from the person himself. In referring to the Ngozo boy in the terms 'he was as the shadow of the *inkosi*; he was as himself', informants emphasized the extreme closeness of the tie between the two men. It seemed as if the royal shadow existed to meet a need for strengthening the Paramount by giving him a second self. It emphasized also the dangerous sphere of life and action in which the Paramount lived, due to the medicines he had used, his powers to protect the land and its fertility, and his power to give strength to the army through the use of the *tonga* medicine. No one else in the royal family shared these dangers and there was inherent in the relationship of royal shadow to *inkosi* the sense of some security through a companionship where protective medicines were shared as well as the hazardous occasions for which they gave protection.

This intense and dangerous ritual relationship was buttressed by the social ties binding the Ngozo boy to the Paramount. We have seen that between them as individuals there was that freedom of a joking relationship, described in terms of brotherhood, and this brotherhood was further emphasized by the ban on inter-marriage between the Ngozo and Maseko clans. The significance of the Ngozo boy, when he became a man, building in the *cigodlo* where the Paramount's sons built, was often stressed by informants. Though his huts were in this *cigodlo* section of the royal village, as if he were a son of the Paramount's family, the Paramount never said 'child' to him but invariably 'brother'.

In all the occasions of daily life, as well as in those of special ritual significance, the Ngozo boy stood or sat next to the Paramount. The Ngoni insisted that the status of a man or woman should be expressed in terms of sitting or standing in order of precedence. Sitting or standing next to the Paramount implied that that individual had the highest possible social status. The leading members of the Ngozo clan in their villages displayed an awareness of their social prestige which was very noticeable. This high rank was, however, in the past bought with a price —that of sharing in the dangers of the Paramountcy. This was acknowledged through the gift of cattle to the boy's family, sent at the time when he 'entered the chieftainship' with the Paramount.

The institution of the royal shadow came to an end with the advent of the Europeans. An Ngozo man acted as a royal shadow on the accession of Cikusi but did not die on his funeral pyre. When Cikusi's son Gomani I was installed as *inkosi*, an Ngozo boy 'entered the chieftainship' with him and stood with him 'in the smoke of the *tonga*' when the army went to war. It was this Gomani I who was killed by the British, and there was no royal ritual at this death, and no cremation in a stream in which the Ngozo boy could share. The royal shadow retired in those troubled days to his father's village, where he died in 1937. It was alleged that no Ngozo man stood in this relationship to Gomani II, either at his accession, which took place during the period of Direct Rule, or in 1933 when his Paramount Chieftaincy was recognized. Informants showed a certain hesitation in answering direct questions on this topic, which was attributable partly to the fact that the Paramount was a Christian, and partly to a reluctance to discuss the continued use of 'royal medicines'. The following account of the royal shadow was given by informants of the Nzunga and Ngozo clans.

℀ When the Paramount entered the chieftainship he stood with a man from the Ngozo clan. The Ngozo people are of one blood with the Paramount, because they stand together when entering the chieftainship. When the Paramount of the Maseko dies, he dies together with one of the Ngozo. It was so when there died Ngwana, Mputa, Cikusi.

When the Ngoni came into this country they stopped killing an Ngozo man when the Paramount died. When the Paramount died a young man of the Ngozo clan just stood beside the body of the Paramount, and when making the funeral pyre of the Paramount, he also was there until they set fire to it. If anyone wanted to kill an Ngozo man by the water and the pyre, he was refusing, saying 'No, not in these days, but formerly.'

When Magona Ngozo was with Cikusi he was staying with him in the daytime. Magona had his own huts and Cikusi his. When eating, Cikusi ate alone, but afterwards he gave food to Magona. When Cikusi was washing it was together with Magona. When he went to the bush, they went together. When Cikusi was washing with the *tonga*, he was doing it with Magona. When the warriors were going out, Cikusi and Magona stood together, and they made fire for the medicines and they stood together in the smoke and then the warriors went out. So, when mentioning Magona, they said: 'the shadow of Cikusi'. When they were eating in the *bwalo*, the *nsima* (porridge) was brought to Cikusi, but if some *alumuzana* came, the wives of Magona cooked *nsima* and gave it to the *alumuzana*. When Cikusi died, Magona could take his wives if he wanted. The Ngozo man could tell the Paramount anything, good or bad, and stay like the mouth of the Paramount.

When the Paramount died formerly, the Ngozo man dressed in his war-dress. When he came near the fire he danced with the shield in his hand. When the fire blazed up he ran and jumped on the fire. So the Maseko people gave cattle to the Ngozo people, to quieten their hearts because they were brothers. And when another Paramount was installed they gave an Ngozo man to stand with him. The father of the man who died with the Paramount received cattle and villages to rule over and gifts. The Paramounts gave cattle because they said: 'Since our brother is going to stand with the Paramount, if that Paramount dies, he also will be killed, so the Paramount ought to give cattle like *lobola* so they may quieten the hearts of his brothers.' Though these cattle are not given for a woman but for a man, any Maseko man ought not to marry an Ngozo woman because there is this brotherhood.

And this man of the Ngozo clan was like a chief because he had men to manage his affairs at his door, as did the Paramount. And if he died his funeral was like that of a chief. But the day the Paramount died the Ngozo man was killed. When the Paramount washed with medicines, he was washing with the Ngozo man. When drinking beer, he was drinking in the same hut as the Paramount. When the Paramount was sacrificing he was together with the Ngozo man, and they did not leave each other.

The Ngozo people have a thanking name (*isibongo*) Maphonya. It is they who were standing with the Paramounts, and the Ngozo people were in the section of Ziyembe. Their avoidances were the same as all the Ngoni, especially fish and elephant. When Cikusi died Gulo stood with Gomani when he entered the chieftainship. Gulo was the son of Magona.

The royal village and the daily routine of the Paramount

In Part I, Chapter II we referred to the process by which each Paramount, after his accession, went out from his father's village to build his own. The Ngoni called this *ukupumisa inkosi* (to send out the Paramount) and the term used for the new village, *lusungulu* (the needle), was said to signify 'the front village where you expect to find the Paramount'.

Dr. Kuper described the Swazi king making his own capital, but referred also to the existence of several royal villages where the wives of the reigning king lived.[1] The Ngoni system of one royal village which went out from the former royal village resulted in a series of social groups, based on residence, which were related to past Paramounts and their widows and to present Paramounts and their wives. The diagram in Chapter III of Part I shows a very much simplified form of the component parts of a new royal village and their relationship illustrated by the siting of the huts.

The following text was given by an elderly widow of a grandson of Zwangendaba, in the head village of Chief Mperembe in the northern kingdom.

❡ When a new village, *lusungulu*, was built the *indlunkulu* was first erected and then followed all the other huts of the *inkosi* in order. Those huts which belonged to the *indlunkulu* took the right-hand side facing the kraal. The second house took the left-hand side, and all huts belonging to this one followed it. Such huts could be counted as belonging to the *indlunkulu* and the second house by the cattle that were taken from such houses. To marry a new wife, if the *inkosi* took cattle from the right-hand house that new wife would belong there. All the huts of each house of the *inkosi* were built at the back of the hut of the owner of that house.

When erecting huts, those of the *izinduna* came next and were built next to those of the *inkosi*. After that they built their own according to their *izigawa* or divisions.

All the huts at the back of the *indlunkulu* and behind the other huts were called *cigodlo*. Huts near the gate of the kraal at the left were called *kwa cikulu*.

This text brings out the fact that each new royal village had three main elements in it: the mothers of the Paramount, his wives, and the *izinduna* and their families. The Paramount was always accompanied to his new village by one or more wives of his father, *ukulondolosa mntwana* (to keep the son). One of these was usually his own mother and she occupied the *indlunkulu*. The text points out that the big wife of the Paramount was on the right of the *indlunkulu*, and closely associated with its owner, the Paramount's mother.

There was no fixed rule for the number of *izinduna* in charge of the houses of the Paramount's mothers and wives. When the Ngoni kingdoms were established in Nyasaland, the royal villages were very large and the divisions of the village, called in the text *izigawa*, were small hamlets. Each division was generally identified with a house, and in that case the *induna* in charge of the house was also in charge of the division. The original composition of royal villages could only be reconstructed by tracing the relationships of separate villages in the 1930's to their former parent village. This will be illustrated in the next chapter on the

[1] Kuper, H. op. cit. p. 41.

royal women. In the royal villages in the 1930's there was one big *induna* and several lesser ones whose position and functions will be described in Chapter IV.

This 'going out' of the new Paramount's village, leaving the former Paramount's village as the *gogo* village, brought about some re-distribution of authority, prestige and material goods. It gave the new Paramount his own village, always to be known as his, even after his death. His village became the focal meeting-place for the territory and for the court and territorial officials who surrounded the Paramount; and it was to the new royal village that the *alumuzana* in pre-European days came frequently to visit the Paramount and report to him on conditions in their areas. His moving out of the *gogo* village, on the other hand, gave his brothers who stayed there, and especially those of the *gogo* house, more freedom and authority within that village as well as responsibility for the conduct of all ritual matters relating to the kingdom. The Paramount's big wife had to take her place as the leading woman in the new village and to order the affairs of the wives attached to her house in consultation with the Paramount's mother. Cattle, beer and food for the royal household became the concern of the new village, and the *izinduna* and the royal women had to plan and manage the economy of a capital where political interests converged and where visitors and hangers-on were constantly turning up.

The following text by Chief Mtwalo Jere in Mzimba district, helped by Cibambo's older brother, describes the daily routine of the Paramount and his royal village as they had known it in their youth before the coming of the Europeans:

❦ The *inkosi* had to wash very early before the people came to see him. The *ingceko* was the servant who took care of washing the *inkosi*. He had to go with the *inkosi* to the bush and hide the faeces to prevent any bad person from getting the faeces. The *ingceko* was anyone whom the *inkosi* called for this, and must be one who walks well with the *inkosi*.

Before leaving his house to go to the kraal the *inkosi* had to eat a little porridge. When he went to the kraal a calabash of beer was brought to him. When any beer was brought to the *inkosi*, the *ingceko* tasted it first to see if it was good. The *inkosi* asked 'Is it good beer?' and the *ingceko* said 'Yes *inkosi*' and gave it to the *inkosi* to drink. When the *inkosi* took snuff the big *alumuzana* could beg from him. The other *amadoda* could only touch their noses. Then the *inkosi* knew they were begging snuff from him. Where the *inkosi* sat a mat was spread, and on it was laid a leopard- or a lion-skin. This was called 'the chair of the *inkosi*'. On arrival the big *alumuzana* went straight into the kraal to where the *inkosi* sat and greeted him '*Bayete*', and sat down in front of him.

The *inkosi* could not eat porridge except that cooked by his own wives. In his own hut he ate alone with one wife to serve him. His mothers also came with food every day. He ate twice in his own hut, early and late, and once in the kraal. When he ate in the kraal all could see him. He could not eat so much as other people. He must leave enough for others or he would be ashamed. He would take a few lumps of porridge from one wooden dish (*ingcwembe*) and then hand the other dishes to those around him. Each day one beast had to be killed from the house of each wife of the *inkosi* in turn. It was their food and they could not cease killing. The *inkosi* had his own great garden. After hoeing the *induna* of the *indlunkulu* called all the village people to come and plant these gardens first before their own. They did this because if a man was hungry, he went to the *inkosi* and said 'I am hungry' and he was given food to eat.

In this account it is clear that the daily life of the Paramount had both private and public aspects. In private he was vulnerable to attacks from enemies. Hence he depended on the services of a trusted attendant to see that no sorcerers could make bad magic from his excreta; and he ate no food except that prepared by his own wives and mothers. On the other hand, in public he appeared as the generous and ceremonious ruler, providing food, beer and snuff for his visitors, and himself practising that restraint in eating which was characteristic of Ngoni good manners both from host and guest.

In addition to the daily routine of sharing food with his immediate entourage and chance visitors, the Paramount had special feasts known as *izipheko*. These feasts, as described by Cibambo, were related to the bringing of tribute, thus emphasizing the reciprocal nature of the gifts passing between the people and the Paramount.

❢ Along with the tribute the *inkosi* had his feasts with which he wanted to feed his people. At an appointed time the *inkosi* and his wives and mothers prepared beer and three or four beasts for his men and women. Men ate their meat in the kraal but the women at the *indlunkulu*. All the people thanked him everywhere, including the women, and the men were thanking with dancing. Even although people were not called by the *inkosi*, yet many people came to his village to beg food from the *inkosi*. Also by telling the *izinduna* the *inkosi* would invite people to eat with him, and many would come from far away. The wives of the *inkosi* and his mothers were cooking soft or hard porridge, with different *imbido* (relishes) so that the *inkosi* could give them to his people. They would all be waiting in the kraal. A generous *inkosi* liked to stay in the kraal so that his food should be sent there in order to feed both notable people and poor people. He would be watching whom to give food to.

In this way although there was tribute (*imitulo*), it was not very burdensome. People did not complain to the *inkosi* about it. It was as if they were playing, because of the dancing. Those who had no wealth came to the *inkosi* and begged him to help them. The *inkosi* gave cattle to these people without asking them to pay again, because he said 'The people and the cattle, they are all mine. They are eating each other.'

There was an apparent contradiction here. On the one hand there was true reciprocity, that of the people who brought tribute or gifts and in turn were invited to eat with the Paramount or summoned to special feasts. On the other hand there were people who seemed to have nothing, and who came in the hope of getting invited to eat food if they just sat in the kraal and looked hungry. Cibambo called them 'the notable people' and 'the poor people'. This contrast in behaviour ran right through Ngoni society and reflected the social standing of individuals who behaved in such different ways. There was a good deal of cadging for gifts and of gate-crashing at feasts on the part of people who had no intention, or no possibility, of making any adequate return. An Ngoni proverb illustrated the public attitude to reciprocal giving as distinct from begging: 'To say: Give, give, is to snatch. The child of a free man only gives.'

The bringing of tribute to the Paramount was only one aspect of the reciprocal relationships which ran right through Ngoni society, namely the bringing of gifts by a man in an inferior social position to his superior, with the expectation of receiving food or favour and of standing well with this superior. It was recognized that tribute was of two kinds, one of which was voluntary. If a *mulumuzana* or other notable wanted to please the Paramount he brought him presents—grain, flour, meat, beer. It was always emphasized that this was a free gift, with the added proviso that the giver wished to keep on good terms with the Paramount. Ngoni informants declared that the only compulsory form of tribute in pre-European days was that whenever a lion or a leopard was killed it had to be brought to the royal village through a succession of intermediaries, as described below.

These two principles of free giving and compulsory giving, and the attitudes engendered, are compared with the feeling about compulsory taxes under European rule in this text by Cibambo.

❡ Although people hate giving taxes to strangers in this land, yet tribute (*imitulo*) was given to their *inkosi* and to other chiefs. Such tribute was given in an indirect way, that is the *izinduna* did not mark out those who gave and who did not give tribute. The Ngoni did not wish that every male should give tribute as is done by Europeans today. They were just pleased if the village headman or *mulumuzana* had given something even though other people in his village did not give anything. Even the *alumuzana* themselves gave something at the time they thought it was convenient to themselves to give. There was no fixed time of the month or year. Much that was given as tribute was beer, meat, ivory, hoes and cloth, also cattle, sheep and goats after raids, and other loot from war.

Power to 'eat' (*ukudla*) lion- and leopard-skins was given to certain people of the Swazi clans, but all the rest were obliged to bring them in. The lion- or leopard-skin had to be given first to the village headman. He went with it to the chief or *mulumuzana*. This one brought it to the *inkosi* along with his *amadoda* or *amajaha* of all his villages, the older men and younger men. This was like going as warriors and they went with dancing (*ligubo*). The one who first stabbed the animal was pointed out, and the second and third, and the finisher, at the place of dancing in the kraal. At such times each one when called rose and danced *umgiya*, repeating his names. This was called *ukubika izinkalipi*, reporting the heroes or the fierce ones. This is still being done today. The *inkosi* thanked the people who brought the skins by giving them a beast or a goat. When they were dressing the meat and eating it, they kept on dancing *ligubo* and crying the war-cry. At such times the women went along with the men to help them dance *ligubo*. They made the responses to the songs and jerked their necks.

All such things the *inkosi* divided among his houses. The big house had a big share, but especially his mother's house. She should have most. Even if his real mother was dead, the big share had to go there, to her house, where her successor lived.

Visits to the Paramount, whether for a particular occasion or as a matter of routine, were hedged about with ceremonial. It was expected that *alumuzana* and other important people who lived near enough would visit the Paramount frequently and, according to some informants, they went every day in pre-European times.

No one could approach the Paramount except through one of the *izinduna* of the royal village, and the correct person to approach was the *induna* of the *indlunkulu*. Visitors were expected to wait at the gate of the kraal and put down their spears. When they were brought by the *induna* to the Paramount, they greeted him with '*Bayete*'. Then they sat down and the Paramount told the *induna* to greet them, and they replied '*Yebo, inkosi*'. This custom of indirect approach to the Paramount has been maintained. Early travellers in Nyasaland spoke of observing it, and when I was there it was considered outrageous manners on the part of any European if he penetrated immediately to the presence of the Paramount, without going through the accustomed channels.

The Paramount was both greeted and thanked for gifts of food, beer or snuff, with '*Bayete*'. If he moved from the kraal, all present said '*Bayete*'. If anyone had to leave his presence, he crouched low and murmured '*Bayete*' as he went out. Cibambo described this punctilious formality of thanking for gifts in the Ngoni manner.

❡ When receiving presents the Ngoni thanked the giver by taking them with two hands, even though it was a small present. Afterwards they thanked the giver by his *isibongo*, clan name, openly. They said that receiving a thing with one hand showed that you derided it and did not put any value on it. When receiving a present from bigger people or from a chief, some words of respect were added to the *isibongo*, such as '*Baba*', '*Nkosi yami*', '*E-Jere*'. Often the receiver if he was much pleased with the present added some *izitokozo* to the clan name, if he knew them. Those near him or some further away helped the receiver by thanking loudly after him. If what he received was food, he thanked at the beginning, and after eating the food he thanked again. If such a present of food was given to a body of people, the leader in the company first led the others in thanking, and then all thundered the thanking together. This included all the rest who were in the neighbourhood though they did not take part in the food or the present. The leader would first thank '*E-Jere*' and then all would follow together, '*E-Jere*', or the clan name of the one who was the giver. The Paramount, if he gave presents to the people, was not thanked by his clan name as other people. He was thanked by '*Bayete*' as was done when saluting him. Likewise those who received the title *Nkomo* were thanked by that title when they gave presents to people.

On ceremonial occasions, visitors to the royal village heard the *izibongo* or praise-songs of the Paramount. These were songs referring to great deeds and notable incidents both in the lifetime of the reigning Paramount and in the lives of his predecessors. They were distinct from the *izitokozo*, which were honorific epithets added to the clan name and spoken when thanking a well-known man or woman for their gifts. The *izitokozo* could be said by anyone, since each person of note had his own which were well known. The *izibongo* could only be spoken or sung by an *umbongi* or official 'praiser'. Such a person was a man of good memory and possessing eloquence. The chest was thought to be the seat of wisdom and eloquence, and a man who composed praise-songs, as distinct from repeating well-known ones, had to have the faculty of finding the right words, since new songs of this kind were generally invented on a sudden inspiration.

The occasions when the praise-songs were recited were when important visitors came to the royal village; when beasts were slaughtered in the ancestor cult; at special dances at the royal village or at the feasts of the Paramount. On such occasions the official praiser stood up in the kraal, everyone kept silence and did not move, and after a pause he began to call out '*Bayabonga inkosi*', 'let us praise the Paramount'. In repeating the praise-songs he began with those of the immediate ancestor of the Paramount, and then went on to those of earlier ancestors. At the end he shouted '*Bayete*' and all the people replied '*Bayete*'. Examples of the praise-songs of Zwangendaba and his father Hlacwayo of the northern kingdom and of Ngwana, father of Mputa, of the central Ngoni kingdom are given at the end of the chapter.

The tension caused by the extreme formality in the behaviour of the Paramount, his courtiers and his visitors was lightened by the presence of a court jester. Informants were agreed that such an individual was usually present to amuse the Paramount with his sallies and gestures and clown-like tumbling about. Dr. Laws referred to such a jester at the court of Mbelwa I when the Livingstonia Mission was making its first settlement in northern Ngoniland.[1] I saw a jester who came with Paramount Zintambira Maseko from Portuguese territory when he and his officials visited Mcakhatha for the war-dance at the mourning for Bambo

[1] Livingstone, W. P. *Laws of Livingstonia*. London, Hodder & Stoughton, 1921, p. 200.

Manga. It was a time of great emotional tension and strain, and the absurdities of the jester relieved the solemnity and formality of the visit. This jester was said by informants to be a man of the Moyo clan, who owed his position not to hereditary right but to a ready and witty tongue.

The death of the Paramount

It is in the ceremonies at the death of the Paramount that we find some major differences between the traditional practices of the northern and central Ngoni peoples, which might be attributed to the separate groups in Natal from which they came. I was living in Mcakatha village in the central kingdom at the time of the sickness and death of Bambo Manga, the most important of the royal women among the central Ngoni. The ritual ceremonies at her funeral were said to be almost identical with those at the death of the Paramount, and I was able to check details of similarity and difference with old men who remembered the death of Cikusi, the last Ngoni Paramount in the central kingdom for whom the full ritual was carried out. I was not able after that to pursue further possible parallels and differences among the northern Ngoni. My general impression from informants was that among the northern Ngoni the ritual at the death of a Paramount differed from that of any other prominent man only in certain details of the period and form of mourning. Among the central Ngoni, as Rattray said in a note on the text which will be given, 'such funerals were more of a military pageant than anything else. All outward signs of grief were rigorously excluded.' I can confirm that from my observations at the death of Bambo Manga.

When the Paramount became ill, a diviner was called to give advice. He might advise that a sacrifice should be made to the ancestor spirits. He might suggest witchcraft as the cause of illness. He might advise calling in a man to give medicine to the Paramount. When, in spite of sacrifices and treatment, the Paramount died, the announcement was made from the edge of his village: *Izulu lidilikile*, 'the heaven has fallen down'. Messengers were sent to all the chiefs and to all the *alumuzana* and other leading men. From the edge of each central village the cry was made, and each chief and *mulumuzana* sent his messengers to make the same announcement in each of the villages under him.

Among the northern Ngoni the actual ceremony of burial does not appear to have been very different from that of any other important man, with one exception, that the Paramount, like other ruling Jere chiefs, was buried at the edge of the cattle kraal in a circular pit of the kind used when digging clay for mudding houses, on one side of which there was a niche where the corpse was placed in a sitting position, facing south-east. This burying in a circular grave on the edge of the kraal was the procedure which I witnessed at the burial of Bambo Manga among the central Ngoni (see below p. 75).

Dr. Steele, one of the early medical missionaries in northern Ngoniland, was present at the burial of Mbelwa I and left an account of it which is quoted by Dr. Elmslie.[1] He spoke of the great crowds of men coming to mourn armed with spears and shields, and some with guns. They came in companies, as if they were the military bands coming for mobilization from the head villages. They marched first with their shields held high over their heads, and then laid them down and clasped their hands behind their heads, advancing towards and retreating from the grave and keeping up a continuous mourning cry of 'Baba be'. Three days elapsed between the death and the burial. During that time two graves were dug, in order that all the Paramount's possessions might be buried with him or beside him. When the graves were ready, the kraal was cleared of all but the married men who had the head-ring. Meantime the wives of the Paramount, carrying his shields, were advancing towards the grave and retreating, a few steps at a time. They finally went back to their houses, dressed themselves in skins, and returned in single file on their hands and knees. They withdrew as the corpse was brought out and placed in the grave, and other women came with the Paramount's possessions, such as pipes, wooden head-rests and shields, and all were put into the graves. The men stood in circles round the graves with their shields over their heads.

Among the central Ngoni Rattray recorded an account of the funeral rites of Cikusi in 1891, which I was able to check with more than one old man who had been present. There was also the funeral of Bambo Manga which I witnessed in 1937, where the ritual followed was identical with that described by the old men for the Paramount Cikusi, with one exception: that her possessions but not her body were cremated by a stream.

The chief differences between the northern and central Ngoni in the funeral rites at the death of the Paramount were that the central Ngoni Paramounts of the Maseko clan were cremated and not buried, and there was no public mourning, but instead a series of war-dances. There were two other distinctive features among the central Ngoni: formerly the individual known as the 'royal shadow' died with the Paramount; and from the time of the actual death to the time of the cremation there was a period of licence and lawlessness called ciponde. This latter phenomenon may have existed among the northern Ngoni, but I did not ask about it specifically when I was there, and I did not hear it referred to. I was made aware of it forcibly at the death of Bambo Manga when my cook and houseboy immediately dumped all their possessions in my hut as the only safe place during the time of ciponde. Rattray's account of the death of Cikusi also mentioned this practice.

In the traditions of the central Ngoni it was recorded that only the Maseko Paramounts in the direct line were cremated, and not the

[1] Elmslie, W. A. op. cit. p. 270.

brothers of the dead Paramount who acted as regents. Thus Ngwana was cremated in Ulozi before crossing the Zambesi, and Mputa was cremated in the river Lichiningo in Songea in Tanganyika. This was confirmed by an informant of the Gama clan who were for a time under the central Ngoni Paramount in Songea and later were allied with the northern Ngoni. He said 'We killed Mputa, the *inkosi*, when fighting, and his people burned him because it was their custom in burying to burn.'

An old woman who came from Portuguese territory to see me in the central kingdom said that when Zintambira I died the Portuguese made them bury him 'in a box'. The onlookers in Mcakatha at the time of my interview with the old woman said 'Yes, they were not allowed to burn him.'

The central Ngoni leaders referred often to the ritual significance of the cremation of their Paramount, followed by the washing of the ashes into the stream 'to strengthen the land'. On my first arrival in the central kingdom I was questioned closely by several of the big *izinduna* and *alumuzana* about the practice of cremation in England. They alleged that, under the influence of the local mission, the Paramount Gomani II had said that he wished to be buried in a coffin with Christian burial rites. They were much concerned about this, because of the effect on the strength and status of his successor and on the country as a whole. 'If he is not burned his children will not be honoured and will only be as *alumuzana*. Is it right that another tribe, the English, should come and change our customs?' Great relief was expressed when I told them that Christians were cremated in England with full Christian ritual, and also when I told them that the ashes of one of the early Scottish missionaries in northern Ngoniland had been brought back by his widow to lie there.

The following account of the funeral of Cikusi was given to Rattray:

⟨ When the chief of the whole country dies, they do not immediately inform the people of his own village. First they send messengers to other villages, to tell them 'the clouds have fallen today'. They do this because they fear, 'if we tell his own men first, they may go and commence to forage and plunder, as is done at a chief's death'. Then all begin to assemble, all the war bands from the different villages, shields in hand. They are decked out in their feather head-dresses, and wristlets and anklets of goat's hair; (the bands) glitter as if it were all for show and not for a funeral. Then some of the old men dress the dead chief for burial. The knees are bent against the chest, and the arms bent, the hands are laid against the cheeks, and they take a small gourd-cup and make him grasp it in his hand. When they bathe him, they take grass from a forest glade. They do not wash the body, but only the face. The water they use they do not draw from the well where people drink, but take water from a running stream. The body is not anointed with oil. Then they take the spleen of an ox and deck his head until it all glitters, and then take the

N.N.—F

skin of an ox, killed that very day, and bind him in it. But do not wrap it round his head, but only as far as the neck, and take the fat from the ox's belly and throw it over him. Then he is set on a stone and the cup filled with beer.

The body remains in the hut four days, and bands of warriors sound their shields without ceasing. When the body begins to stink, oil is brought and poured in a dish and set fire to. On the fifth day they lift the body, the child whom the dead chief had named as his successor leads, and all the relations follow, and the wives of the dead chief. The warriors come in companies, village by village. Very old men bear the corpse. It is carried upright. When they come with it to the water, if it be running fully they do not dam it up, should it be low they dam it across with stones and mud, and down stream becomes quite dry. Then they begin to lay firewood on some rock in the stream, and bring the corpse and put it on the pile and take more wood and prop it up on the sides. When they have finished piling up the wood an old white-haired man makes fire, and when the hot ashes fall blows it into flame and sets fire to the pyre and the flames go roaring up. They place the child [and heir] where the smoke is blowing to. He stands on one leg, his shield is in his hand. When the fire bursts out in sparks the men clash their shields, and chant their war songs . . .

The shield of the chief, which he was wont to carry . . ., they burn on a fire on one side, and all his household belongings. When the fire has burned out, and the corpse is also consumed and turned to ashes, water is splashed over (the spot). Should the stream have been dammed they pull down the barrier, and all the ashes go down the *Mawi* (a river). When they see all is finished a sheep is killed, they take a wooden spoon and catch the blood and place it on the rock. Then they skin the sheep, cut it open, take the stomach, turn out the contents on the rock, and smear it over. The elders only eat the meat. When they have done this they go off to the village and kill many oxen, the people still keeping up the rolling sound with their shields. All the ornamental tufts of grass from the hut roofs belonging to the chief are removed. Next morning all the headmen shave their heads, and then the people from the different villages. The widows put on the red head-bands.

Additional details and slight variations were supplied by Habuya Dube, an old man who was official praiser of Paramount Gomani II. He was also at the funeral.

⳾ After some time Cikusi began to be ill and of that same illness he died. And we danced *ligubo* for one month, and over a hundred beasts were killed. For a whole week [1] he was in the house, and then soon he began to smell because he was decaying. The grave-diggers, they of the Ngozo clan, burned the fat of the cattle and roasted it on the fire, doing it as if to prevent the smell. And they made him hold a cup of beer in his hand. On a certain day we lifted him up and went with him to the water. Then

---

[1] Compare the previous account which gave four days between death and cremation. At Bambo Manga's death it was three days.

we dammed the stream and made a pool and a mound. And we put him on a rock, and on top of him we put cowhide shields and left them so. And we put firewood above. Then Ngwazi Ngozo took fire and lit that fire. Then *ligubo* was danced and the women were singing. They sang songs of *ligubo* and the *amadoda* danced (*anagiya*). The owner of the country did not cry, no, and the big people did not cry. Only the wives and other women cried.

Habuya Dube added later that everyone came with one piece of wood and put it on the pyre; and that they killed a cow and took the fat and put it on the wood, and used the skin to wrap the body in.

In discussing the ceremony of cremation with informants among the central Ngoni, there was no reference to the suggestion made by Dr. Kuper, that cremating was a substitute for embalming to avoid the corruption of the body of the king. They regarded the act of burning as an essential element in the continuing strength of the royal line, since the heir stood in the smoke from the pyre, and in the continuing fertility and strength of the country, since the ashes were swept into the river. The concept was that the royal ruler had been strengthened with the *tonga* medicine, and thereafter his body and its strength was the symbol of the unity and strength and fertility of his country.

On the question of mourning or no mourning they were equally emphatic. 'Death cannot cut life' was an expression often on their lips during the funeral ceremonies of Bambo Manga, when great care was taken to carry out the traditional ritual as far as possible in every detail. They were shocked at the idea of mourning and wailing at such a time by any of the big people. The leading Ngoni women were expected to join the *ligubo* dances in the courtyard. Some old women of lower social rank in the village, together with the daughter of Bambo Manga, sat in the house with the corpse sobbing and crying '*Mayi, mayi*' and many of them became quite ill and others hysterical with prolonged sobbing. The leading Ngoni men were contemptuous of this display of grief. They admitted it was correct behaviour for her daughter because of the close kinship tie, but of the behaviour of the rest they said 'Ha, just like the Ntumba people.' The only behaviour which was considered correct was to dance in the courtyard openly before the house of Bambo Manga, or to slip off quietly home and rest before returning to take up the dance.

The traditional ritual procedure at the death of the Paramount, with the exception of the cremation of the corpse, I saw in all its details at the death of Bambo Manga. The corpse was placed in the same position in the hut as described at Cikusi's death, and was wrapped in a sheep-skin first with a cow-skin over, the spleen, gall-bladder and fat decorating the head and neck. The dancing of *ligubo* by the men with shields and spears, and by the women, was continuous from the moment of death to the burial, and afterwards whenever fresh companies from the central kingdom and from Portuguese territory arrived to mourn. The grave was made at the edge of the kraal and the kraal fence enlarged to take it in so that the cattle might walk on it.

In this chapter I have tried to bring together some of the chief elements in the position of the Paramount, and in the performance of his duties, which were remembered by the old men as having been characteristic of pre-European days. Some of these features, as I have indicated, had disappeared in the 1930's. Others survived and will be illustrated in Chapter V. Chapters III and IV on the royal women and on the officials in the kingdoms will illustrate the importance of the leading women in the Ngoni kingdoms, and the hierarchy of officials already mentioned in Chapter II of Part I.

The texts of the praise-songs which conclude this chapter are given because in the 1930's they were still recited in the royal villages and were a feature of all public ceremonies. Most of the allusions in the texts were obscure. Cibambo, who translated them for me and who consulted other older men, did not recognize some of the names or the meaning of the attributes. Some names corresponded with those given in Part I in the texts about the departure of the Ngoni in their two groups from Natal (see pp. 7, 8), such as the Nqumayo people whom Zwide ruled over, Nqaba who left with Ngwana, Nyathi who tried to prevent Ngwana from leaving. But in the way in which they were used in the 1930's these praise-songs had little meaning for those who heard them except as a form of salutation to the Paramount.

Praises of Zwangendaba, son of Hlacwayo

Zwangendaba whose intention it is to be black who denies it to be light.
Go away, let us go, you the rejected one.
We are like a man of the Ntungwa, a fat one; there the people die as fat ones.
Nqaba you must eat people. Leave the cattle.
Nqaba son of Lushwana, there was confusion.
There he is, there he is, where do they see him? They see him in the fences of his mothers.
One who is angry because the cattle have gone with the calves.
His great cunning overcomes the magic stones of the doctors.
I have gone away until I have seen Lebombo Mountains.
We are suffering on account of the great dispute with the Nqumayo people.
You are seeing the hoes which are waiting for you, the hoes which cannot be used for hoeing.
He saw it, the short grass, he was biting it hastily.
He saw it, the ditch, his foot slipped into it.
He who divided the water with a stick at the Zambesi.
He who remembered the cattle of the Balunjana.

Praises of Hlacwayo, son of Magangata

Hlacwayo the dwarf who cannot trail his cloth
Whereas the tall people trail their cloths.
Meat eaten with knives of axes,
If it is not eaten with forks it is rotten.
Hlacwayo whose bodily vigour is finished off compared with Hlacwayo
of former times.
Grass of deep red colour is not burned with burning; it burns very
slowly, drop by drop.

Praises of Ngwana, son of Goqweni

You who cut the trees and who cut the mouths,
You the locust, the grasshopper who fixed in your hair the feathers of
the locust,
Who went below and climbed up, and went to bring the morning star of
the dawn,
You go, since you are rejected; you go and bring the armlets of wild
animals; those of cattle will be much disputed.
You who remember the fault of long ago.
In descending, you descend together into the mountains.
You who drank the blood of cattle,
You who separated from the people of Shaka, Shaka of Mbelebele kraal,
You who separated from the people of Nyathi the son of Mashobane; it
thundered, it was cloudy.
Thou resemblest cattle which were finished by wolves.
You who originated with the people of Mzilikazi,
You who originated with the people of Mpakana son of Lidonga,
You who originated with the people of Ndwandwe.

CHAPTER III

THE ROYAL WOMEN

An early traveller in central Ngoniland in 1886 remarked on the number
of 'true Ngoni women' to be found there, who were 'easily distinguished
from the other women by their light colour and by being taller and
stouter'. He went on to say: 'The king's houses at Livisini were 30 feet
in diameter, built within an enclosure with other huts where the attendants lived. All were kept very clean and well swept.' This tribute to the
appearance and achievements of Ngoni women of high rank was borne
out by my own observations in the 1930's in central and northern
Ngoniland. There was a definite physical type, light in colour, with
high cheek-bones and orthognathic profile, tall with an upright carriage
of the head. Women with these physical characteristics were in all cases
of leading Swazi or trans-Zambesi clans, and their influence on their

surroundings, their families, and the behaviour of those for whom they were responsible was most noticeable. Not all of these women were in the category of royal women, nor did all the royal women conform to this distinctive physical type, though the association of high-ranking family, physical appearance and pride of bearing was striking.

There were three main classes of royal women, all associated with the Paramount in a special relationship. These showed some parallels with the classes of royal women among the Swazi described by Dr. Kuper. I have not adopted her terms for distinguishing them, with the exception of the term Queen Mother, which I have used in the English sense of the widow of a former ruler and mother of the existing ruler. The chief women associated with the Paramount in the Ngoni kingdoms were the Royal Sister, the Queen Mother, and the big wife. This same association of three leading women with a ruling chief or *mulumuzana* was found in the subordinate chieftainships under the Paramount, and in the head villages of the Swazi and trans-Zambesi clans. It was a definite Ngoni pattern, associating women of high rank with the men who carried political responsibility. Their positions in the Ngoni patrilineal and virilocal social structure was markedly different from the position of the leading women in the matrilineal and uxorilocal societies of other Nyasaland peoples, especially in their relationship to their husbands, sons and brothers.

The relationships of the Queen Mother and the big wife to the Paramount were of a different character from that of the Royal Sister to her brother, since she was of the royal clan and they were not. We shall first consider the position in the Ngoni kingdoms of the Queen Mother and the big wife, since reference has been made to them already in the previous chapter. In the new *lusungulu* village of the Paramount there was a close connexion between the Queen Mother, who moved out with him, and his own big wife. His big wife was of the same house as the Queen Mother, since the cattle for her *lobola* had been taken from the herd of the Queen Mother. At this time of moving out into the new village the big wife began to be head of her own house. Other wives, married with cattle from the herd which had been built up for her, and kraaled with those belonging to the Queen Mother, were attached to her house, and their huts were built near her own. She was the mother, actual or potential, of the future Paramount. If she failed to have a male child, or if her sons died, a male child would be taken from another wife's hut and brought up in her hut and would be known as the child of her house. Since she was the mother of the heir she had a special relationship to the *induna* appointed to look after her house. It was the house of the Paramount elect and also she would probably, when the Queen Mother died, succeed to the ownership of the *indlunkulu* hut. Her *induna* would then become one of the most important men in the village as he would receive all guests and strangers.

When the Queen Mother, who had in her husband's lifetime been the big wife of his village and the head of his big house, moved out with her son to his *lusungulu* village, she had the unrivalled distinction of occupying the *indlunkulu*. While her hut was the centre of all hospitality and of ceremonials such as marriages and funerals, she was aware that her daughter-in-law, her son's big wife, was the leading lady of that village by right of being the Paramount's big wife and the mother of his heir. Such a situation could have produced friction between the big wife and the Queen Mother, but informants were shocked at the idea of two women in such positions not being able to control their tempers and adjust any differences which arose. I never saw any visible signs of friction. The Queen Mother and her co-widows in the village seemed aware that their time of active participation in royal village or national affairs was over, and the Queen Mother appeared content to occupy the *indlunkulu*, provide a meeting-place for all the women, and give advice and counsel when invited to do so. Part of her duty in occupying the *indlunkulu* hut was to keep the ritual vessels for sacrificing to the ancestral spirit of her late husband, the former Paramount, and when the sequence of ceremonies after his death had been completed, she looked after his spirit which had been 'brought back' to that hut.

In the central kingdom, when the Paramount Mputa died in Tanganyika, a regent took care of the kingdom while his son Cikusi was a minor. During that period the royal village built by Domwe mountain was a very large one divided into hamlets. The position of Queen Mother was then held by NaMlangeni, formerly the big wife of Mputa, who had a daughter Manga, but no son. A son, Cikusi, born to the next wife, was put into the house of NaMlangeni and brought up there. Golozela Nzunga, the *induna* in charge of her house, was also in charge of the section of the royal village called Ziyembe. When the royal village divided, its constituent hamlets spread out from Domwe and the section called Ziyembe moved to the east towards the escarpment. The head village of the Nzunga clan was built there, and Golozela continued as *induna* for NaMlangeni. She went with him, while Cikusi's own mother went into his *lusungulu* village in the section called Liwisini sited near the Kirk Range. NaMlangeni took care of the spirit of Paramount Mputa in the Nzunga clan head village of Mcakatha. Her hut in that village was the *indlunkulu* and after she died her daughter Manga came to live in that hut and look after her father's spirit.

This brief account of the succession of a Queen Mother in the central kingdom brings up the question of succession, which was a vital element in the office [of the Queen Mother, in respect both of her occupancy of the *indlunkulu* and her guardianship of the spirit of the dead Paramount. In the case of a successor to the Queen Mother of a recently deceased Paramount, two alternatives were open. The reigning Paramount's big wife could succeed to the *indlunkulu* and to the guardianship of his father's spirit, or she could take over the *indlunkulu* while a co-widow of the Queen Mother inherited the guardianship of the spirit in her own hut. The second alternative was the one followed in all the instances remembered by informants. In both kingdoms the spirits of the main line of the Paramounts were guarded by someone appointed to that task, chosen on the grounds of reputation and reliability. There was yet another variant in the central kingdom, where, as we have seen, it was Manga, the daughter of Mputa, who succeeded to her mother's guardianship of his spirit. The one principle which emerged from a number of cases cited in both kingdoms, was that occupancy of the *indlunkulu* and guardianship of a spirit might be undertaken by the same person, but generally it did not work out that way.

The Royal Sister, a title equivalent to the English Princess Royal, was the older full sister of the Paramount by the same mother, or his older sister by his father's big wife if she had borne no son. She was always referred to as 'the one who would have been chief if she had been a man'. She stood in a special relationship to the reigning Paramount and to the Paramount-elect. She was in constant touch with the Paramount's children who used the name *dadakazi* (female father) when addressing her or referring to her. Dr. Kuper [1] reported that the Royal Sister among the Swazi was addressed by the same term, and that she came next in rank to the big wife and the leading wives. My informants and my own observations in both Ngoni kingdoms put the Royal Sister next to the big wife and before the other wives. She visited the royal village at frequent intervals to see her brother and his children, and was consulted about their affairs. She took a leading part in the puberty ritual for the daughters of her brother and was prominent at *ligubo* and other dances, and at mourning ceremonies. She was married with an exchange of cattle to a man of a leading Swazi or trans-Zambesi clan, and during his lifetime lived in his village, visiting the royal village often.

The position of the royal women in the Ngoni kingdoms has been discussed in terms of the sister, mother and big wife of the Paramount. The same relationships were found in the families of the chiefs and *alumuzana*. There the equivalent of the Royal Sister was the older full sister by the same mother of the chief or *mulumuzana*, and his own big wife and his father's big wife played similar roles, within their own spheres, to those played in the Paramount's village by the Queen Mother and his big wife.

Five texts follow which illustrate the life and activities of leading women who filled roles equivalent to those of Royal Sister, big wife and Queen Mother. One of the texts is by a Royal Sister—Bambo Manga, who was the sister of Paramount Cikusi in the central kingdom. Margaret Jere was the elder full sister of the heir to the chieftainship of

---

[1] Kuper, H. op. cit. p. 59.

Chief Mtwalo II in the northern kingdom. Two texts are by former big
wives of leading men. NyaNsangu was the former big wife of a grandson
of Zwangendaba, a member of the royal clan but not a chief, though he
owned many villages. NaNdumbu was the former big wife of the head
of the Nzunga clan in the central kingdom. The last text by Cibambo
gives details of the clothes worn by royal women and leading women in
pre-European days, some of which were still in use in the 1930's.

LIFE OF THE ROYAL WOMEN
by Manga Maseko

daughter of Mputa, former Paramount of the central kingdom

❡ Formerly I was just staying for I did not work. I had many slaves and
their work was especially to thread beads. Up to today I have not worked
except to cook. Our hair was anointed with the fat of cows and of milk.
Our food was milk and we drank it in a wooden cup. We were getting
cloth when they sold slaves to the Arabs. For honouring each other, the
big men were telling the youths: 'You should honour the big people that
the country may be rich.' Only the big women were dancing *ngoma*,
msindo and *ligubo*. If a man married the child of a chief, he gave many
cattle, and the poor man could not marry the child of a chief.

When NaMlangeni was alive she was a well-known chief and was
greatly honoured. When speaking a case, they called her that she might
judge. When people went to war and captured slaves and cattle they were
giving them to her, and she divided them. For thanking her they said:
'*Zaithwa Mai.*'

LIFE OF THE ROYAL WOMEN
by Margaret Jere

*granddaughter of Mtwalo I, daughter of Johanne Jere in the
northern kingdom*

❡ When I was a child I was not allowed to go out quickly in the sun, and
when crawling I had to stay in the house. I was very light coloured. The
mlezi (nurse girl) took me to my mother, UNsulazi Nzima, to be suckled at
special times. I slept in the house of Magodise Moyo, my grandmother,
who was the widow of Chief Mtwalo. The *isidandani* (attendant) also
slept there. My grandmother and others, the *manina* (senior women), were
telling me how to behave. A special *isidandani* living in Magodise's house
was told by my grandmother to speak specially to me when I had reached
puberty. This *isidandani* could speak to me about anything. When nearing
marriage a woman was chosen, Hlamseya Nzima, and sent to reveal to me
how I was to live in my married state. The sisters of my father, Tinzira
and Sayeya Jere, also came and spoke to me at the time of my marriage.
Hlamseya Nzima was sent by my grandmother to examine me (for
virginity) before marriage. I was allowed to play with those children who
lived in the same section of the village and who were known to my mother
and grandmother. The *izidandani* did all the work but sometimes I used
to pound and fetch water, but not too hard and just for pleasure.
When strangers came, I came and saluted them and then went out of

the house. If my father came to my mother's house, I would go out, but if he sent for me I would return and he would talk to me and play with me. We learned how to behave well, and were rebuked if we behaved badly. My father would beat a child for not behaving well. My father did not allow his children to be spoiled by being treated differently from others. He said: 'They are all my children.'

LIFE OF THE ROYAL WOMEN
by Mdingase Nsangu
widow of Chinombo Jere, grandson of Zwangendaba in the northern kingdom

❡ The *amakosikazi* were not working. During the day they kept dressing their hair, both the young women and the old. The old women no longer kept their *isihlutu*, or high chignon, but wore the *umzoco*, or long curls. For the *umzoco* the hair was cut short and not allowed to grow very long. Instead of dressing it upwards they took a blade of grass and kept it pressed down after oil and scent were applied. Their other work was to go to the river and wash.

They also drank beer and some gruel, and afterwards danced *ngoma* in the house where beer was brewed. The men and chief also joined in the *ngoma* and the women were responding to the singing. They began to drink in the morning until the afternoon, but not in the evening. Other people went on drinking until evening, and even some of the *amakosikazi* who were *izidli* (gluttonous) but the rest were sleeping or resting.

When drinking in the house the chief always sat by the right-hand door-post, and the big *inkosikazi* by the left-hand post. They sat near the door to draw breath easily because there were many people inside. The beer-pot being set halfway between the door and the hearth-stones in the centre, a man was chosen to pour the beer in the gourds for drinking. He was *umtele wocwala*, the beer pourer, and was often the village *induna* or one who was favoured by the chief. When the gourds were full he told the chief, and the chief told him to distribute them. Sometimes there were four or even six for the different classes in the house. They sat in order, the *inkosi* with the *izinduna* and *amadoda*, and the *inkosikazi* with the other wives of the chief and the wives of the *izinduna* and *amadoda*. The chief and the *inkosikazi* kept on inviting the common people to come and drink. Such invited people thanked the person at the beginning and at the end, others joining him. The *inkosikazi* or other wives of the chief were thanked '*Nkomo*'.

The *amakosikazi* never worked at all, but the lesser wives worked, and pounded grain and fetched firewood. These were the ones who had not yet got attendants in their houses. All the chief *amakosikazi* had attendants who performed all the work of the house. The *amakosikazi* often sat in the verandah or outside under the platform of branches supported by posts. There they ate their food which was *ilambazi* and *umnjinji*, thick gruel of millet; *izinkwa ze nyauti*, bulrush millet ground to a paste; or *izinkobe*, whole grains of maize boiled and pounded. The meat was eaten as a feast on the *egcekeni*, the smeared place in front of the house, and all the chief's wives joined in. A mat was spread for the big *amakosikazi* where they sat when eating meat. The lesser wives sat on the ground, which was cleaned and smeared often with cow's dung.

The second *induna* of the village was the one who put the meat on the *ingcwembe*, or big platter of the *inkosikazi*, and placed it before her. She herself or her *nhlanzi* (co-wife) divided the meat for the other women, the wife of the *induna* helping her. After they had eaten, each *inkosikazi* called for an *ingcwembe* from her house for the meat to be given to her attendants.

THE LIFE OF THE ROYAL WOMEN
by NaNdumbu
formerly the big wife of the late Chief Njolomole Nzunga I in the central kingdom

℄ Old Njolomole had many wives, great and small. His huts were well made, and in the middle was the 'big house'. They made a fence to go round all the huts, and its appearance was very good.

He was fond of sitting on the *bwalo*, and all his wives cooked *nsima* and took many baskets to the *bwalo*. He himself ate alone, but afterwards gave food to the big people and they in turn to the children who were waiting on the *bwalo*. If a stranger came, he did not lack food, for the chief gave food to strangers and beer. So all strangers praised his behaviour. And he was known far and wide in the land for his comely behaviour.

When the days for *ngoma* were near he was going to the stores to buy many cloths to divide them to all his wives. Especially he was giving them to NaNdumbu his big wife to divide. Those cloths were all of one kind. On the day of dancing *ngoma* all the women wore these cloths and came on the *bwalo* with the chief. The people were astonished to see the women dressed alike. Njolomole excelled among all the people, and all praised him.

In the hut of NaNdumbu there were girls to sweep and to pound, and NaNdumbu was just sitting, no pounding for her.

Njolomole was very fond of hunting and when he killed animals in the hunt he divided them among his wives. Then he died and left his wives. From that time his wives have been very poor, and some have gone away to their own homes. Those who are here have been married by other men. Although the men dance *ngoma*, those women cannot dance it because they were greatly praised when they danced with fine cloths, but they cannot dance with poor cloths, no. So when people dance they just look on. Those women can dance *ngoma* in other villages, but here in their own village, no. Because they grieve very much to see the tomb of their husband who was dancing with them.

THE CLOTHING OF WOMEN
by Yesaya Cibambo

℄ Today Ngoni women are not easily recognized because they have taken foreign customs of clothing. Long ago Ngoni women were easily distinguished by their hair. They did not shave their hair except when their husband died. It was washed carefully and oiled and combed upwards to the top of the head in the *isihlutu*. The oil was *ipehla*, clarified butter. This was done every two or three days, or every day if they were grand women. They decorated it with small strings of beads dangling from a thorn stuck at the top of the *isihlutu*, and round it they put narrow bands of beads (*intuyeya* and *isincwayo*) arranged in layers. Royal women wore leopard and lion claws among the beads. Round the neck and on the arms they wore coils of brass wire (*amasongo*) which they got from the Arabs, or *izipote*, strings of beads wound round a piece of cloth. The kilt of soft dressed leather (*isidwaba*) reached from the waist to the knee, and wrapped well over. A long piece of soft leather (*ingcayi*) was fastened on the left shoulder and reached a little below the knees. On the edges of the *ingcayi* were fastened small bells made of brass (*mgomani*). Ngoni women did not like to cut their bodies with tattoo marks. They said it was ugly. The *inkosikazi* might decorate other wives at the *ngoma* dance because she had a large store of beads and wire and leather cloths.

The common features of the life of leading women as illustrated in these texts were: the number of attendants and servants in their households and their consequent freedom from manual work; the etiquette surrounding life in the *indlunkulu* and the big house, and the formality of hospitality, beer-drinks and dances; relationships with their *induna*, and with their husbands, and, as illustrated by Margaret Jere, with the paternal grandmother who supervised their upbringing when they were young.

In addition to the *induna* in charge of the big house, the royal women and leading women in the villages of chiefs and *alumuzana* were surrounded by a number of young girls and serving women. These were known in pre-European days as domestic slaves or servants (*micetho*), girl companions (*izidandani*), nurse girls (*alezi*) and older women attendants (*agogo*). Informants said that in pre-European days there were fifteen or twenty girls in each royal household and the number was constantly being added to when female slaves were captured in war and allocated as servants to the Paramount's wives. All the texts in this chapter refer to the fact that the royal women and the leading women did no work, and there was always a nostalgic refrain from senior women informants about the time devoted to hair-dressing and beauty treatments, to 'just sitting', and to dancing and drinking beer, while all the household tasks and the care of the children fell to the servants. The Ngoni royal women, even in the 1930's, commanded the labour of six to ten women and girls in each household. The hard physical work of fetching firewood and water, pounding grain, preparing vegetables and often cooking too, was done largely by servants in the Paramount's and chief's villages where I stayed. There were young nurse girls and older women to help with the children and with the adolescent girls. There were no longer any domestic slaves, and the domestic helpers, who were often distant relatives of the wives, appeared to enjoy the prestige of being attached to an important house.

The royal women in pre-European days were distinguished by the clothes and ornaments they wore which were reserved for the royal

clan and for women of leading Swazi and trans-Zambesi clans. Two of
the texts emphasized the distinction conferred on the royal women by
special clothing. Cibambo described the use of well-dressed soft skins
and of beads and wire, the beads brought with them from the south,
the brass wire obtained from the Arabs. In NaNdumbu's text she mentioned cloth bought from the stores. After the Ngoni women gave up
wearing soft leather for skirts and the long piece of leather draped from
the left shoulder, they used strong cotton cloth of dark blue or black,
originally brought by the Arabs and later stocked by the stores. They
tied the main cloth under their arms in a draped knot over the breast
and on ceremonial occasions they added another fastened on the left
shoulder like a plaid. A woman who had been a young girl in the village
of Paramount Cikusi, but was not of a leading clan, said that in this
village there was a great difference between the royal women and the
rest: 'Only the daughters of Cikusi and his big wives could wear dark
cloth as the Ngoni do. The others would have been killed if they tried
to look like the big women'.

The royal women and the big wives and widows of chiefs and
alumuzana were treated by all with whom they came in contact with
the distinction and respect due to their prestige. They were addressed
and thanked by the term *Nkomo*, with the clan name and the honorific
prefix added, except where, as in the case of Bambo Manga, a title had
been conferred. She was thanked '*Nkomo Bambo*'.[1] *Ukuhlonipa*, and its
Nyanja equivalent *kulemekeza*, meaning to honour and to behave in a
respectful manner towards senior people and those of superior rank,
was an expression constantly used by the Ngoni and by the other peoples
in the Ngoni kingdoms. The forms of showing respect were partly
verbal; partly in the position adopted, with the eyes cast down and a
slight curtsey by the women when facing someone; partly in the tone of
voice when speaking; and partly in the deliberate and controlled behaviour noticed by several early travellers in Nyasaland. A particular
verbal form of respect practised by the royal women was the use of the
hlonipa vocabulary. I found this practice surviving only in the Emcisweni area in northern Ngoniland where the Ngoni language was still
spoken, but informants said that it had been common to all married
women of trans-Zambesi clans in the northern kingdom when they had
spoken Ngoni among themselves. The *hlonipa* vocabulary consisted
of the substitution of special words, known only to the women, in order
to avoid using a word in which the main syllable of a man's name
occurred—a man with whom they were connected by marriage or by
affinal relationship.[2] Thus Zwangendaba's wives and widows could

---

[1] *Bambo* (father) was a term of respect used for important senior men.
[2] *Hlonipa* as a form of special vocabulary was widely practised among the Nguni
groups in South Africa. Hoernlé, A. W. 'Social Organisation', in *The Bantu-speaking
Tribes of South Africa*, pp. 74, 77.

never use any word in which *indaba* (meeting or affair) occurred. They substituted *incayo* for *indaba* and spoke of him as Zwangencayo. The women of the Ngomezulu clan could never use the word *ilanga* (sun) for which they substituted *ijiko*, since Langa was the name of the father of Zwide who had married into the Ngomezulu clan.

Though the particular verbal form of *hlonipa* which the Ngoni royal women brought from the south survived only in one area of northern Ngoniland, the concept inherent in it and the attitudes of honour and respect which it implied were expressed in the use of *Nkomo* in thanking and in the other non-verbal forms already mentioned. Manga, the Royal Sister of Cikusi, was as we have seen, thanked '*Nkomo Bambo*' but also with the formula '*Zikomo mntwana wenkosi*' (thanks, child of the Paramount). Among the central Ngoni there were two expressions of thanks which were probably a relic of *hlonipa* vocabulary since they were used only by the leading women. The customary form of thanking, and of taking leave after a conversation or after getting a reply to a question, was '*Zikomo*' with the clan name and honorific prefix added. The royal women in this area, when making the response to this form of thanking, always replied '*Zaithwa*' with the clan name, and they thanked each other by '*Zimata*' with the clan name instead of '*Zikomo*'. When I observed this and used it myself, they nudged each other and said 'She also is one of us.'

We have discussed so far the outward signs of respect shown to the royal women, and the visible marks of distinction in their clothes and the number of their attendants. We shall now examine the way in which the authority of the royal women was exercised. This will give some indication of their relationship to the political organization of the kingdoms, in so far as they had certain responsibilities to the people as a whole, and to their husbands and sons within the royal village where they lived. At the royal village the Queen Mother and her co-widows shared with the wives of the two leading houses to the right and left of the *indlunkulu*, the responsibility for preparing and serving food and beer for the Paramount and those whom he called to eat with him. The text by NyaNsangu[1] describes the etiquette of beer drinking in one of the chiefdoms in the northern kingdom, of sending food to the chief when he ate in the cattle kraal, and of assembling the wives in order of precedence according to their houses to take their food. The formality of this etiquette was characteristic of Ngoni eating and drinking, and it was maintained by the organization and forethought of the royal women, the big wives and mothers of the Paramount, who planned the work of their own households and supervised that of the lesser wives who were attached to the two main houses.

---

[1] The procedure described in the text applied equally to the Paramount's village and to the villages of ruling chiefs. The Ngoni in that area used the term '*inkosi*' for chief as well as for Paramount.

The responsibility of the royal women went beyond the sphere of domestic economy, fundamental though that was in a largely subsistence mode of living. They were expected to maintain good relations and settle all disputes among the women under them, except in cases where a dispute had to be taken to court, and such instances were generally regarded as a failure on their part to use their judgement and exert their authority. In pre-European days, when the Paramount and the chiefs held their judicial courts in the kraal, the royal women generally sat outside the kraal fence and listened, and were asked by the chief in the evening what they had to say about the judgements given. Some of the royal women had a great reputation for wisdom and intelligence, though they never spoke in public. They were still acting as unofficial advisers and critics to the chiefs during my visits in the 1930's, though it was recognized and often said that this kind of wisdom in judicial affairs was an unusual gift among women.

The title 'royal women' was adopted for this chapter in order to show the relationship of three particular women to the ruling Paramount in both kingdoms. It was difficult to discover whether the existence of an older full sister was accidental and she was given *ad hoc* recognition, or whether the relationship was considered so important that it was provided for by adoption if there did not happen to be an older full sister. The example of the Swazi, as described by Dr. Kuper, points to evidence of a recognized institution, by which in the case of the Paramount, a woman of the royal clan was always associated with her brother who was the ruler, with the same provision in the case of reigning chiefs and *alumuzana* of Swazi clans. Informants were able to give the names of Royal Sisters of former Paramounts prior to the establishment of the kingdoms in Nyasaland. It seemed, therefore, that this relationship was a permanent institution and that its chief significance lay in the public acknowledgement of a woman of the royal clan in a position close to her brother who was the ruling Paramount. The fact that she was of his clan, and that she had a special relationship to the Paramount's children, was a check to the power and authority exercised by the Queen Mother and the big wife, who were of other clans, over the Paramount's children of the royal clan.

In the case of the Queen Mother and the big wife, since the big wife in course of time became the Queen Mother, the permanent element in their positions was the setting up and maintenance of houses in the royal village and in other important villages. This will be discussed more fully in Chapter III of Part III. They shared with the Royal Sister the supervision and responsibility for the children of the Paramount, as Margaret Jere shows in her text; and in the royal village, and hence in the kingdom as a whole, they occupied leading positions in daily affairs as well as on ceremonial occasions.

CHAPTER IV

COURTS AND OFFICIALS

THE Ngoni claimed that when they established their kingdoms in Nyasaland they introduced a new idea of law, a different system of courts, and a different procedure for conducting cases in those courts, from those found among the local peoples. Within their kingdoms they imposed on all their subjects these ideas, courts and legal procedure as part of their government, applied to the conquerors and the conquered alike. We shall consider in this chapter only those aspects of the courts and the legal system which were related to the political structure. The categories of crime, the degree of punishment, the sanctions for enforcement of the law, and the effect of the judicial procedure on the balance of equilibrium in the community, all belong to a specialized study and are not included here.

THE NGONI CONCEPT OF LAW

We begin with two texts, the first from the northern kingdom by Cibambo, the second by Ishmael Mwale the Treasurer of the Paramount in the central kingdom.

¶ (1) The Ngoni seem to have been born with a gift for leadership or rule. Though they were a wandering tribe, yet there was one Paramount from whom proceeded the laws for the good government of the people. All the lesser chiefs and headmen received from him the leadership of the people. Though they had no way of writing to each other, they kept their unity by messengers passing between them. The Paramount had power to call gatherings from time to time, in which they talked of the affairs of the country. In these gatherings the old men and the men of repute who had a point to make were heard in criticism and made suggestions for the building up of the realm. By this means the Paramount and his counsellors learned of and understood the thoughts of their people. It was in such large gatherings that the laws of the country were delivered to the people, so that they might hold fast to them and not be punished unreasonably for breaking them in ignorance. After they came back from these gatherings, the headmen and men of standing gathered together their villages to tell the people what had been spoken in the great council of the Paramount, and told them carefully about the laws which had come from the gathering.

(2) Before the Ngoni came to this country the villages were small and isolated from one another. There was constant pouncing on people to catch them as slaves. It was unsafe to go even a quarter of a mile from one village to another, because a man might be in hiding and pounce out and catch you and take you off to his village as a slave, and there was no redress and no case was heard. Most people never went beyond the

boundaries of their own village, and they were afraid to travel even in a large party of twenty or thirty. So no one had any wisdom beyond that of his own village and family. When the Ngoni came they had one law for all people and they had courts to hear cases where this law was enforced. There was freedom to travel in the land where the Ngoni ruled, because they had peace within their boundaries. Therefore, we say: this was the kind of peace we had.

In these two texts we have one major concept of Ngoni law with three chief ways in which it was implemented. The concept was that there was 'one law for all people' and that the knowledge of and enforcement of this law brought internal peace and resulted in good government in the country. There was one source of law as there was one source of political and military authority—the Paramount. As Cibambo points out, the Paramount delegated his authority for carrying out the law to chiefs and headmen and depended on his 'old men and men of repute' to keep him in touch with the thoughts and desires of all his subjects, so that he might adjust the enforcement of the law to bind the people to him. He also called large gatherings of all the chiefs and *alumuzana* and headmen in order that they might hear from him any new laws and regulations and understand them so that they in turn could make them known to their people. In the intervals between the holding of these large gatherings, which took place not more than once or twice a year, messengers passed constantly from the Paramount's village to all the areas of the chiefs and *alumuzana*, reporting to them about decisions taken at the royal village on matters affecting the country as a whole, and taking back reports to the Paramount on what was happening in the outlying districts.

I attended two of these annual meetings of the chiefs and *alumuzana* and headmen in the central kingdom. They took place not at the Paramount's village but at a more central spot for the whole territory. The people were drawn up in a square formation, with the Paramount at one end supported by his 'mouthpiece' (*mlomo wenkosi*), who always spoke for him, with the six Subordinate Native Authority chiefs beside him, and the councillors (*izinduna*) messengers and other officials of his court and of the S.N.A. courts arranged in order of precedence, facing the crowd as they did during court sessions. On the three sides of the square in the front ranks were the *alumuzana* and the headmen of their villages, sitting in territorial groups, and behind each headman were the *madoda* or senior men of the village, and behind them again the *amajaha* or young men. I watched this assembly of 3,000 to 4,000 people being arranged, as they arrived, by the *izinduna* of the Paramount's court and the *izinduna* of the six chiefs. They took up their places as though on a military parade, and once placed there was no further movement. The effect was that of a barrack square in the straightness of lines and orderliness of behaviour. After all was in order the Paramount arrived, and there were deep-throated shouts of '*Bayete*' until he sat in his chair. The proceedings were under complete control from beginning to end. After a brief introductory speech, delivered for the Paramount by his 'mouthpiece', the matters for the assembly were introduced one by one by the councillors of the Paramount and were spoken to first 'from the platform', that is from the group round the Paramount. Then it was open for any of the *alumuzana* or headmen to speak 'from the floor'. They did so vigorously but respectfully, and there appeared to be no hesitation in putting forward views which were divergent from those expressed 'from the platform', and questions were asked with freedom.

The topics covered a wide range of subjects and dealt partly with matters sent on by the Administration and partly with the enforcement of regulations emanating from the Paramount for his area. A letter from the health authorities about the incidence of bubonic plague in Southern Rhodesia was accompanied by an order to kill all rats and rabbits. Several headmen stood up and said they had heard by letter from men in the south about this. The Agricultural Department sent a notice exhorting men to take up gardens, and to go and settle and build villages below the escarpment where cotton and tobacco could be grown for sale. Those who went there as a group under a leader, so the notice said, would have that leader recognized as a headman. This drew a number of comments from the audience, some warmly supporting the scheme, others opposing it. The supporters welcomed the chance of earning money from cash crops and of having new headmen recognized in the new villages. The opposers repudiated the idea of setting up new villages. 'Why should we divide ourselves? We have our chiefs and our headmen. Let us stay together' was their theme, adding as a significant afterthought: 'If we go to those hot lands, our cattle will die'. The Paramount had introduced a marriage certificate for which a shilling had to be paid at the chief's court when the marriage was registered. Very few shillings were coming in and the Paramount wanted to know why. A number of men leaped to their feet and wanted to speak, and the *izinduna* had to keep order by pointing to individuals: 'You, what are your words?' The gist of that discussion was that Christians had to pay a shilling to the mission for being married in church, and they wanted to know if they must pay another shilling to the Paramount. His verdict was that Christians would have to pay twice because it was his law that marriages must be registered in the courts. There was much talk among the audience during and after this discussion and the *izinduna* had to call for order several times.

Two well-received items on the agenda were that permission had been given by the Government for villagers living on the Portuguese boundary to go and hoe gardens over the frontier. This use of lands over the frontier, both as grazing-grounds and as gardens, had been going on for years. The land was apparently unused by anyone on the Portuguese side of the boundary road, and the need for extra land for villagers living on the British side was urgent. The Portuguese authorities had been charging rent for the gardens, a shilling or so per small plot, which the Nyasaland men had paid after being threatened with confiscation of their crops. This prolonged struggle had tried everyone's temper and endurance, and when it was announced that it had been arranged that gardens might be hoed without payment, there was a great roar of applause. The *izinduna* gave them time to talk among themselves after this announcement, to work off pent-up feelings. The other popular item was that the Paramount would have his own agricultural show at Ncheu in the coming year. He had asked Government permission to hold it, which had been granted, and he had money in his treasury to pay the expenses. European officers would come and judge the exhibits and the best would be sent on to the all-Nyasaland show at Blantyre. This announcement was greeted with cheers, a number of questions were asked and much talk went on in the ranks.

This account of the Paramount's annual gathering illustrates several of the points made in the two texts quoted. It was the only formal occasion when the Paramount met as one body all those who bore authority in his territory under him. The kind of laws and regulations which were promulgated at these meetings were previously discussed by him with his officials and the chiefs, and their presence at his side, facing the assembly, made it clear to the people that the laws came from the Paramount and had the support of his subordinate chiefs. The freedom of discussion in the council gave anyone who had something to say the opportunity to stand up and say it. There was no sense of the business being put over quickly. The *izinduna* gave speakers time to express themselves, and allowed time to elapse for other speakers to get up. They were more lenient with the speakers at this meeting than they were with witnesses in the courts, and only once or twice in the sessions, which lasted six or seven hours, was a man addressed from the platform and told: 'Speak well that we may hear your words.'

This method of putting new laws and regulations before the people illustrated the concept of one law for all, and of one source of lawmaking within the territory, namely the Paramount, whom they saw before them as the centre of the group of chiefs and leaders. The procedure therefore gave strong support to the political structure, for it was only on the occasions of this assembly of all the Paramount's officebearers that all those in authority could be seen together as an authority-wielding group, their relative importance being indicated by the order in which they sat. The procedure also gave support to the policy of political assimilation, for in that assembly of several thousand people, the great majority were not of trans-Zambesi clans, and therefore not acknowledged as Ngoni so far as tribal origin was concerned. They were, however, and they realized it at such assemblies, the people of the Paramount, and he was to them the visible symbol of their unity in one kingdom.

The Court System of the Ngoni

The enforcement of the laws as announced and discussed at these assemblies was the business of the courts, where the laws themselves were interpreted and often elaborated on occasions of an open breach.

The relationships of the courts in the kingdom followed the hierarchical pattern of the political organization. All minor cases were heard and, whenever possible, settled at the village level. If the plaintiff failed to get satisfaction, or if the village headman was unable to get his judgement accepted, he had to go with the litigants to the chief's court, and if he failed there, the case could be taken to the appeal court of the Paramount. There were certain cases, such as murder and witchcraft, which in pre-European days could only be dealt with in the Paramount's court.

Some confusion arose over the use of one term 'court' for every type of institution which exercised judicial functions. The Nyanja term used in central Ngoniland for the courts at the lowest level was *bwalo*, literally the open space in front of the *indlunkulu* in any Ngoni village. Nothing could be apparently more informal than the discussion among a group of senior men called together by the headman, on a verandah or under a big tree, in order to settle quarrels and hear complaints. No formal records were kept, there was no clerk, and there was no summing up or pronouncement of judgement. There was, if the meeting was successful, general agreement about the action necessary and about who ought to initiate action. Above the level of this village headman's court were the courts of the *alumuzana* held at their head villages, and above them again the chiefs' courts. After 1933 the courts of the *alumuzana* gave place to the courts at the head villages of the chiefs. The proceedings there were more formal and included presenting evidence, defending the case and pronouncing judgement on cases rather than, as in the villages, talking things over and appealing to certain principles to re-establish equilibrium and resolve disputes.

The Ngoni nevertheless always recognized these courts at the village level as an integral part of their system. It was the mark of a good headman that he should be able to settle the minor cases in his village without constant reference to higher authority. The majority of villages under Ngoni rule were villages of local tribes who had surrendered to, or been conquered by, the Ngoni. The headmen were therefore of the local tribe, as a rule surrounded by their kinsmen, and their position carried with it the necessity of relating local tribal custom, especially in matters involving marriage and family affairs, to the legal principles and procedure of the Ngoni courts. Many cases came before the courts in central Ngoniland in which Ngoni law and usage differed from local usage in such matters as the custody of children, the right to 'leave the village' and the ownership of cattle.

Above the informal courts of the village headmen were the courts held in pre-European days at the head villages of the *alumuzana*. A *mulumuzana* was called 'the owner' of those villages surrounding his head village, consisting of his own clan members, local people and captives. The *mulumuzana* had a double interest in maintaining justice in his area. If he failed in a case, there was in the central kingdom only one court above him—that of the Paramount—though in the northern kingdom the areas ruled by the leading Jere chiefs had courts which came between the *alumuzana* and the Paramount. Except in cases of murder and witchcraft, which he was obliged to take to the Paramount's court, the *mulumuzana* was anxious to prove to the Paramount that he was a man fit to hold and wield authority over a number of villages. He was also concerned to maintain his authority among his own people, and this was recognized most clearly in the conduct of cases in his court. The system of checks and balances in the Ngoni political organization required that the Paramount should always dominate, but at the same time delegate authority to his chiefs and the heads of leading clans. The authority exercised by a *mulumuzana* derived from his leadership of a Swazi or trans-Zambesi clan in a particular area, but he had to maintain his position in pre-European days by constant vigilance over his people. In the process of holding together villages of mixed tribal origin the courts of the *alumuzana* and the administration of law in them played an important integrating role.

The conduct of cases in Ngoni courts

Informants in the northern and central kingdoms made it clear that there were certain common elements in Ngoni procedure in pre-European days which were carried on in the courts in the 1930's. The one who brought the case to court, the plaintiff, was called the owner of the case (*mwini wa mlandu*). Those who were called as witnesses were those who were present at the time of the quarrel who might have seen or heard something which bore on the case. The Ngoni practice of legal procedure was not to call witnesses to support either side, but to appeal to the public to give evidence about what had occurred. I heard Ngoni counsellors press a witness to say exactly where he or she was at the time of an assault. On other occasions they addressed a witness in these terms: 'Now you are from X's family. Here in this court you must tell us truly what happened. Do not be afraid. Do not remember your kinship (*cibale*) but remember what you saw, and speak well.' There was explicit in this approach a definite appeal to the public to take their part in seeing that justice was done and so restoring equilibrium and good feeling in the village. If the counsellors who were conducting a case suspected a witness of lying, they accused him of doing so after he had told his story. If he persisted in his version of the events, and they still thought he was lying, they cross-questioned him, and when the point where he contradicted himself was reached they turned on him and said: 'You lied. Now you have said you lied. You do not speak well.'

In the following account of Ngoni law by Cibambo there are two main emphases. One is on the existence of law, in the sense of a norm of good conduct, conformity to which was expected and enforced. The text at the beginning of this chapter showed how the law was made known to all the inhabitants of the country, so that ignorance could not be pleaded as an excuse for law-breaking. The other emphasis is on decorum and the regular and accepted pattern of behaviour expected in the courts, and on the Ngomi hatred of bribery, which was claimed by them, and on the whole endorsed by Europeans.[1] Respect for the law, for the court in session and for the judgement, are expressed in Cibambo's account of the proceedings, and the winner of the case (though formerly it was the loser) expressed his thanks, after judgement was given, to the Paramount or the chief, and to the elders.

❡ The laws and the power to punish disturbers of the peace were in the power of the Paramount and those who were under him. If there was a bad case in which the guilty man deserved death according to the law, such a matter was in the power of the Paramount and the lesser chiefs who helped him, and of them only. It was the same in the case of anyone who deserved to be despoiled of all his possessions because of his wrong-doing. The law was a protection for the people who might have been killed cause-lessly by their masters if they had had the power. People who were in danger from those who were above them, in danger of confiscation or of death, ran to the younger brothers of the Paramount or to the Paramount himself or sometimes they ran to the great *izinduna*. Praises had been added to those of Chief Mtwalo for this very reason that he had saved many whom Mbelwa had wanted to kill '*Isifuba esinamazwi, sitsho nkokutetela abalumuzana*' (a chest with words which spoke for the men of noble birth).

If people quarrelled in a village and could not be reconciled it was the work, as it is today, of the headman to try and bring them together, and if he thought that one had wronged the other he ordered him to bring something to recompense the other. Such recompenses were small things, from beads to a goat, perhaps an axe or a hoe. If the headman found he could not settle the business he went with them himself to the next court, to the head of the group of villages, and the standard of the payment increased. Serious cases went to the courts of the chiefs but these cases were few and not like today. People were very much afraid of each other

---

[1] On the walls of Paramount Mbelwa's court in Mzimba district in north Nyasaland were painted three sayings in English and in Tumbuka. Over the Paramount's chair was written 'Justice is blind'; by the place where the witnesses stood to speak, 'The law has no respect of a person'; and over where the general public sat 'Everyone is equal before the law'.

and appeals were uncommon. Chiefs did not allow a man to come by himself with his case to them, he had to come with his headman. Even those
in danger of death went first to the headmen and these brought them to
the chiefs.

The Ngoni hated bribes. If any *induna* was found to have taken bribes
from people he was condemned and punished.

The hearing of the cases was like what it is today. The one who brought
the case to the court spoke first, then the one with whom he was quarrelling. If there were elders there from their village they also spoke telling
out how these people quarrelled, saying so-and-so began to quarrel in
such-and-such a way, and then showed how they had been unable to
judge it in the village. They did not go into details of the quarrel, that was
done by the men themselves. After those who had quarrelled had told of
the beginning of the case any who knew of it were asked to say how it
appeared to them in the village. These were the witnesses both for and
against.

When this had been done, all who were implicated or interested in the
case remained silent. It is the custom of the Ngoni that all who spoke in
a case should stand and have a stick, and as they spoke they should walk
about and limp with the stick or sometimes stand all together, but in that
case the hand which held the stick should shake and stick it into the
ground. Only women spoke seated. No one at the hearing of a case was
allowed to lie down, everyone, even the Paramount, sat. They did this
because they were afraid that otherwise the case would not finish quickly.
The court was held in the cattle kraal. Women were not allowed into the
kraal for cases, but sat outside opposite where the old men were gathered,
even though they were the wives of the Paramount.

After the litigants and the witnesses had spoken it was the turn of the
elders of the court. They questioned and agreed with or criticized the men
who had quarrelled but they did not pronounce judgement. They waited
for the Paramount who first of all sat silent and noticed those who
unravelled or twisted the case. Afterwards when the people had finished
speaking, the elders delivered the story to the Paramount or judge. The
judge then delivered his judgement and condemned those who had
twisted the case. He delivered his judgement sitting not standing like the
other people and when he had finished all thanked him, or rather saluted
him with a loud '*Bayete*' or with the surname if to lesser chiefs. Sometimes
he sent an elder to tell the court the judgement. When the case had been
judged no one criticized the judgement. The one who began to give
thanks for the judgement was the one who was found guilty: this he did
to show submission and repentance. The custom of today that the one
who wins the case gives the thanks is not good because the man who has
lost goes away in resentment and threatening and often the case crops
up again.

If an *induna* or man of standing went secretly to the Paramount to
accuse somebody that he deserved death (perhaps for witchcraft), very
often the Paramount sent a man in secret to warn the condemned man to
run to a chief's village and hide his head. In this way many left their
fathers and went to build with the chiefs and when they went they took

all their things. Even when the Paramount agreed that a man should be killed he ordered that all his possessions were to come to him, stock, slaves, wives and children. These were called *izizi zenkosi*, the things of the Paramount, and they were divided among the houses of the Paramount, and the master of the man killed got nothing. This was done to teach the fathers of the villages that they should not sentence their people to death because they coveted their goods or people. The Paramount taught them by taking all the belongings of the one killed and they got nothing. Of course the Paramount's and chiefs' villages grew quickly in this way. At the beginning the punishment for adultery and murder was death; in adultery both the man and the woman were killed. Beginning from the time of Mbelwa and Mtwalo the penalty for adultery has been changed. The man who did it was despoiled of his goods or paid compensation. The courts agreed that any man wronged by such adultery could go with a war-party to the village of the guilty man and take what he wanted, but not kill any person. The Paramount took no notice of such an affair.

No account of the conduct of cases in Ngoni courts would be complete without reference to the popular interest in and support for the law. After a day in the courts the *izinduna* and the *amadoda* talked of almost nothing else. They went over and over the details of the cases, and recalled former cases of a similar kind and compared the judgements given. They criticized each other sharply for the handling of cases, and such criticism was taken well on the whole, as a contribution to the process of interpreting and enforcing the law rather than as a personal affront. The attendance of the public at the court sessions was encouraged so long as they observed due decorum. When talking broke out among the onlookers, the *induna* in charge bellowed 'Silence' in a voice of thunder. If a group of women continued to chatter and giggle after the *induna* had called for silence, he told them to go home. The interest in courts and cases extended to the play of children and to the conduct by the boys of their own affairs in the *laweni* or boys' dormitory. I often saw the young son of a chief or *induna* organizing his playmates into a court and allocating roles to them and in his play imitating the voice and gestures of his father.

NGONI OFFICE-BEARERS

In Chapter II of Part I we stated that the main element in the Ngoni political system in the 1930's was a ruling aristocracy supported by a hierarchy of officials. In this chapter we shall first look at two texts, one by Cibambo on the northern kingdom and the other by a big *induna* in the central kingdom, explaining the relationship of the different office-bearers to the Paramount. We shall see how there were in effect two groups of office-bearers, one related to the territorial divisions of the kingdoms, and the other consisting of state or national officials and those connected with the royal village. There was no set of terms which could be used exclusively for either group, and in fact there was considerable overlapping between them.

We begin with the text by Cibambo which emphasizes the hierarchy of office-bearers in the northern kingdom in pre-European days and illustrates the correlation between the courts and the political administration.

℧ The former government of the Ngoni was based on the following:

(1) Above all was the one called *Inkosi* or *UBaba*, because they thought of him as the father of the country, the head.

(2) After him came the *izinduna*. Sometimes these were two or perhaps four. These were very highly honoured and the Paramount feared them greatly: he called them *Bobaba* and their words had great weight with him. They were the ones who gave advice to the Paramount and if any grave matter arose he called them to hear what they thought. The Paramount in his village had also his old men who helped him with everything small that did not need to go to the *izinduna*. If there was word that the Paramount was meeting with the *izinduna* he first of all met with the old men and asked for advice to place before the *izinduna*. And these old men had the right to speak when the Paramount took counsel with the *izinduna*.

(3) After the *izinduna* came the *amakosana*, or lesser chiefs. These were perhaps the younger brothers of the ruling Paramount, and had their districts under him. They also had their *izinduna* and were responsible for their own districts. When the Paramount met with the *izinduna*, the *amakosana* were also there if it was considered fitting.

(4) Then there were the *alumuzana*. These were over villages or smaller districts. Their villages were called *amakanda* (heads) and they had power in their small districts to carry out the laws and they looked to the *izinduna* for instructions.

(5) Lastly the old men (*madoda*) who wore the head-ring (*cidlodlo*) but not all of them; only those who had good sense and understood the ways of the tribe.

All these five divisions had their share in the government of the country. If there was a great court of justice, all these were to be found at it, and took part in the discussions. If fresh matter arose, or new laws, these delivered them to their villages. Also there were men called *amanxusa*, messengers. These were men chosen to run with messages from the Paramount to the *izinduna* or *amakosana*, to go with and return with news. Almost every village or little district had its chosen messengers. All the types (2), (3) and (4) had their messengers. When anything happened, the messenger in the village of the Paramount made a general proclamation and called the *amanxusa* together. When the *amanxusa* had heard the message they scattered throughout all the country. So in the districts and by this way news travelled very quickly.

In the central kingdom one of the big *izinduna* explained the change in their system which occurred after crossing the Zambesi:

℧ When the Ngoni were coming from the south they chose lesser chiefs and *izinduna* from the *amakosana*, who were the Paramount's brothers, sons of his father and of his father's brothers. These *amakosana* were honoured next to the Paramount. The *alumuzana* were for justice in the courts, and for being the 'ears of the Paramount' in all the country. The change was made by Mputa because he saw that if the *amakosana* were given power they claimed to be big chiefs themselves. Therefore he chose for the courts and for the leaders in war and for lesser chiefs the *alumuzana* and *izinduna* who were clever and whom they could trust.

The diagram on p. 99 relates to the period between 1933 and 1939 and sets out first the officials in the territorial divisions of the Ngoni kingdoms from the Paramount to the headman of a village. In the northern kingdom only the Paramount and the six chiefs had recognized courts, the chiefs' courts operating for their districts and the Paramount's court for the whole kingdom. There were two sets of office-bearers who had no courts but who exercised authority over groups of villages. One group consisted of members of the Jere clan who were not recognized chiefs but were *amakosana*, literally 'children of the chief' but used as a rule for all members of the royal clan. Only certain *amakosana* had villages under them. The other group consisted of the heads of Swazi and trans-Zambesi clans who owned several villages and sometimes had authority over a large area. Cibambo put this group below that of the chiefs, and other informants confirmed this as the pre-European pattern. But the informants also said that many of the powerful *alumuzana* formerly had their own courts and did not have to bring their cases to the chiefs' courts as they did in the 1930's. At the bottom of the territorial hierarchy came the headmen of single villages. In some cases the village headman had formerly been an *induna* in a large village which had broken up. Some were of the royal clan or of Swazi clans. The majority belonged to the local tribes and were owners of villages which were for the most part villages of one kinship group.

The text about the hierarchy in the central kingdom shows that a deliberate change had been made in the traditional pattern to avoid a struggle between the Paramount and his brothers when they had recognized positions as chiefs. The *alumuzana* who appear in the diagram as chiefs were the six who were recognized in 1933 as Subordinate Native Authorities. There were other *alumuzana* who were not so recognized, and certain members of the royal clan, all of whom owned a number of villages but had to take their cases to the recognized courts. The division caused by setting up the Portuguese boundary in the 1890's left many of the leaders of the Maseko clan on the Portuguese side, with the result that the number of *amakosana* owning villages and taking any prominent part in the life of the kingdom was very small; and another large group of the Maseko clan were in Dedza district under Chief Kacindamoto. The majority of village headmen in the central kingdom were of local tribes, and their villages were as a rule much larger than those in the northern kingdom.

Ngoni territorial office-bearers.

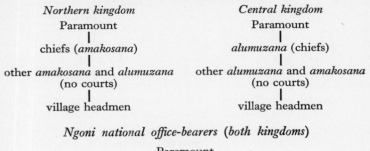

Northern kingdom	Central kingdom
Paramount	Paramount
chiefs (*amakosana*)	*alumuzana* (chiefs)
other *amakosana* and *alumuzana* (no courts)	other *alumuzana* and *amakosana* (no courts)
village headmen	village headmen

Ngoni national office-bearers (both kingdoms)

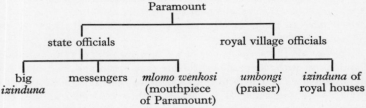

Paramount

state officials — royal village officials

big *izinduna* — messengers — *mlomo wenkosi* (mouthpiece of Paramount) — *umbongi* (praiser) — *izinduna* of royal houses

In the description of the annual gathering in the central kingdom to discuss new regulations, reference was made to those on 'the platform' at one end of the great square. There the Paramount sat with his state officials, the big *izinduna*, the messengers, and his spokesman or mouth-piece. These have been called state officials in the diagram to distinguish them from the officials of the royal village. It is a distinction which is one of convenience rather than of importance. The Paramount's spokes-man lived in the royal village, and the praiser often did not. But the spokesman appeared with the Paramount on all occasions in every part of his kingdom when he went visiting, whereas the official praiser only recited the praise-songs at ceremonies in the royal village.

The big *izinduna*, as Cibambo points out in his text, were very close to the Paramount, advising him on matters of state, and speaking to the cases in his court. The *izinduna* of the big house and of other houses in the royal village were not concerned with matters of state, but with day-to-day affairs in the village. Illustrations of their work will be given in the next chapter. The work of the messengers, described by Cibambo, was that of keeping close touch between the royal village and the chiefs. He describes also how each territorial office-bearer had his messengers to send out to the heads of the next group below his. By this use of mes-sengers for intercommunication between officials, the *alumuzana* and *amakosana* who had no courts received messengers from the chief above them and sent out their own messengers to the villages which they owned.

The only group mentioned by Cibambo which is not included in the diagram is that of the *madoda*, the older men who wore the head-ring. Probably in pre-European days they received more recognition than was apparent in the 1930's after the head-ring had been given up. The *madoda* will be referred to in the next chapter on the royal village and in Chapter V of Part III on age sets. In the appeal court of the Paramount and in the chief's court there was always a group of these senior men sitting behind the *izinduna*, to whom the *induna* speaking to the case sometimes turned for advice and consultation.

Reference was made to an overlap between territorial office-bearers and national office-bearers. The big *izinduna*, the spokesman of the Paramount, and sometimes the messengers, were members of Swazi and trans-Zambesi clans, and often were *alumuzana* who had no courts. This was a method by which in the 1930's those *alumuzana* could be drawn into the circle of officials and receive a small salary for their services.

This set of office-bearers which we have considered in relation to the Paramount, with the exception of his spokesman and his praiser, was duplicated for the chiefs in both kingdoms, whether they were of the royal clan or *alumuzana*. The account of the royal village in the central kingdom which follows in the next chapter will illustrate how these officials functioned in the day-to-day affairs of the Paramount's headquarters.

CHAPTER V

A ROYAL VILLAGE AFTER 1933

The Paramount and his village

FOR some weeks in 1935 and in 1936 I lived in the Paramount's village of Maganga in the central kingdom. The central kingdom included all Ncheu district, consisting of 1,092 square miles, a total population of 88,446, and a density of 80·99 per square mile. The village was 300 yards off the main road running from north to south of Nyasaland, and was approached by a hoed motor road flanked by huts. It consisted of three main sections: the Paramount's large brick residence and the surrounding buildings within a palisade or reed fence, including the huts of his daughter and son-in-law, and of his brother-in-law and sister; the huts and kraal in the section of the *induna* of his big house, Kalilombe Mbewe; and the huts and kraal of the original village 'owned' by the headman, Lazaro Dzonzi. On the south of the village was the large open space where the weekly market was held, and where several Indian stores faced the main road. On the north was the dispensary building, and the circular court-house in a commanding position on a small hill with a big open space all round it.

There were several places in this village which were referred to as the *bwalo*: they included the open space within the reed fence of the Paramount's section, the much larger open and unfenced space round the court-house, and the more restricted spaces round the huts of the *induna* and of the headman. The meaning of the term *bwalo* was always slightly ambiguous in this village since it was often used for the verandah of the royal residence, as well as the open space in front of it. The central Ngoni custom of surrounding the huts of important men and women with high reed fences with a narrow opening, made it easy to say '*ali pa bwalo*', 'he is on the *bwalo*', so that it covered either the verandah of the hut or the space inside the fence. The local usage of *bwalo* by the Cewa people more often denoted the open space in the middle of the village where the men congregated to sit and talk and drink beer.[1] The connotation of *bwalo* in Ngoni villages in the central kingdom was usually in terms of the big house and the space in front of it within the fence.

In Maganga the place to which the name *bwalo* was most often applied was the space within the reed fence surrounding the Paramount's large brick residence and the outbuildings. When I lived in one of the outbuildings at the back of the house, I was said to be living *pa bwalo*; and it was also alluded to as *pa cigodlo*, that is in the enclosure where the Paramount's children lived behind the big house. His daughter's hut was in this section, on the north side, and beyond her hut was that of the *mlomo wenkosi*, who was also the Paramount's brother-in-law, since he had married the Paramount's sister and was the brother of the Paramount's wife. In the other buildings within the reed fence lived several servants of the household, and at the kitchen end of the brick house lived the girls who assisted the Paramount's wife with cooking and looking after her younger children.

When the Paramount built his court-house, he built some offices as part of it for himself, his *mlomo wenkosi*, his treasurer and the court clerk. The intention had been that official business would be carried out there, and relieve the big house of some of its many callers, and also ensure some measure of privacy for those who lived there. It proved very difficult to achieve this separation of public and private affairs, since the tradition that the Paramount was accessible to all his people at all times was persistent.

The entrance to the enclosure or *bwalo* of the big house was guarded in the traditional manner. If strangers (and all visitors were called *alendo* or strangers) arrived on the side road leading off the main road, they inquired from one of the huts there if the headman was present and waited till he arrived. The headman then went to tell the *induna* or the *mlomo wenkosi* that strangers had come, while they waited till the reply

[1] Scott, D. C. *Mang'anja Dictionary*. Edinburgh, 1892.

came. One of these two officials usually came to greet them. He then informed the Paramount that strangers were present and took back the Paramount's greeting to them and asked their business. This was in turn reported to the Paramount, who arranged for their business to be taken care of and, if they were important people, sent an invitation for them to come to the *bwalo*, to which they were escorted by one of his officials and given seats. In due time the Paramount came out of his house and they gave him the *Bayete* and then he greeted them. As a rule he carried on all conversation through his *mlomo wenkosi*, and, after staying for a short time, often went back into the house and left his officials to entertain the guests. If the guests were visiting chiefs and *alumuzana*, word had gone round when they first arrived, and the senior men of the village, the *madoda*, gathered to greet them, and sat in a group as they did for court cases. Such conversations of a social nature took place as a rule in the courtyard where chairs and mats were placed. If it rained or was very hot they went onto the verandah which ran the whole length of the house. Never, so far as I could discover, did visitors come into the house unless they were close relatives of the Paramount or his wife.

Women visitors who came with the men or by themselves went through the same procedure of announcing themselves and stating their business. Then, if they were important people, they were escorted to the courtyard at the back of the big house where they were greeted by the Paramount's wife and by her daughter, who then settled down to talk with them, either out of doors or on the back verandah, according to the weather. It was usual for the Paramount's wife and daughter also to go and greet the men visitors on the front verandah or in the courtyard. They did not stay, however, and if the visitors had come from far the Paramount told his wife, after she had greeted them, to 'catch a fowl'. When she returned to the back courtyard, children chased hens and there was squawking and yelling until the right number had been caught and killed. Pounding of maize began, the fowls were dressed and put in pots on the fire and other 'relish' was prepared of vegetables and groundnuts, and the flour was cooked to make porridge (*nsima*). The Paramount's wife and her helpers prepared the best pot-roast of chicken I have ever had. Food thus prepared was served to the guests on the front verandah in the traditional style, the porridge in food baskets (*nsengwa*), the chicken and other relish in small covered pots. The Paramount offered the food to his guests and then withdrew into the house. When they received the food, as well as when they had finished eating, they thanked him with the traditional *Bayete nkosi*, adding, if they were of Swazi or trans-Zambesi clans, some of the praise names or *izitokozo* of the Maseko Paramounts. To European visitors, and occasionally to Christian Africans, tea was offered with milk and sugar.

Viewed from the back *bwalo*, where I lived and watched all this happening and listened to comments, it was evident that the never-ending hospitality involved both planning and expense. The Paramount's wife had to keep enough food stocks on hand not only to feed her own large family and household, but also to be able to respond to expected and unexpected guests. The Paramount's personal annual salary at that time was £60, out of which he had to keep his family and household in food and clothes and school fees, and pay for the upkeep of his house. The bulk of the cereals and some of the beans and other vegetables used in his house came from his fields worked by hired labour. Another source of food supply was the market 'custom', a small toll levied on the produce sold in the weekly market, which was paid chiefly in kind and put in the storehouses on the Paramount's *bwalo* to be used to feed his guests.[1]

The Paramount not only gave food and drink to the expected and unexpected visitors to the royal village. From time to time he gave a feast to which the Christians of the congregation of the mission church were invited, as on one New Year's Day when I was staying there. He gave a feast to all the neighbourhood on the occasion of his daughter's wedding. From time to time he invited all his people to dance *ligubo* or *ngoma* at the royal village and provided beer for all and food for the *alumuzana* and the chiefs and their wives. The organization of these big feasts demanded planning on a generous scale and a large outlay in maize for porridge and meat for relish. No feast at the Paramount's village was complete without meat enough to satisfy everyone.

The visitors, the feasts, the dances, all had their focal point in the royal residence in the royal village. There were two other focal points in the village where large numbers of people came regularly, and made the place where the Paramount lived a centre which brought his people together and brought him before them as their ruler. These were the market and the court-house which also housed his offices.

Before 1939 the market in the royal village was unique in the area for its size and the service which it rendered to the countryside. At any one time on a Saturday there would be 600 to 1,000 people present. In 1938 a second market was opened by the Paramount at Nsipe at the southern end of his territory. They were definitely his markets in that he allotted space for them; fixed the days on which they were held; controlled the policing of the market and the strangers' huts where sellers arriving overnight could sleep; fixed the prices according to seasonal variations in supply; and, as we have seen, collected 'custom' in lieu of rents for sites. The market at Maganga served an area extending roughly 15 miles to the east, 15 to the west and 10 miles to the north and south. It stretched in the east to below the escarpment whence came bamboo and

---

[1] An average weekly amount of custom reckoned over several weeks was 10s. in cash, and a quantity of bananas, sugar-cane, vegetables and cereals amounting to two sackfuls and sometimes three. The cash was levied on meat, 1s. 9d. per cow, 1s. 6d. per goat or pig; and on mats, baskets, etc. at roughly 1d. in the 1s.

sugar cane, and fish from the lake. From the west came sellers of food-stuffs, mainly maize and vegetables, from the villages in Portuguese territory. Whether by accident or design the sellers took up their stands in the market-place on the side to which they first came. Thus on the east side were the fish-sellers, who had carried their fish up the two escarpments from the lake during the night. Near them were the sellers of bamboo and bark-rope, reed and raffia mats, baskets of all kinds, wooden spoons and hoe handles. The vegetable sellers mostly from Portuguese villages were on the western edge of the market. In the centre under some trees were the butchers selling meat and cutting up the cattle, pigs and goats which they had killed in the early morning. Pottery was in another section, thread for bead-work and grass hats and bangles in another. On the edge of the market site were the Indian stores where, on market days, people with cash in hand from their sales bought cloth and had it made up by the tailors sitting with their sewing machines on the verandahs of the stores.

The Paramount's early life and marriage

The officials surrounding the Paramount in the central kingdom were aware that he had begun his rule under difficulties owing to the death of his father. Two texts on this follow, the first by the *induna* of the royal village, Kalilombe Mbewe, and the second by Ishmael Mwale the treasurer of the Paramount, neither of them members of trans-Zambesi clans, but both imbued with Ngoni sentiments and sense of values and devoted to the royal clan.[1] The first text emphasizes the action taken by the two big *izinduna* of the Paramount to hide and protect the young heir to the Paramountcy, and to look after the wives of the big house.

⦗ Formerly we were on Domwe, and when we left there, we built the first village here and its name was Lizulu. When Gomani I was taken by the Europeans his *izinduna* Cakumbira Ndau and Mambeyu Moyo were here at Lizulu. When Gomani I was taken, his son Phillip Gomani was a young child. He stayed with Cakumbira Ndau, so did the big wives of Gomani I. Other wives of Gomani I went to their own families. Cakumbira took with him from Domwe his own cattle and those of the Paramount. When Gomani I was killed the Europeans did not ask about the child who would enter his place. Later when the people were accustomed to the Europeans, the Europeans asked: 'Who is the child who should enter his place?' And the senior men brought him out from hiding and said 'This is he.' The senior men revealed this because they knew that the war had finished and that he could not be killed.

The text by the treasurer takes up the story from the times when the existence of the heir to the Paramount was made known, and covers

---

[1] The fathers of both these men had been taken by the Ngoni from near the Kirk Range, and trained as warriors in Songea before returning to Nyasaland to the royal village on Domwe mountain.

his boyhood, schooling, marriage, conversion to Christianity and accession to the Paramountcy. The first paragraph refers to the action of a European who had made contact with the young heir because of his friendship with his father.

¶ When Mr. Walker returned to Lizulu on another journey he told the big people, 'Today I am taking the big child and I will bring him up in my home.' He took Philip Gomani and he looked after him very well, in the same way as a black man would bring up his child. He engaged a man to teach the child until he knew Cinyanja well and could read and write it. Altogether he took care of him for five years, and then he brought him back to Lizulu.

When the children were back at the village they were thinking and thinking about the European schools. When they were thus thinking, another European came who lived at Nsoni in the Mang'anja country. He came to recruit men for work. When he saw the children he asked them 'Why do you children just stay here without learning anything?' The children said 'It is school that we want, but we have no means by which we can be helped to go to school'. This European said 'Where I live there is a school of the Blantyre Mission. If you come I will take care of you and pay your school fees.' In very truth when those children went to him, he took care of them well, fed and clothed them and paid their school fees as he said.

In 1915 when he was still at school the Paramount married NaNdau. And the big people said 'The child of the Paramount who ought to enter the chieftainship ought not to marry only one wife.' Because they spoke thus he also married two other women, NaNungu and NaMilanzi, whose home was in the Portuguese country in Mpanyila in Chief Zintambira's kingdom. The Paramount did not want these three wives, and only took them because of the words of the big people. When he had stayed with them only one year, he sent away those two wives and said 'I want to join the Church', and so began in the Bible Class at Blantyre Mission to learn there.

In 1917 before he had finished school they began to build his house in the village which was called Maganga. It was his coming out of the village of Chief Cakumbira. When he left Blantyre in 1918 he went to live in his village because he had finished school. He came with a letter from the Bible Class. But the elders of the church of the Dutch mission in that country did not believe that it could be true that the child of the Paramount would join the church. Before he had been received by the mission, there came to his house at Maganga a European woman who said 'This house is very good. It ought to belong to a Christian'. The Paramount said 'I changed my heart long ago. I brought my letter from the Bible Class and gave it to the elders of the church but they said nothing to me.' Then she said 'Tomorrow you come to my place and let us talk.' The Paramount went. When they had talked she told the minister of the mission station. He said 'All right, next week you come and I will examine you.' That week the Paramount was tested and showed that he believed all the teachings.

N.N.—H

In 1921 he was baptized by the Rev. J. Botes in the year in which he entered the chieftainship, when Cakumbira, the one who took care of the chieftainship, had died. For entering the chieftainship there was not much to be done. The people gathered together, and the Paramount just stood up and grasped his spear and pointed to the south-east. The people danced *ligubo* and praised the Paramount.

The people began to consider and said 'Seeing that he is a young man, how will he know how to judge the cases?' Ha! But there was confusion in their minds, because his judgements excelled those of the big people who had judged formerly. From 1921 to today in all matters he has the chieftainship and Christianity. He holds both these in his hand to strengthen him.

The texts bring out several points relative to the royal village which arose from the circumstances surrounding the early life of the Para-mount. Reference has already been made to the large royal village on Domwe which broke up when Cikusi entered the Paramountcy and built his *lusungulu* village at Liwisini near the Kirk Range. The section of the royal village called Lizulu moved out almost due east from Domwe under its big *induna*, Cakumbira Ndau. When Gomani I was killed after a brief reign of five years, the Ndau clan brought to their village the big wives of Gomani I, including NaMagagula his first wife, in whose house the child Philip Gomani was brought up. With the big *induna* of Lizulu of the Ndau clan was Mambeyu Moyo, one of the big war *izinduna* of Cikusi. Lizulu, with NaMagagula living there, was regarded as the *gogo* village of the Paramount, and from there his own *lusungulu* village went out to build at Maganga where there was already a village under a headman of the local tribe. One of the reasons given for building on a village site already occupied was that the Portuguese frontier restricted all movements to the west, and round the village of Lizulu to the east and south a number of outlying villages were already in existence. Proximity to the main north to south Nyasaland road was also considered a good reason for building the Paramount's village on the site at Maganga. Lizulu village had two important aspects. It was the *gogo* village of the Paramount, and it was also the head village of the Ndau clan, and the court of Chief George Ndau who was one of the S.N.A.

The conversion of the Paramount to Christianity was a severe blow for the older officials in his kingdom. They feared that much of the ritual associated with the office of the Paramount would necessarily dis-appear and that the Ngoni kingdom would become weakened in con-sequence. Three events partly allayed these fears though the older men were never wholly reconciled. One was his marriage to NaNdau, daughter of Cakumbira Ndau who had hidden him, thus binding the royal line to the powerful Ndau clan which had protected him in his childhood. Another was the recognition in 1933 by the Nyasaland government of the Paramountcy with its Appeal Court. The third was

the Paramount's interest in modern aspects of administration, especially
after his visit to the course for chiefs held at the Jeanes School in Zomba
in 1934. The old councillors, sceptical though they were of many modern
innovations, recognized that they were in line with European ideas of
administration, and also that they appealed to the younger educated men
in the kingdom who had travelled and seen other countries and ways
of living.

The Paramount married NaNdau as his big wife, and though, as the
text mentions, he married two other wives when urged by the senior
men, he sent them away after a year or two and NaNdau remained his
only wife. She had an assured position since she bore him five sons and
two daughters, the first-born being a daughter and receiving all the
respect due to a Royal Sister. One of the brothers of NaNdau was chief
of a division, and another was *mlomo wenkosi* to the Paramount. She
succeeded in maintaining much of the traditional pattern in the royal
village and the big house. Her personal supervision of the household
was thorough and competent. She exercised complete authority over the
girls and women belonging to the household and arranged that the
Ngoni custom of examining the young girls, including her own daughter,
at regular intervals should be maintained. Her knowledge of Ngoni songs
and dances, and her own skilled and graceful participation in the dances
on state occasions, brought her before the people in her role as the big
wife. At the feasts given by the Paramount she moved about among the
people to serve them, and listened to complaints from the women about
affairs in their villages which she then handed on to her husband.

The back verandah and all the outbuildings were the domain of the
Paramount's wife. When I was there, she had some ten or twelve girls
and women as well as several men working for her. They came and went
if they had homes elsewhere, and the personnel changed often. All the
household work was done by them: bringing water and fuel, pounding
maize, and a good deal of the cooking, though this was closely supervised
by the Paramount's wife. No beer was made in the household as it was
against the rules of the church to which they belonged. In other Ngoni
households of subordinate chiefs and *alumuzana* who were not Christian,
the brewing of beer was a time-absorbing part of the household tasks
and was shared by the different wives under the supervision of the big
house. In Maganga, when the Paramount was entertaining unexpected
guests and wanted to offer them beer, he inquired from his *induna* if
anyone was brewing beer in the village, and sent for some for which he
paid. When he knew beforehand that guests were coming who would
expect beer to be offered to them as part of the Paramount's hospitality,
he told his *induna* to see that beer was made in one of the village households, and he paid for it.

The cooking which went on in the big house kitchens was always
extensive. The Paramount, his wife and six children had two meals a

day, and so did all the regular helpers in the household. The stream of
visitors was incessant, especially on Saturdays when the market was
held, and on the days when the Appeal Court was in session at the
court-house adjoining the village. Not every caller was given food, but
if they came from a distance it was always offered. In the setting of a
modern brick house and a Christian household with only one wife, the
Paramount had to provide a great deal of hospitality. The old tradition
that *alumuzana* and other important men visited the Paramount daily no
longer held. But the weekly market and the court meetings, and the lorry
service on the main road bringing callers from north and south, as well as
administrative affairs which had constantly to be discussed and settled,
made the Paramount's house and *bwalo* a very busy place.

Officials of the royal village and state officials

When I lived in the royal village for several weeks I was aware of a
never-ending stream of persons coming to consult or to work with the
Paramount. Well protected as he was by the Ngoni method of indirect
approach and the surveillance of the village and *bwalo* by the *induna* of
the big house and the *mlomo wenkosi*, the Paramount was still subject to
constant inquiries from his office-bearers who needed his counsel, and
from persons great and small from all over his kingdom who believed
that he could help them. Among the village officials the *induna* of the
big house worked closely with the headman of the village, and displayed unremitting efforts to see that all affairs in the immediate neighbourhood of the Paramount should go smoothly. They were constantly
on the *bwalo* of the big house, or near the gate of the fence surrounding
it. These two always turned up when visitors came, and sat on the
verandah or in the *bwalo* with the other senior men, and kept an eye on
all that happened. If anything went wrong in the village or the com-
pound when the Paramount was away they were in great distress, as on
one occasion when a man ran amok and threatened people with a knife.
There was a strong tradition that around the Paramount and his living
quarters everything and everyone had to be orderly and peaceable.

The *umbongi*, or praiser of the Paramount, was among the royal village officials, though he only appeared on the *bwalo* when ceremonies
took place there. He sometimes came when important visitors arrived if
their visit was known in advance. He always came to the big dances and
feasts held at the royal village. He was an old man, tall and spare, lean-
ing heavily on a long staff, and many of the onlookers who listened
attentively to his praise-songs showed nervousness when he began
making personal remarks, for he had a sharp tongue and a flow of
language.

Of the state officials the *mlomo wenkosi* was seldom away from the big
house or far from the person of the Paramount. He had married the
Paramount's sister, and was own brother to the *inkosikazi*, and his

kinship links strengthened and facilitated his official relations. If the Paramount went away visiting, he generally went with him, and if he were very busy or resting, then the *mlomo wenkosi* would act as his assistant and endeavour to meet the needs of the applicants. He was known on the register of Native Administration employees as the Paramount's assistant.

The other state officials who were constantly at the royal village included the clerk of the Appeal Court, the four councillors, the three messengers, and the treasurer. The clerk was in his office on most days, and when the court was sitting he kept the records. He also came to the big house when important visitors arrived and sat with the senior men. The four councillors and three messengers were all senior men, five of them of trans-Zambesi clans. The councillors conducted the cases in the court and reported to the Paramount, and spoke for him when he gave judgement. They and the messengers always came to the big house before the court opened, and returned there to eat food after the sessions were over. This was invariably an occasion for discussing cases and judgements and the general state of the country. The fact that the court was an Appeal Court, to which cases were referred from the six subordinate courts, enabled the councillors to estimate the efficiency of these courts in various parts of the country. Their private comments on the abilities of the respective chiefs to maintain order and judge cases in their courts were often caustic.

Several references have been made to the treasurer of the Paramount, a title assumed by Ishmael Mwale in view of his financial responsibilities for the central kingdom. The District Commissioner in his report for 1935 said:

❡ During the year the financial responsibility of the Native Authority was increased: he was handed over the keys of his safe at the Boma, and the District Commissioner only handled his cash for the purpose of checking. Gomani's clerk has acquired or given himself the name of 'Treasurer', and in this capacity frequently visits the Subordinate Authorities to make a financial inspection of their books, and to collect money which is surplus to their needs and bring it on charge in the main account. The District Commissioner's role has in consequence become akin to that of an auditor.

Ishmael Mwale, the 'Treasurer', has shown ability for his duties. Not only is he capable of abstracting the revenue and expenditure of the Subordinate Authorities into a common ledger, but the time has now come when he should be fully capable of preparing draft estimates for the consideration of the District Commissioner.

The treasurer knew the country and the people of the different regions in a way that no other official of the Paramount knew them, and was therefore often called in for advice when petitions were brought in or complaints made. His eldest son married the Paramount's older daughter, and there was therefore a close tie between the two families.

He was a student of Ngoni history and custom, and used his travels as treasurer to collect new information. He always intended to write a history of the central kingdom as Cibambo had done for the northern kingdom, but his public duties never gave him time.

In making contact with his people and keeping in touch with his officials the Paramount did not rely only on their visits to the royal village. Two or three times a year he toured his kingdom, accompanied by his *mlomo wenkosi* and the treasurer, and stayed at the head villages of the chiefs and also of other *alumuzana*. The treasurer spoke enthusiastically of the Paramount's habit of making himself known to his people and enabling them to present petitions to him in person. He met village headmen on their own ground, and *alumuzana* who were unostentatiously directing the affairs of their villages and areas, as well as the official chiefs or Subordinate Native Authorities. He saw for himself how his own regulations were being carried out and how the measures for agricultural improvement and cattle-dipping which the Government was promoting were being adopted. These visits in his own territory were followed by visits to Blantyre and Zomba and to the mining centres outside the country where his people were working. He was thus able to check on the conditions in the subordinate chiefs' areas which had been created by the prolonged absence of men from the villages.

The Paramount and changes in law and custom

Through his school education at Blantyre, his membership of a Christian church, and through attending the chiefs' course at the Jeanes School in Zomba, the Paramount stood between the old and the new in the changing conditions in his kingdom. After the 1933 Ordinance one of the changes in administration was that a Native Authority had to budget for income and expenditure in his area. The income for 1935 for this area was £959, made up of a share of the taxes; fifty per cent. of the yearly rental of stores; court fines and fees and beer licences. The expenditure was £832, under items of salaries to the Paramount and subordinate chiefs; salaries for messengers, councillors, clerks and policemen; payment of fourpence per tax to the headmen of the villages so that it was to their advantage to collect the full amount; and a small sum for uniforms, office expenses and such items as cash boxes and handcuffs. This budget for the central Ngoni kingdom was drawn up in consultation with the District Officer by the Paramount and his treasurer. It was a source of great pride to the treasurer that he had, as we have seen, his own key to a safe in the District Office where he put the tax money collected in the area, and drew out sums needed for expenditure in the Paramount's office.

In 1933, as already mentioned, a meeting of subordinate chiefs, *alumuzana* and headmen heard the Paramount's proposals for new regulations about village improvement and agreed to them. These regulations were

called 'to make a clean village', and were one of the results of the Paramount's visits to his area. They included building latrines, sweeping the
open spaces round huts, disposing of rubbish, mending roofs and fences,
smooth mudding of houses, digging wells. The Paramount appointed
three men who were called *masanitari* to go round the villages to inspect
and report to him, and instituted a system of fines for failure to carry out
these measures. In addition to promoting clean villages, he ordered that
cattle were to be dipped regularly, cultivation was to be carried out by
a ridge system instead of mounds, and all sick people, especially women,
were to attend hospital. He sent his own daughter to hospital for her
confinement, and she attended the baby clinic regularly with her child.

Some of the changes in local customs which the Paramount ordered
were not so easy to enforce as the newer practices in relation to health
and hygiene. He forbade drinking at night when quarrelling became
rife; he prohibited Cewa dances such as *vinyau* and *malombo* and the
Cewa female puberty rite of *cinamwali*. The only dances allowed were
the Ngoni dance *ngoma*; the *ligubo* or war-dance at his village; and the
individual hero's dance (*ligiya*) when a lion or leopard was brought to
his village. Marriages had to be registered, and births and deaths
recorded and reported to the Paramount when he visited the villages.

It was always possible to start an argument among the senior men
sitting on the Paramount's *bwalo*, or on the steps of his court-house,
either on the subject of how far Ngoni law and custom had replaced
local Ntumba and Cewa custom, or on the advantages and disadvantages
of the modern reforms of the Paramount. Some of the older men were
anxious to establish that the Ngoni, meaning those of the trans-Zambesi
clans, had not only achieved a political conquest but had also changed
the practices of the local peoples and made them observe Ngoni customs.
They used to assert, among other things, that the local people had
become patrilineal, and had adopted a *lobola* form of marriage—statements which could easily be disproved and were laughed at by the
onlookers. On the other hand, they were right when they said that Ngoni
laws and court procedure were universally approved and followed, and
that the younger generations at least were willing to carry out the welfare measures of the Paramount. One constant feature of all such discussions of recent changes was the steady support given by the Ntumba and
Tengo clan leaders to the Paramount and his rule. This, more than any
other feature, proved that the trans-Zambesi pattern of political rule had
triumphed, and that in their loyalty to the Paramount and their practice
of Ngoni custom the village headmen and their families could be counted
on to support the rulers.

PART III
NGONI SOCIETY

CHAPTER I

NGONI SOCIAL ORGANIZATION

A BRIEF review was given in Chapter III of Part I of the main elements of Ngoni culture, analysed into 'patterns' covering kinship, village lay-out, ritual, ceremonial, and language. In this section we shall be con-sidering the principal social institutions embodying Ngoni culture: their clans, houses, families and age sets. We shall find evidence in the two kingdoms of an extensive common element in the social organization which the Ngoni brought with them from the south. Some important diversities will be evident also, such as the variations in virilocal resi-dence found in the central kingdom, and the less widespread practice there of *lobola* marriage. Those elements which were common to Ngoni social organization in both kingdoms were often those which distin-guished Ngoni culture from that of the neighbouring peoples. Patrilineal descent, the house system, the ranking of clans, the *laweni* organization of boys' life and activities—these were all distinctively Ngoni, practised by families of Swazi and trans-Zambesi clans, and sometimes adopted by individuals and families of other clans who had been associated with the Ngoni over long periods. Nevertheless, in many of the villages of the central kingdom there were clearly two cultures existing side by side: the Ngoni culture being that of an aristocratic minority and the local culture that of the majority, who in the kingdom were equally sub-jects of the Paramount but in their villages possessed inferior social status.

Indications were to be seen, even in the more conservative and more isolated northern kingdom, that modern influences were affecting Ngoni social institutions. We have already noticed some of the effects of the cessation of warfare on a social system founded on military traditions. The exodus of young men from Ngoni villages to seek work elsewhere was very extensive, especially in the northern kingdom, where the level of education was higher but employment was not available, and this had repercussions on the age of marriage, the distribution of wealth, and the undertaking of family responsibilities, including the care of the old people. The gradual decline in polygyny, largely but not entirely due to the work of missions, was beginning to have its effects on the working of the house system and on the interrelations of the generations within the family group.

In the 1930's many of these modern changes were appearing but the traditional institutions were still functioning, and the Ngoni leaders themselves were clear about those forms and activities which were distinctively their own.

CHAPTER II

CLANS

In Chapter III of Part I we saw that the Ngoni clans had a particular role in their political and social organization. These clans had certain characteristics which distinguished them from the clans of the local peoples, and which they had in common with the Nguni group of the South-eastern Bantu. The use of the clan name in address and in thanking for gifts, the strict exogamy in the clans, and the hierarchy of rank among the clans—these were all of southern origin. Mrs. Hoernlé,[1] writing of the social organization among the northern Nguni, said that the clan was called *isibongo*, 'a word referring more particularly to the name of the group'. The Ngoni spoke of their clan name as their *cibongo*, and they generally added 'that is my thanking name'. Dr. Kuper [2] used the term clan for 'the furthest extension of kinsmen traced through the father or the mother'. She referred also to the sub-division of clans among the Swazi—a process of fission by which a section of a clan was known by a double name, so that the Nkosi clan became the Nkosi Gininza, the Nkosi Mamba, with other sub-divisions. These divisions eventually became recognized as separate clans, so that marriage could take place between them, and so that the heads of the sub-clans could achieve independence from the head of the original clan. It is possible that some development of this kind took place after the Ngoni left Natal for, as we shall see later in this chapter, there were among the Ngoni a number of clan names which they said emphatically were Swazi but which were not among those noted by Dr. Kuper [3] or by Bryant.[4] In tracing the early history of the Swazi Dr. Kuper [5] distinguished between two periods: the first, when small patrilineal clans were migrating southwards, and the second, when rival clan heads became petty chiefs having non-clansmen among their subjects. At the beginning of their northward march Zwangendaba and Ngwana, in addition to being military leaders, were petty chiefs of this type, each including among his followers members of his own clan as well as others.

The Swazi became a heterogeneous nation composed of people from over 70 clan descent groups, of which one-fifth were true Swazi, one-seventh were prior inhabitants of the territory, and the rest were migrants into the kingdom. The clan hierarchy which was part of the structure of the nation showed, as Dr. Kuper [6] pointed out, 'some connexion between the rank of a clan and the period at which it was

---

[1] Hoernlé, A. W., 'Social organisation', in *The Bantu-speaking Tribes of South Africa*, p. 80.   [2] Kuper, H. *An African Aristocracy*, p. 11.
[3] Op. cit., p. 111.   [4] *Olden Times in Zululand and Natal*, pp. 681–97.
[5] Kuper, H. op. cit., p. 11.   [6] ibid. p. 113.

incorporated into the nation'. This, as we saw in Chapter I of Part I, was what took place in the Ngoni kingdoms. By the time they settled in Nyasaland, a hierarchical relationship had been built up between the clans based on the length of time they had formed part of the Ngoni kingdom. As the Swazi had their true Swazi, 'those found ahead', and late comers, so the Ngoni had their 'Swazi' clans, others from across the Zambesi, those who joined from this side, and the local peoples.

Dr. Kuper [1] summarized her description of the Swazi clan hierarchy by saying that it was 'neither precise nor static . . . a certain degree of mobility is recognized amongst the élite'. The Ngoni too had their own ways of adjusting a somewhat rigid system to suit their needs in spite of their recognition of the ranking of clans, and the fact that in the 1930's, the kingdoms were ruled by an aristocracy. As among the Swazi, officials were appointed who did not belong to Swazi or trans-Zambesi clans. Much importance was attached, as also among the Swazi, to 'marrying up' and a number of instances of this were recorded, particularly in the central kingdom. In such cases a man, when explaining who he was, often gave the name of his mother as well as that of his father in order to impress upon the inquirer that he came from Swazi stock on one side, though his clan name, being his father's, did not show it.

Since some discussion of clans comes into every section of this book it will be useful to summarize here the main characteristics of the Ngoni clans in the two kingdoms. We shall be referring exclusively to the Swazi and trans-Zambesi clans, except when others are specifically mentioned.

Each clan was primarily a group of people with a common name. The families bearing this name might be found throughout the Ngoni kingdoms and states, in the towns and elsewhere, as the census figures quoted in Chapter I, Part I show. Their kinship was recognized firstly through clan exogamy, and secondly through the fact that when Ngoni people met a fellow clansman, they greeted him with particular warmth and both individuals were prepared to render each other mutual service. I met a number of the younger educated Ngoni who set out on a journey in Nyasaland, or to Northern or Southern Rhodesia, with the express purpose of looking for fellow clansmen, getting hospitality from them, and inviting them to visit Nyasaland and receive return hospitality. I was present at one or two such meetings in Nyasaland between Ngoni from the two kingdoms and the conversation began by establishing what branch of the Moyo or Gama clan they belonged to, and where the head village was situated. Within each kingdom each clan had a head village, and the head of that village was the head of the clan. In most of the Swazi clans the head of the clan was acknowledged as a *mulumuzana*. This correlation between being head of a Swazi clan and being a

[1] ibid. p. 233.

mulumuzana was not invariable. Some informants said that *alumuzana* were appointed by the Paramount. Others said that if the ancestor of a Swazi clan was known by name to have crossed the Zambesi with Zwangendaba or Mputa then his descendant in the direct line was always a *mulumuzana*.

It was the criterion of having a known ancestor and knowing the genealogy of the clan that was most widely accepted in acknowledging the head of a Swazi clan as *mulumuzana*. At the clan head village prayers were addressed to this ancestor, his cattle were sacrificed, and the names recited as far back as tradition and memory could recall. Later we shall see that there were said to be about 25 Swazi clans in the northern kingdom and 29 in the central. Among these about 15 in the northern and 12 in the central kingdom had head villages where the ancestor cult was performed. In the central kingdom several of the leading clans had their head villages in Portuguese territory, and therefore did not carry out the cult in the central kingdom.

In the hierarchy of the clans the Swazi clans were the acknowledged leaders. In village and national life this leadership was accorded to the royal clans and the clans of the chiefs, and was the reason for the respect shown to *alumuzana* who had no direct political power. Only the heads of Swazi clans possessed *izitokozo* (honorific epithets) which commemorated events in the past history of the clan leaders. On all ceremonial occasions heads of Swazi clans, whether in national or in village affairs, took precedence over the rest when walking in procession, standing for dances, taking part in ritual, or sitting down at feasts. Certain forms of burial, such as the use of a sheep-skin, and placing the corpse on a shelf in the grave, were observed only for members of the Swazi clans.

In arranging marriages, there was, in addition to strict exogamy within a clan, a prohibition on marriage between clans which had *cibale* (brotherhood) relations. In the central kingdom the royal clan, Maseko, had *cibale* with the Ngozo clan which provided the royal shadow, and with the Nzunga clan. The Nzunga and the Maseko clans shared the same taboos, notably elephant and fish. As well as prohibited marriages between certain clans, there were preferred marriages between certain others. In general there was a preference for marriage between the families of leading Swazi clans. In the northern kingdom the Nqumayo clan had a preference for marrying into the Thole, Nhlane, Maluleka and Pakati clans. It was alleged that formerly they could marry only into these clans, but in the 1930's exceptions were found in a number of villages.

The following lists of the names of Swazi clans were collected from informants in the two kingdoms, who were questioned closely about which names should be included under the title of Swazi. This was the grouping claimed by the Ngoni in both kingdoms. They said emphatically 'These are Swazi clans.' The first set of names on each list, 17 in the northern kingdom and 12 in the central, occurs in the lists of clan names given by Kuper [1] and by Bryant.[2] Very few, however, were enumerated as names of actual Swazi clans either by Kuper or Bryant, and they related, in fact, to several tribal groups which were found in the early nineteenth century in Natal. The Ngoni made no attempt to separate these so-called Swazi clans into constituent tribal groups, as they did the Karanga, Tsonga and Venda clans. I have therefore accepted this classification of these clans and used the name of Swazi as it was used by the Ngoni.

Swazi clans in the Ngoni kingdoms occurring in the lists of Kuper and Bryant

Northern kingdom	Central kingdom
Thole	Maseko
Nkosi	Magagula
Gama	Mlangeni
Nzima	Manyoni
Sibande	Maganeni
Ngomezulu	Mashabana
Ndabandaba	Tabete
Tsela	Pahla
Nkambule	Maziya
Mdluli	Magininda
Pakati	Dube
Maluleka	Nqumayo
Madise	
Mlangeni	
Mabaso	
Ndlovu	
Nqumayo	

Swazi clans not occurring in the lists of Kuper and Bryant

Northern kingdom	Central kingdom
Jere	Magwagwa
Nyambose	Ngozo
Nhlane	Nhlahla
Mkalipi	Ngwana
Madlopa	Ngqongwana
Ngqongwana	Ziphondo
Gausi	Gwati
Muyeni	Nzunga
	Mhlambi
	Phungwako
	Ndumbu
	Mauya
	Likhuleni
	Manokera
	Maile

---

[1] op. cit. p. 233   [2] op. cit., pp. 681–97

The Ngoni were, as I have said, emphatic that the names on this second list should be included among the Swazi clans. It was headed in the northern kingdom by the royal clan and in the central kingdom by one of the most honoured clans, and all the clan names were in fact held in great respect. There are three possible explanations for their non-occurrence in the Kuper and Bryant lists. One is that the clan name and the *isitakazelo*, the ceremonial or address name, may have been interchanged, and the original clan name forgotten. Another explanation may be that fission of the clans took place on the march, and as a result new clan names appeared. Both these were likely and may account for some of the omissions. The third reason may be that on the march and after settlement the Ngoni may have forgotten the correct pronunciation even of their famous clan names, and the anthropologist may have made mistakes in transcribing them.

Reference was made earlier in the chapter to the fact that social mobility was found among the Ngoni aristocracy. One form in which this took place affected the position of individuals belonging to the royal clan. In the northern kingdom the chiefs as well as the Paramount all belonged to the royal clan, and descendants of the sons and grandsons of Zwangendaba and his brothers were found all over the kingdom. In the central kingdom, where none of the chiefs were of the royal clan, the descendants of Cidyawonga, the brother of Cikusi, were in the secession state under Chief Kacindamoto, and the children of the brothers of Cikusi and Gomani I were most of them living in the Portuguese Ngoni kingdom. Thus there were large numbers of the royal clan in the northern kingdom, some in the family groups of the chiefs, others living in their own or other villages; while in the central kingdom members of the royal clan were comparatively few in number and were excluded from all political power unless they were of the Paramount's immediate family. Members of other Swazi clans in the north felt they had to assert themselves against the dominance of the royal clan in social as well as political life. In the central kingdom it was the royal clan who asserted themselves socially because they had no political rights in the chiefdoms.

There was a general opinion that individuals bearing the royal clan name who were not of the immediate family of the Paramount or, in the north, were not among his subordinate chiefs, ought not to trade on their name. This meant in effect expecting to get hospitality and other formal recognition when visiting other villages. As one informant said 'If they come to a village they like people to tremble and say "A chief has come".' They wanted to be recognized everywhere as *makosana*, children of chiefs. The popular resistance to these claims came from two sources. One was the general public who did not see why an ever-increasing number of people bearing the royal clan name should get free food and beer—gifts which they would not hesitate to give to people they acknowledged as rulers or direct sons of rulers. The other opposition came from the heads of the Swazi clans who saw their claims to recognition threatened by large numbers of these *makosana*. When such a person was announced a *mulumuzana* might comment to bystanders 'Who is this man? We do not know his father.' Then to save his face as well as that of the visitor, he would send a greeting to him and order beer to be supplied, while avoiding any elaborate form of entertainment. This subtle form of resistance to what were considered undue claims from lesser members of the royal clan was found everywhere.

In both kingdoms the Paramounts and chiefs, especially after 1933, appointed as officials for the kingdom and for the royal village, members of Swazi clans, but also, and increasingly, members of cis-Zambesi and local clans. This practice brought together in the royal villages and in the chiefs' villages men of the ruling aristocracy and men of the lesser clans, to share administrative responsibility, to assist on ceremonial occasions, and to take part on an equal footing in giving and receiving hospitality. This mingling on the official level was one of the reasons why marriages became more frequent between girls of Swazi clans and men of non-Swazi clans whose fathers had been promoted to official positions. The marriage of Paramount Gomani II's daughter to the son of his treasurer was an illustration of this. The daughters of families of Swazi clans were also sought in marriage by men of non-Swazi clans who, through their education, had got well-paid work in the Government or in commercial firms, and could therefore afford to give cattle for *lobola* for the girls. These were two instances of the type of marrying up which in the 1930's was lessening the sharp division in social life between Swazi and other clans. We shall see in Chapter IV, pp. 137, 140) that Ngoni fathers of daughters married to non-Swazi clansmen found a way of keeping their married daughters, as well as their sons, in their villages, particularly in the central kingdom.

Though the Ngoni clan system in the 1930's was, in Dr. Kuper's phrase, 'neither precise nor static', it was an integral part of Ngoni social organization. It was closely related on the one hand to the ruling aristocracy, and on the other to the social hierarchy. Both in the villages and in the national life of the kingdoms individuals belonging to Swazi clans played a leading part in social and ceremonial life, and carried on those distinctive Ngoni practices which their ancestors had brought with them from the south.

CHAPTER III

HOUSES

Writing of the social organization of the northern Nguni among the South-eastern Bantu, Mrs. Hoernlé[1] referred to three divisions of the typical village: the *indlunkulu* section where the principal hut was that of the mistress of the village; the *ikhohlo* section on the left-hand side of this hut, and the *inqadi* section on the right. The terminology used by the northern Nguni expressed right and left hand from the point of view of someone looking up from the gate of the kraal. I found that among the Ngoni they used right and left the other way as if the person were at the top of the kraal looking down at the gate, and I have adopted their usage.

Ngoni villages, which were royal villages or the head villages of Swazi and trans-Zambesi clans, also had a tripartite division into houses related to leading women, as we saw in the village plan in Chapter III of Part I, but there was a major difference between them and the northern Nguni grouping described by Mrs. Hoernlé. In Ngoni villages the *indlunkulu*, the hut at the head of the kraal, was occupied by the mother of the owner of the village, who had 'come out' with him from his father's village. In the right-hand section of the huts round the kraal was the hut of the owner's big wife, and on the left the hut of his next important wife. These three huts, representing three houses, were the focal points of the main divisions of the village. In fact in most villages the owner of the *indlunkulu* had the huts of other widows of her late husband beside her on each side, and the *cigodlo*, or section where the sons of the owner of the village lived, spread over a wide area behind the *indlunkulu* and behind the huts of the two chief wives. The plan used in Chapter III of Part I was necessarily simplified in order to bring out the main points. The grouping of huts in typical Ngoni villages showed varying degrees of elaboration, and it was not always easy at first to trace their connexions with the houses.

Houses in the Ngoni kingdoms could be considered as divisions of the village, though they did not always cover all the divisions. If we look at the membership of a house, as it was illustrated in a typical Ngoni village, it is clear that it had in it three elements connected by ties of kinship, affinity or association with the owner of the house, who was either a wife or a mother of the male owner of the village. The kinship group related to the *indlunkulu* comprised the male owner of the village, his mother and classificatory mothers with his brothers who had joined him. In the big house and in the second house of his wives the kinship

[1] op. cit. p. 83.

group consisted of himself and the mother and her children, including her daughters only until they married.

The affinal element in a house consisted of the other wives associated with the owner of the house as co-wives, and the wives of the sons of the owner. Both the kinship group and the affinal group were bound together by their rights in the cattle of the herd which was known as 'the cattle of the house of X'. From that herd were taken cattle for the *lobola* of the wives married after the house was founded, and for the wives of the sons and adopted sons of the house. Into that herd came the cattle received for the marriages of the daughters belonging to the house and the gift cattle sent to wives by their fathers after marriage. When the *lobola* had been fully paid up for a daughter of the house, then her relationship with it ceased and she was thenceforth known as belonging to her husband's mother's house.

Associated with the house in the villages of the Paramounts, the chiefs and the leading *alumuzana* were two other groups of people. One was the *induna* appointed 'to take care of the house' and his family. In the 1930's the *induna* was in charge of the cattle and of the many activities connected with the house, including the organization of male labour in hut-building, in kraal construction and in cultivation; he was consulted by the male members of the house about the selling of cattle and the use of the goods accumulated in the house. The other group associated with the house in pre-European days consisted of captives taken in war and allocated to the house who worked as labourers. The servants who worked for a house in the 1930's assisted with cooking, beer-making and minding the children, and they had huts near that of the owner of the house to which they belonged, placed on the right- or left-hand side of the kraal according to their affiliation with the big house or the second house. Informants said that in the past such association with a house included giving a beast from the herd of the house for the marriage of a servant. The *induna*, through the marriage of his daughters, built up his own herd, which he frequently kept at first with the cattle of the house in the main kraal, later building his own kraal.

A new house began when a man married his big wife. Although at first he built her a hut at the back of his mother's hut in his father's village, as soon as he moved out to his new village after his father's death, the big wife's hut had the next most important site in the kraal after that of the *indlunkulu*, and the second wife had the third place of importance. In some of the larger villages of the central kingdom, the custom of moving out into a new village after the death of the former owner had been given up, partly because of pressure on the land. The house grouping in relation to the siting of huts then became very complex, but the pattern was nevertheless discernible. The two sections under the big house and the *gogo* house, which had formerly divided into two villages, continued to exist together, and at Mcakhatha this dual pattern covered two generations including the houses of the former chief and the reigning one.

The houses served several purposes in the organization of village life on the one hand, and on the other, provided an important instrument for regulating succession and inheritance, and for carrying out traditional ceremonies and ritual. It was the eldest son of the second house who would, if the *lusungulu* practice was followed, remain behind with the *gogo* village; and he was responsible for conducting traditional ritual and was expected to be able to carry out ceremonial procedure correctly. This was the main function of the *gogo* village and of the man who was head of the male members of the *gogo* house. The corresponding head of the male members of the big house was the owner of the village, and it was his eldest son by his first wife who would normally succeed him as chief or *mulumuzana*. The members of each house had a stake in the property of that house, particularly in the herd of cattle owned by it, and in any goods, such as cloth, bought by the sale of the cattle of the house. The house united the male members who belonged to it through this common ownership of cattle. In Chapter II of Part IV we shall examine further this aspect of belonging to a house.

In the organization of village life in villages belonging to chiefs or *alumuzana* the houses established the status of the wives of the owner of the village, and the status of those of his mothers who had come with him. His mother in the *indlunkulu* hut ranked first among her co-widows. The big wife came next, and the wife of the second house after her. Wives attached to the big house ranked above those attached to the second house.

The houses fulfilled their most prominent role in the day-to-day activities of the households associated with them. It was in these daily affairs and in planning for future events that the house organization provided the chief channels of authority. The exercise of this authority ranged from instruction in household tasks and emphasis on good standards of housekeeping to settling minor disputes arising from marital quarrels over property and over the custody of children. These minor cases could be settled out of court if the senior women showed that they knew how to listen to complaints and give advice which was accepted, with the result that good relations were restored. The main topics of discussion among the senior women on the verandah of the *indlunkulu* were the ingredients of these minor quarrels and disputes. If, by judicious handling, they could keep the cases out of court, they knew, and so did the village, that their authority was enhanced and their prestige more firmly established.

The authority of senior women was further reinforced through their organization of women's labour in household work and in cultivation. This authority in domestic affairs covered a woman's own household and the women and girls attached to it as household servants, the households of her co-wives who were junior to her in the house, and the households of her sons' wives. These women also decided when to undertake certain work in cultivation or in harvesting crops, when to brew beer, when to re-polish the floors of huts and the sitting place in front of the huts, when to replenish the stock of cloth, ornaments and beads, baskets and mats, which were part of the wealth of the house. Other occasions for the exercise of authority were attending and super-intending women's confinements and the private puberty rite of the girls, advising on matters of health, and supervising the training of children.

All these activities of the owners of the houses were so much part of the day-to-day life of a village that they could pass almost unnoticed unless a detailed analysis were made. The position and authority of owners of houses was, however, immediately evident on ceremonial occasions. These included the pre-marriage ceremony of *umsindo*, which was abandoned after the Europeans came; the series of visits and ex-changes leading up to the marriage ceremony, *mtimba*; brewing beer on a number of occasions, for dancing *ngoma* and *ligubo*, for funerals and subsequent ritual shaving, or for entertaining important visitors whose coming was expected so that beer could be prepared in advance. On all such occasions, the courtyard surrounding the *indlunkulu* was a scene of great activity. Men put on their war-dance equipment there; the beer pots were assembled there; meat and blood for feasts were cooked there, while the less important maize porridge (*nsima*) was cooked in subor-dinate households. From the courtyard of the *indlunkulu* a procession of the *manina* (senior women) led by the owner of the house went out to greet visitors, to go to the beer drink, to take part in the dances, and to perform the ritual connected with births, deaths and marriages.

MARRIAGE IN NGONI SOCIETY

Earlier in this chapter it was said that a new house derived from the marriage of a leading man to his big wife. Since marriage was so closely linked with the continuance and development of houses, and since a new wife when married separated from her own mother's house and became a member of her husband's mother's house, I have included a discussion of marriage in this chapter on houses.

There were three main principles in Ngoni marriage. It was a binding contract sealed by the exchange of cattle; it established succession in the male line; it formed a link between leading Swazi clans. When we examine in detail the organization of Ngoni marriage we see that its objectives were to build up a series of inter-clan and inter-family rela-tionships. These began with inter-marriage between the leading Swazi clans, in order to strengthen the political and social relationships within that inner circle of Ngoni society. The political allegiance of leading individuals from clans of non-Swazi origin was strengthened by marriage with men and women of Swazi clans. There were two Ngoni practices which could be regarded as directly contributing to marriage as a binding process within the society. One was the inheritance of widows by a man's brothers. No formal marriage ceremony took place and if the widow was elderly it was primarily a method of providing for her needs. If she was still capable of bearing children, however, this inheritance ensured that she would continue to produce offspring for the family she had married into, and that her relationship with that family would be maintained. Thus ties which appeared to have been broken by death could be re-established. There were two stages in the reintegration of his widows into a man's family and clan after his death. The first was the ceremony of widows 'seeing their brothers-in-law' after the mourning was at an end, when beer was brewed and they took off and burned their mourning caps. The second was the ceremony of being inherited, when the widows offered snuff to one of their husband's brothers whom they were willing to marry.

Another Ngoni practice was that of giving an *nhlanzi*, a substitute or additional wife. If, after a marriage had taken place and cattle had been handed over, the wife appeared to be barren, her family might give another daughter as *nhlanzi*, without further transfer of cattle, to bear children for her older sister whose house she entered. These children were always referred to as children of the house of A, the earlier married wife, even if they were borne by B, her *nhlanzi*. Sometimes, even if the first daughter given in marriage bore children, an *nhlanzi* might still be given without additional cattle being transferred, because the bride's family were pleased with her treatment in her husband's village and wished to compliment the man as a good husband.

There were four main stages in Ngoni marriage, in all of which the houses played an essential part. The first was the selection of partners and securing the consent of the families; the second the negotiations from the betrothal onwards, centring round the transfer of cattle; the third the series of feasts culminating in the marriage feast itself; and the fourth the assimilation of the new wife into her husband's family, house and village.

The selection of a marriage partner might take place in more than one way. There was direct courtship by the man; there was an indicated choice by the girl; there were marriages arranged by the parents; and there was direction of a son by his parents towards a suitable partner. In addition to clan exogamy and parallel cousin prohibition, there was in pre-European days a prohibition upon marriage between children of age mates in the same village. For girls of Swazi clans marriages were generally arranged, though informants insisted that in most cases the personal preferences of both partners were considered. A young man of a Swazi clan was told that in one village there was X, in another Y, with whom a suitable marriage might be made. Having taken this hint, and found opportunities for visiting the village and looking at the girl, and having decided in her favour, he then proceeded to court her along the following recognized and definite lines:

1. He courted the girl and if she was willing she eventually agreed to marry him.
2. He informed a member of the *gogo* house of his father's family, usually an older brother of his father.
3. This elder informed the man's father.
4. At the father's request, this elder went to the girl's village and sought out a corresponding elder of her family, usually an older brother of her father and always someone belonging to the *gogo* house.
5. This elder in the girl's village informed her father and mother and, when this was done, told the elder from the man's village, who then went home.
6. The girl's parents asked her if she agreed to the marriage and, if she gave her consent, they considered the matter and finally gave their consent.
7. The man's elder returned to the girl's village and the girl's parents told him they had consented and he then went home again.
8. He returned soon with a beast, called 'the snuff box', as a gift from the man's father. This elder now had several companions with him, but no one from the man's immediate family circle or from his house.
9. The beast was killed and the betrothal feast was held in the girl's village, after which her parents and the elders of her village said, 'We have snuffed.'
10. The man's father sent another elder to 'call the girl' and she was then addressed as 'daughter-in-law'.
11. The girl's father and his brothers decided what the *lobola* should be and informed the man's parents how many beasts they wanted.

Men of the *gogo* house in each village played the major part as go-betweens in the negotiations between the two families, opening the way for the new relationship which was felt to be full of difficulties. Once the betrothal feast had been held, the leading function of the *gogo* house gave way to more direct participation by the man's house, where the male members had now to find the cattle for the *lobola*, the amount of which had been fixed by the girl's family. This amount was in direct relationship to the status of the girl's family and clan. In the 1930's for a girl of the royal clan it was up to fifteen beasts; for girls of other Swazi clans from three to nine beasts; and for girls of non-Swazi clans from one to three—the variation depending on the status of her father in his village, and on the house from which he came. It was to the herd belonging to this house that the cattle of the *lobola* were allocated. The period within which the handing over of cattle was completed varied according to the demands of the girl's father and the capacity of the man's father to find the required number. Informants agreed that when only a few beasts were demanded, the transfer took place before or immediately after the main ceremony. In addition to this formal transfer agreed on and carried out as part of the marriage contract, there was also an informal reciprocal transfer which had two main purposes. At the time of the main ceremony the bride's party brought with them a beast, called *mcando*, which was put into the herd of the bridegroom's mother's house to which the bride would henceforth belong. Later, when the two families ate together for the first time, one or more additional beasts were brought from the girl's former house and put into the herd of the house to which she now belonged. In this way, the new wife began to have cattle in the herd of her mother-in-law's house which were known as hers and which would be taken to form a new herd when she went out with her husband to his *lusungulu* village. As soon as these cattle were in the kraal of the house to which she now belonged, the new wife was able to eat *amasi* in her husband's village, which she had not been allowed to do since leaving her father's village.

In the series of feasts which marked the stages in the marriage relationship and which facilitated the coming together of the two families, the major part was played by the *indlunkulu* in each village. Many households in the girl's village shared in the preparation of food for the betrothal feast, but it was assembled when cooked and divided out by the woman owner of the *indlunkulu*, assisted by the men and women belonging to the girl's father's house. The next feast was in the man's village, and formed part of the main ceremony, before the bride's party returned to their home. The third feast was to celebrate the 'showing of the hearth-stones', when the young wife was allowed to cook in her husband's village for the first time. The food was collected in her parents' village and carried to her new village, where it was cooked by the women of the house into which she had married, and served in the courtyard of the *indlunkulu*. In the two final feasts—the *umncengo* which was a beer drink, and the *izinyongo*, a feast of beer and food—the beer was brewed and the food collected in the wife's village and cooked and eaten in the courtyard of the *indlunkulu* in the husband's village. These two feasts finally broke down the barrier between the parents-in-law and were the first occasion on which they ate and drank beer together.

The main ceremony (*mtimba*) had three distinct parts.[1] The first part included the preparation of the girl in her own village (*ukuconga*); the entrance of her party into the man's village and the presenting of snuff

---

[1] I was present at an *mtimba* in Ezondweni in the northern kingdom when the traditional ritual carried out in full was combined with a church wedding. The bridegroom was a man of the Dlamini clan from Swaziland, who had been adopted by Chief Mtwalo and had built a hut in the *cigodlo* of the big house.

(*ukuqandisa*). The middle section, the main part of the ceremony, took place in the husband's village while the bridal party was there. In the last part the bride was left in her new home and three ceremonies marked her gradual integration into her new social group.

After the number of cattle had been decided upon in the final stage of the betrothal, the initiative was left to the girl's parents to announce the date of the *mtimba*. Eventually a message was sent through the *gogo* house of the girl's village to say that the bridal party would arrive on a certain day. Before the day came, the girl, now addressed as *umlobokazi* (the bride), was called to the *indlunkulu* in her village. There the leading women, her father's mothers, who had called in her father's sisters, gave her final instructions on how to behave in her new home. Ngoni women said that they were told at this time: 'Our child, we are putting you out of our family. We are handing you over to the other people. You were free and now your freedom is over for you are under other people. Where you are going you will meet with many troubles. They will say of you many things which you did not do. It is good to be patient.' During this instruction the girl cried and so did her mother. On the morning of the departure the girl was dressed in freshly prepared skins, her hair was arranged in the *isihlutu* (chignon) to which the gall bladder of a goat was pinned, and the gall bladder of a cow was tied to her elbow. Then, still sobbing and whimpering, and surrounded by her age mates and the female members of her house, she set out for her bridegroom's village, the young men of her village driving a bullock (*mcando*) as a present from the bride's parents to the mother of the bridegroom, in whose herd it was placed.

This part of the ceremony, the entry of the bride's party (*ukuqandisa*), was held to be of great importance, since it was the first time the bride's family and friends as a group had met the husband's family. The bride's procession waited by the kraal gate, singing *mtimba* songs, and every now and then a woman of the bride's party, one of her father's sisters, sang the praises of the bride's clan. As the young men driving the bullock entered the kraal, the bridal party joined them and they began to dance in the kraal.

Now the first overtures were made between the bride's party and the people of the bridegroom's village. The older women of the village approached the older women of the bride's party, greeting them and exchanging, in the Ngoni phrase, 'words which were good and proud and showed the quickness of their tongues'.

After these advances, the men of the village came into the kraal or gathered by the *indlunkulu*. While the bridal party began to sing with their heads bowed, the chief woman from the *indlunkulu* of the bride's village came forward, bending low, and on her knees presented to the *induna* of the *indlunkulu* of the husband's village a basket containing snuff boxes and beads. She made a speech, in which she said, 'Here is our child who is now leaving her home. She has no father now. She is leaving his care. We expect you to cherish her now as her father would.' In reply the *induna* assured them, 'Now she is here we will cherish her, but she must respect the owner of this house and be under her in all things.' Speeches about the absence of disease in either village were then made and the men took snuff. The bridal party and the villagers all remained seated and began to sing *umbedlo* songs (songs to be sung sitting).

At the marriage at Ezondweni, where I was present, the girls of the bridal party began to shiver as night fell, and a woman of the village brought a sleeping mat as an invitation to go into the huts. Singing as they went, the women of the bridal party were shown a place to sleep, and the bride slept among them for that night. The bride's party went off the next morning to the church at Elangeni for the church marriage service, while the bridegroom with a party from Ezondweni went by a separate route. In the days before the mission came, they used to spend the morning dancing in the kraal, while the husband's family killed a beast, or more than one, for the feast. During the day's dancing in the kraal, the leader of the village women took the husband's spear, came into the kraal with the village party and touched the bride gently on the shoulder. This was a sign that the bride was now one of the village group, and the correct response was for her party to turn their backs and weep to show their grief because she had left them.

In Ezondweni, when the parties returned from church in the afternoon, a large crowd had assembled. The bridal party danced and sang in the kraal and outside the *indlunkulu* and now and then a leading woman of the bridegroom's village joined in. The bride and two supporting friends were given a mat to sit on, the husband and the *madoda* also sat down, the minister from the church prayed and they sang a hymn. Then the food, bowls of *nsima* with large pieces of meat on top, was divided. The names of the divisions of Ezondweni were called out and the leaders of the divisions of that village and of other villages came to get the portions for their people.

Dancing continued after the feast until the bride's party took the bride to the husband's hut and left her there. The next morning the bridal party returned home singing. Formerly the bride came to the door of the hut where she had slept with her husband, and called out the praise-names of her father. She then sang the *ummekezo* song (song of the deflowering) and the husband stood in the doorway behind her. Then he went into the kraal and sat facing the bridal party, who were singing. When the bride came in with a gourd of water there was silence while she poured water for him to wash his hands, mouth and eyes. This was the first public act of service for the husband after the consummation of the marriage and ended the main part of the ceremony, after which the bridal party went home.

The three final acts of the *mtimba* were performed for the new wife by the women of her new village. The first took place about two days after the end of the main ceremony and was the occasion for her instruction by her husband's relatives. She sat on a mat by the *indlunkulu*, while the woman of that house dressed her *isihlutu*, anointed her with oil, and clothed her in fresh skins and new beads taken from the store of the house to which she now belonged. They then instructed her in her behaviour to old and young, telling her to avoid selfishness and quarrelling and to be friendly with everyone.

The second act, called *ukufumisa umlobokazi* ((bringing the wife out), took place thirty to forty days later, during which time the wife had been sitting by her hut being watched. All this time she had eaten only a little food, sent to her from her mother-in-law's hut, had been afraid to speak to anyone, and had wept often. Now she was told that she might go anywhere and talk with anyone. She could help her mother-in-law by fetching firewood and by lighting her fire. A pot of water was given to her and an axe to cut firewood, and her mother-in-law gave her the *indlekuza* bead, a sign that she might speak and eat in front of her parents-in-law. But her testing time was not yet over. She was told to fetch a huge bundle of split wood and to lay it down carefully before her mother-in-law's hut without dropping any. As the bundle was on her head, it meant kneeling down and bending forward slowly until she could gently ease the wood on to the ground. Other tests included stripping large quantities of maize, soaking them, and pounding them into stamped maize (*izinkobe*). This testing was called *ukulinga umlobokazi* (watching the new wife), and was in most cases far more exacting than anything she had been made to do in her own home.

The culminating act of the integration process, *ukupekisa umlobokazi*, in which the new wife's hut was recognized as the starting-point of a new house, was the ceremony of making fire in her new hut to cook food for her husband. Two or three months after the marriage, a woman from her father-in-law's *gogo* house suddenly appeared in the doorway of the new wife's hut, carrying three hearth-stones. She fetched fire, kindled it, and began to cook boiled maize. The astonished young wife was expected to cry because she had now been turned away from her mother-in-law's cooking-place, as if she were being put out of the house. The maize cooked on this first fire in the new hut was regarded as having been cooked by the bride, and was divided into portions, one being taken to each section of the village attached to a house. Meanwhile the young wife sat nearby, hanging her head and showing the conventional signs of grief. Nevertheless she was so excited that she went back to her own home as soon as possible to tell them the news. The response of her own people was to prepare food for a feast and bring it to her new village to express to her husband's people their appreciation of this token of confidence in the girl's ability to cook for her husband.

The prolonged series of interviews, exchanges and ceremonies emphasized the Ngoni conception of the marriage contract and its binding nature. They also underlined the severance of the new wife from her former family and house, and her gradual assimilation into her mother-in-law's house. This relationship between Ngoni women within the houses provided an effective means of integrating them into a village to which they were strangers.

CHAPTER IV

NGONI FAMILY STRUCTURE

'THE Ngoni have power and authority over their women and their children.' So began one of the texts on *cingoni*, 'the thing that is Ngoni', by a man of the Ntumba people whose grandfather had been born among the Ngoni when they were in Songea. There was a recognized ideal pattern of an Ngoni family which covered both the individuals included in the family group and the place where they lived. This pattern was patrilineal in descent, virilocal in residence, polygynous in marriage for all men of standing who were not Christians. Other recognized and often-mentioned characteristics were the continued residence of widows in their husband's village after his death, the grouping of families by houses, and the *laweni*, or dormitory system for boys and unmarried young men.

The young wife wept on the day of her marriage because she was leaving the security and known relationships of her own family for the hazards and uncertainty of entering as a stranger into her husband's family group. The dramatization of these sentiments in the protracted marriage ceremony, and the allusions in the *mtimba* songs, brought out clearly the continuity of the man's relations with all members of his family and the sudden sharp break in the woman's relationship when she married. When her first child was born, and a new individual family group launched, her final integration into her husband's family began. As a mother who had borne a grandchild to her husband's parents she had thenceforward a direct part in the relationships within her husband's family, but as a wife she was always a stranger. The marriage negotiations and ceremonial express the closeness of the family ties, showing on the girl's side the anxiety of her family on parting with her to live among strangers; and on the man's side the hesitancy of the husband's family at taking into their midst an unknown and untried stranger. In addition, the protracted exchanges of cattle and feasts, delaying the final ceremony and building up relationships between the two family groups, illustrate the Ngoni attitude towards marriage as a binding contract. In theory at least the girl left her family for good once the agreed *lobola* was handed over, and the responsibility for adjustment to the family she had entered was hers, first as wife and then as mother.

Investigation of the terminology associated with the Ngoni concept of family immediately poses problems of relating group structure to individual and group relationships. Dr. Kuper did not refer to any single term for family among the Swazi. The nearest was the term *umuti* used for homestead[1] which covered a recognized leader and his dependents, in terms of common residence, mutual relations and economic activities. The Cewa term *banja*,[2] widely used in Nyasaland in the 1930's to translate 'family', in its general use was more akin to the Swazi *umuti* since it denoted the relationships of a group of people to one man, and their common residence in a single village or a section of a village. *Banja* was used to express relationship to one man by kinship and marriage, but when it was used among the central Ngoni it also applied to other individuals, such as his age mates and the descendants of his father's former captives who lived in the same village. Another Cewa term *mbumba* was used in two distinct senses. The common use was to express the relationship of one man with his sisters and their children who inherited his position and his property and looked to him for assistance. A much less common use of the term was found sometimes in central Nyasaland and occasionally in north Nyasaland to cover the group of a man and his children and his brothers and their children—a patrilineal concept of a kinship group which was usually but not always associated with common residence.

There was one major difference between the Ngoni concept inherent in their use of *banja* and that of the Cewa and other matrilineal peoples. When an important man or woman died among the Cewa, someone always 'entered their place' in the kinship system, and this acquiring of a new position involved a shift in actual relationships and in terminology throughout the group of kin. There was no such change among the Ngoni in the use of kinship terms. When a man or woman among the Ngoni entered a dead person's place it was in order to perform his functions and not to assume the dead person's kinship relationships.

The village lay-out in different types of Ngoni village illustrates the way in which family grouping could be recognized in the sharing of the same hut, in the grouping of huts, and in the relations with neighbouring villages. Later in this chapter illustrations will be given from the northern and central Ngoni kingdoms to show how certain patterns of residential grouping on a family basis were evolving from the divisions of mixed tribal groups characteristic of the former large villages of pre-European days. The general tendency in northern Ngoniland was to

---

[1] op. cit. p. 36.
[2] Scott and Hetherwick in their dictionary translate *banja*: house, home, household, family.

break up into smaller villages, and there were on the whole more villages in the north said to be *wabanja limodzi* (of one family) than among the central Ngoni. On the other hand, the *lusungulu* pattern of village division had almost disappeared among the central Ngoni.

A man on his first marriage built a hut for his wife behind his mother's hut, where his brothers by the same mother or by mothers of the same house also built. The family grouping by residence was therefore determined by house affiliation. Associated with this residential group based on kinship, there were the residences of the *induna* and his family which had separate alignments on a kinship basis, though for certain common purposes they combined with the family groups related to the house by kinship. The children of the families belonging to the house and the children of the *induna* who took care of it began to intermarry when the prohibitions on marriage within the village ceased to operate. In this way kinship bonds were created within a group which formerly had only residence and certain activities in common, and this process was recognizable in a number of the larger villages, especially in the central kingdom.

Within the different types of family groups determined by their residential basis there were certain outstanding relationships between members of the same family. The most important of these was that between father and children; the father, as the biological parent and also the symbol of authority, was the focus of honour and respect, and the one who helped his children when they were in need. The relation between the father and his children among the Ngoni was always a balance between affection and care, and respect and authority. The ideal pattern of a father, as described by informants, included all these elements and also wisdom. This concept of the father relationship was extended to the head of a *banja*, to the headman of a village or a section of a village, to a *mulumuzana* in charge of an area, to a chief, and to the Paramount himself. The Ngoni greeting to all older men, and the most respectful form of address to a man of any seniority, was *baba*, father, or its Nyanja equivalent *bambo*.

The mother, on the other hand, had a more limited relationship within the family circle. To her own children and to the children of her co-wives, especially of her house, she was the provider of food, and the affectionate 'cherisher'[1] of young children; but she was also treated with respect and, when she reached some seniority, she had considerable authority over her daughters and her younger co-wives. She could never compete, however, with the sisters of her husband or with his mothers, who expected to exercise authority over her children and to arrange for the ceremonies connected with birth, puberty, and marriage. In villages where virilocal residence was the rule, the husband's sisters were married elsewhere and were only present in the village during

---

[1] *kulera*, lit. to cherish, is the word used for bringing up children.

visits or on special occasions. In the central kingdom, where an important man's sisters often married in the village and stayed there, it was evident that they often exercised authority over their brother's children.

In polygynous Ngoni families the relationship between siblings was marked by strong attachment. Among the boys in the *laweni* brothers united to protect their younger brothers from other boys, and in the families of Swazi clans brothers showed many signs of youthful intolerance and arrogance towards boys of other clans, especially in matters concerning cattle and their herding. Sibling rivalry among boys was to a large extent controlled by two factors. One was the *laweni* system where the age-set principle predominated. The other was the division into the big house and *gogo* house, where the children of the *gogo* house knew that they stood in a different relationship to succession and authority in the village from their brothers and sisters in the big house. Within the big house itself, sons of the big wife knew that succession was regulated by seniority, and that the eldest son would expect to get priority when he married and it was necessary to allot cattle for *lobola*. The brother-sister link between children of the same mother was, as we have seen, a very close one, especially with the older sister of a man who was heir to a high position. This sister in her relation to his children carried almost the same authority as he did. Among sisters of the same family there was less apparent cohesion, except among very high-ranking Swazi clans where the girl children were looked after by special nursemaids and had their instruction in correct behaviour together from the older woman known as their *gogo*.

Ngoni grandparents on the paternal side showed little of the joking relationship with their grandchildren sometimes associated with this tie. When children went to visit their maternal grandparents in another village there was noticeably more ease between them and more indulgence was shown. In their father's village children were always aware that his parents were persons of standing and authority. Girls over six or seven often slept in their paternal grandmother's hut if she was a widow, and were aware that, though she showed kindliness in providing for their needs, she was a firm disciplinarian in all matters of behaviour.

Within the family group the male role of leadership was unquestioned. Honour and respect were a man's due from wives as well as from children. In difficult relations within his family, as in the case of divorce, he could count on counsel and support from his brothers, who were also ready to help him if cattle were needed for his own or his son's marriage or for payment of court penalties. This male circle of father and sons, father's brothers and their sons, was a closely knit group which functioned in regulating family affairs and in buying and selling cattle for the house to which they belonged. An obligation to help his sons was recognized by the father of a family and this obligation extended to his brothers' sons, especially if their father was dead. Following the same pattern, a man's sons who were away at work sent back money to their father who bought cattle with it, or spent it as the sons asked. It was clear in the 1930's that Ngoni men rarely sent money directly to their wives, though they frequently asked their father to give money to their wives and to buy for them cloth or needed household equipment.

Within the larger orbit of the male family responsibilities women had their more restricted but clearly defined sphere. At a woman's confinement she was looked after by her husband's own mother, aided by his other mothers and by his sisters if they were present in the village. At the 'coming out' of the new member of the family, ten to fourteen days after birth, the woman and the baby, bathed and ritually cleansed, were seated on a mat outside the hut and presented to the male members of the father's family who gave small gifts to the baby. If it was a boy, the father's mother generally carried it to the gate of the kraal where the men were sitting, to present it to them as one who would eventually herd the cattle. On this occasion, or soon after, the child's name was chosen, usually by the father's father, who prepared and gave to the mother a calf-skin or goat-skin for carrying the child in. The meat of the animal was cooked by the father's mother and a small feast was held for the father's mothers, sisters, brothers and their wives, and any others of the father's family who had helped in the confinement.[1] After the child had thus been acknowledged in its father's family circle, the mother took the baby to visit her own family, who also gave it presents.

During the rearing of the child, its father's female relatives assumed responsibility for giving the young mother advice. The father's mother was expected to note the stage at which the child should be weaned, always if possible before the mother's next pregnancy. If the father's mother was unobservant, the other senior women of the husband's family would rebuke her and say 'Look now you are foolish because the child has been endangered. You are like an enemy to it.' These women then took the initiative and insisted on weaning the child. They said to the baby's mother 'We want to wean the child.' They made a paste of ground chillies and put it on the mother's breasts and covered them with a skin or cloth. The child was taken from her after it had tried to suck and had been refused, and given to the father's mother or sister, who looked after it with the help of a nursemaid. It was fed on cow's milk, *amasi* (milk curds), and gruel.

The publicity given to the weaning and the initiative taken by the senior women of the husband's family were intended to inform others in the village that the parents were now free to have another child. This was one aspect of the old Ngoni form of family planning and, in describing

---

[1] This feast was also held when a carrying cloth was given instead of a skin.

what took place, informants were anxious to point this out. They also admitted that its successful carrying out depended on several factors which no longer operated. The former Ngoni households with a number of servants and nursemaids were only to be found in the families of the Paramount and subordinate chiefs. The rigid separation of the girl from her own family at marriage was no longer usual in the central kingdom where Ngoni marriages often took place in the same village, and where daughters of important men stayed in their fathers' villages at marriage instead of leaving.

In Ngoni households family sleeping and eating arrangements depended not upon the small individual family but on the extended family group and on the boys' dormitory (*laweni*). As a general rule small children slept with their mother in her hut, but when her husband was sleeping with her it was considered wrong to have any but very young children in the hut. Boys up to the age of seven, when they went to the *laweni*, and girls up to their marriage, usually slept in the hut of a mother or a widowed sister of their father.

Each wife, after she had been 'shown the hearth-stones', had a granary built for her by her husband or her husband's brothers where she stored grain. On the rafters in her hut, and in pots and jars on the enclosed verandah, and in pits dug under the eaves, she stored other foodstuffs, such as chillies, beans and sweet potatoes. From these supplies, supplemented by fresh 'relish' from the gardens or bush, she cooked daily meals which she served to her husband, and which her younger sons in the *laweni* fetched to eat there, while she ate with her young children. Her husband's meals and the older boys' meals were taken in company with the male members of his kinship group and other villagers at the men's meeting-place by the gate of the kraal. His wife sent his food by a child in a covered basket with the small pot of relish on top. The publicity of the men's eating habits made them critical among their fellows of their wives' cooking, and this was a strong incentive among Ngoni wives to maintain a high standard of cooking. In addition to sending food to her husband, an Ngoni wife was expected to send a basket of food now and then to her father-in-law, or to any of her brothers-in-law who had assisted her to mend a roof or build a granary.

Within a wife's hut, not only food but other possessions, both personal and household, were stored. Clothes for daily and ceremonial use; mats for sleeping on and for drying grain; pots for water, cooking, and beer-brewing; ornamental jars for storing beans; baskets for carrying grain; food baskets embroidered with beads—the Ngoni wife of good family expected to possess all these and to keep them carefully. Many of them she brought with her on her marriage or had given her later as presents by her own parents and family, in order that she might not appear poor or of low rank among her husband's people. For the same reason, she was instructed before marriage how to keep these household possessions in good repair, and how to smear the floor and walls of the hut with cowdung so that they presented the shining surface typical of Ngoni buildings.

The tables which follow show the total population of three villages in each kingdom at the time they were visited in 1938 and 1939, including such data as the number of widows, of plural marriages, of wives for whom *lobola* was given, and the number of men away at work.

	1 Huts	2 Men	3 Women	4 Children	5 Total	6 Men away	7 Widows	8 Plural marriages	9 Lobola marriages
Northern kingdom									
Eswazini .	23	10	21	28	59	10	4	4	21
Endindeni .	15	9	21	21	51	4	1	4	15
Eluhangeni	37	19	36	54	109	11	4	5	32
Central kingdom									
Cinkwita .	39	22	39	54	115	13	5	4	2
Mangozo .	60	41	65	78	184	9	18	2	4
Mcakhatha	122	71	112	68	251	30	16	14	12

Earlier in this chapter reference was made to the patterns of residential grouping on a kinship basis, which had evolved from the mixed tribal groups in the very large villages of pre-European days. The choice of these six villages as examples was made mainly on the grounds that they had a considerable proportion of members of Swazi or trans-Zambesi clans and therefore illustrated the traditional Ngoni pattern of kinship grouping. The northern kingdom villages showed the *lusungulu* and *gogo* pattern still extant. It had disappeared in the central kingdom villages with the result that the villages were much larger, and included groups based on house affiliation which would have been divided into separate villages in the north. On the other hand the sub-division of a village in the central kingdom into *banja* was not found in the north.

The data concerning these villages have been analysed to illustrate the households associated with the chief man in the leading clan in the village. These households were those of his wives, his mothers, his brothers, his sons, sisters and daughters. In the north this man was in one case a *mulumuzana*, in another a son of a great war *induna*, and in the third the head of a collateral branch of the royal clan. In the central kingdom the chief man in one was a *mulumuzana*, in another a grandson of a great war *induna*, and in the third the head of the clan of the royal shadow. The proportion of households belonging to the leading clan was much higher in the smaller villages of the north than in the rest, since they were approximating to a one-family village.

Households[1]

	Total	Leading clan
Northern Ngoniland		
Eswazini	23	15
Endindeni	15	12
Eluhangeni	37	21
Central Ngoniland		
Cinkwita	39	18
Mangozo	60	26
Mcakhatha	122	37

The proportion of persons of Swazi and trans-Zambesi clans in the central kingdom to the total population was lower than in the north. The figures given here, however, do not show the total number of persons of Swazi and trans-Zambesi clans, but only the households related on a kinship basis with the leading clan head.

Eswazini and Endindeni were both built in traditional Ngoni style in horse-shoe formation round a single kraal, with the *indlunkulu* at the head of the kraal, and a recognized right-hand and left-hand grouping. Eswazini had become the head village of the Sibande clan since its owner, Samson Sibande, on his father's death had gone out from his father's village and made this his *lusungulu* village. His big wife, of the royal clan, was in the *indlunkulu* to which she had succeeded on the death of his mother, and there was another wife on the right and left hand. Of the older generation there was only one widow of his father, belonging to the same house as his mother. Of his generation there were five brothers, one of the same mother as Samson, and four sons of the surviving widow of his father. There was also the widow of a dead brother by the same mother. Two sisters of Samson were in the village, one married to the *induna* of his mother's house, whose family lived on the right-hand side of the kraal, and one a deserted widow who had returned to her brother's protection. All the village was one house, that of Samson's own mother.

Endindeni was a *gogo* village owned by Zibekere Makwakwa who was the son of a famous war *induna* and was of the *gogo* house of his father. His brother, who was the son of the big house, had moved out to his own village. The village was composed entirely of his family with the exception of an age mate with whom he had an *ubale* relationship, who lived with his two wives on the left-hand side of the kraal. Zibekere's big wife was in the *indlunkulu* to which she had succeeded on the death of his own mother, and his second wife was also of her house. Of the older generation there was one widow of his father, and one widow of his father's brother; of his own generation, one younger brother of the same mother. There were four sons of his big wife and two of his second

---

[1] In all six villages the total number of households included two or more *laweni*.

wife. The village with its single kraal was 'of one house', and it was widely known as a good village by Ngoni standards, because, as the local people said, 'all the men are Makwakwa men'.

Eluhangeni was a *gogo* village where the spirit of Mtenje Jere, the son of a brother of Zwangendaba, was guarded. The kinship group of Mwanamdoko Jere, the owner of the village, were all of one house, that of his mother who was dead. Her place in the *indlunkulu* had been taken by his big wife who also inherited the guardianship of the spirit of Mtenje. There was one widow of his father in the village, but she had become a Christian and therefore could not guard the spirit. Mwanamdoko had two wives, and three widows of his brothers by the same mother were also in the village. One brother by another mother was the only one of his generation still alive and he had two sons and two grandsons living in the *cigodlo* behind the *indlunkulu*. All Mwanamdoko's family were grouped round one kraal. There were two other kraals with family groups round them in the village, one belonging to the *induna* of his dead mother, and one to an age mate who had been in his regiment. The *induna's* group belonged to the same house as Mwanamdoko, but the pattern of the three distinct groups each with its own kraal was more like that of the *banja* in the central kingdom.

In the central kingdom the relationships of the various groups in a village followed a different pattern from that in the north. Instead of the *lusungulu* and *gogo* characteristics where the family groups were integrated into houses, the southern pattern was that of a conquered village with the Ngoni element superimposed. In Cinkwita and in Mcakhatha the village headman and his family group had originally been conquered, then established as an outlying village, and finally chosen for the permanent settlement of a family group belonging to an Ngoni clan when they left the royal village after it broke up. In Cinkwita there were three kraals associated with three *banja*. Two of the *banja* belonged to kinship groups of Ntumba clans, and the head of one was known as the headman of the village. The head of the *banja* of Cinkwita Ndau, the Ngoni clan group, was his eldest son Wilkinson, whose wife was of a leading Swazi clan, the Magwagwa. His family group consisted of his wife, two sons and three daughters; a brother and his two daughters; the widow of a dead brother and his two sons and a daughter; three sisters, one of whom had married the brother of the village headman and one who was a widow; and a widowed sister of his father. This family grouping expressed in terms of households illustrates what has already been referred to several times, namely the tendency of the heads of leading Ngoni families in the central kingdom to keep, in addition to their sons, their sisters and daughters in the village after marriage, even when *lobola* had been given. It also illustrates the comparatively small number of plural marriages in the south among the younger men.

Mangozo, as its name suggests, was the head village of the Ngozo clan. It had been originally settled by Ngwazi Ngozo who brought with him two family groups of Ntumba clans who had been with him in Songea. These two Ntumba family groups each formed a *banja*, and one had a kraal. The other two *banja* belonged to two elderly Ngozo brothers, sons of Ngwazi and of the same house, who had one kraal between them. The senior of these, Mbiri Ngozo, had in his *banja* a widow of his father, not his own mother, and nine widows of a dead older brother; his own wife, two sons, two daughters, three grandsons and three granddaughters; and his sister. The *banja* of Cinyama Ngozo included two widows of another brother; his own wife, two sons, two daughters, one grandson and one granddaughter. The two brothers between them had to support eleven widows of dead brothers.

Mcakhatha had a dual foundation. The village site was originally one of the outlying villages of the section known as Ziyembe. It was also the head village of the Nzunga clan. Three of the five *banja* into which the village was divided belonged to Ntumba family groups, and the head of one of these was known as the headman of the village. Of the two *banja* belonging to the Nzunga clan, one was a *gogo banja*, the other that of the ruling chief who was a Sub-Native Authority.[1] Within the *gogo banja* was the house of Bambo Manga in whose hut the spirit of Mputa was guarded. Two other houses in the *gogo banja* were associated with the guardianship of the spirits of the grandfather and father of the ruling chief. There was therefore a house and a *banja* formation existing together, in which the *banja* predominated. The two Nzunga *banja* consisted of two family groups, one associated with the ruling chief and one with his paternal uncle in charge of the *gogo* section. The chief's *banja* included his own five wives, one sister and two brothers by the same mother, and two sisters and four brothers by other mothers. The *banja* of the head of the *gogo* section included his own five wives and two widows whom he had inherited from the former chief, his older brother; three brothers and two sisters by other mothers; three of his sons. It also included a widow of his father, and nine widows of his dead brother who had not been inherited; and the households of Bambo Manga and her daughter and granddaughter for whom the father of the ruling chief had assumed responsibility. The Ngoni family pattern of this village was more complex than that of Cinkwita or Mangozo because of the clearly marked *gogo* section existing alongside that of the ruling chief. It showed, however, the general characteristics of Ngoni family grouping in the central kingdom, keeping sisters and daughters in the village after marriage while retaining responsibility for widows of fathers and brothers. There were three Nzunga kraals, two in the *gogo banja* and one in the chief's *banja*, but the cattle were always referred to

[1] In northern Ngoniland the ruling chief would have moved out of this village on his father's death, leaving the *gogo banja* as the *gogo* village.

as belonging to the houses. The relatively large number of cattle and the high ranking of the Nzunga clan accounted for the number of *lobola* marriages.

Family structure in individual and group life

As individuals and in family groups members of leading Ngoni clans claimed and exercised leadership in their villages. The leading families in the area of a *mulumuzana* owning a head village, and the small Ngoni family groups in a larger non-Ngoni setting, all expected and received 'honour' (*ulemu*). The tendency in the central kingdom to marry up, and in the northern kingdom to marry into the clan of the mother if it were a high-ranking one, emphasized the importance attached to the rank and prestige of certain clans. This attitude towards family prestige was more noticeable in the central kingdom where individuals were quick to announce who was their mother or wife if that information would enhance their reputation.

The leadership of high-ranking families was not only a matter of claiming prestige. It carried with it, on the male and the female side, responsibility for regulating the affairs of the village and the house and the *banja*. Quarrels had to be composed, if possible before they came to court, troubles over deserted wives looked into, provision made for hospitality and for keeping the village premises in order. Informants emphasized again and again that in Ngoni villages where many men and women were of Swazi clans, order and cleanliness were to be expected. This was not always the case, but it was strikingly illustrated in two of the villages referred to in this chapter—Endindeni in the northern and Mangozo in the central kingdom.

In day-to-day village affairs much mutual help was given by members of Ngoni families to each other, especially by the men to widowed mothers and sisters, and by the husband's brothers to wives whose husbands were away at work. The dislocation caused to the village economy by the emigration of males called for considerable organization on the part of those who were left. Ngoni male leaders of families and heads of a *banja*, and the women heads of the houses, all had to include the needs of these 'deserted' women in their own planning. In the northern kingdom, in spite of its relative poverty, better care was taken of wives whose husbands were away because the strong virilocal tradition emphasized this type of help.

In rearing and training children the Ngoni family structure and relationships provided direction and responsibility. We shall discuss in the next chapter on age sets the significance of birth and puberty ceremonies in Ngoni life. More significant, however, than any ceremony was the continuous provision for the training of children, adolescents and young adults in correct behaviour. This duty fell on the women as far as young children and girls were concerned, and on the men for the boys and young men, so long as they were in the village. Ngoni men insisted that their children should be correctly trained, and they were contemptuous of Cewa and other tribal groups who left it 'all to the women'. The handing on of correct behaviour by the mother-in-law to her daughter-in-law was, they considered, essential, and one of the reasons why young men in the central kingdom liked to 'marry up' was that they could count on the careful grounding in all the canons of behaviour which their wives had received.

CHAPTER V

AGE SETS

THE Ngoni brought with them to Nyasaland an age-set system akin to that among the South-eastern Bantu, which was an important element in their social structure. In pre-European days the division into cattle-herders or pre-warriors, warriors, and post-warriors or senior men, regulated the tasks and responsibilities of boys and men in other spheres besides those of warfare. At the beginning of this section, when reviewing age sets as one of the constituent forms of Ngoni social organization, I said that some features of an age-set system had persisted. In comparison with age-grouping in the other Nyasaland tribes it was distinctively Ngoni in form; it influenced behaviour patterns in inter-group and intra-group relations; and in it were recognized certain responsibilities and activities belonging to the different groups based on age.

Among the distinctively Ngoni elements in the age-set system were the private nature of the puberty ritual and the absence of initiation schools; the organization of boys' life in the *laweni*; the strong ties between age mates up to marriage; the selective principle in designating senior men and women as *madoda* and *manina*; and a different kind of selective principle in the formation of friendship pacts between individuals of the same age. In observing the role of age sets in Ngoni village society, the two main groups which were constantly in evidence as groups were the older boys and girls and the senior men and women. These groups not only carried out activities together, but also showed evidence of the strength of the internal ties linking members of an age set. There were, however, no sharp edges to these groups, either in terms of actual age or physiological development or of exclusive membership. The following list of terms applied to age sets in the two main Ngoni areas shows primarily the difference in designation between males and females according to broad age grouping, but it illustrates also the fact that the terminology applied to the age sets did not always coincide

with the main activities of the groups, though it did to some extent
illustrate mutual relationships.

Age-Set terms

	Northern Ngoni	Central Ngoni
All children	abantwana	ana
Young men even if married . .	amajaha	anyamata
Young girls before puberty . .	inkakazana	mabuthu
Young girls past puberty . . .	izintombi	anamwali
All married women	abafazi	akazi
Senior men	amadoda	madoda
Senior women	amanina	manina

One of the most characteristic forms of Ngoni village organization
was the *laweni*, or boys' dormitory. It included the older boys in the
group called 'children' and the young men until they married, who were
in fact called *amajaha* after they had left the *laweni* and married and had
huts of their own. The age for entering the *laweni* was approximately
seven years, and was as a rule determined by the age when a child began
to get his second teeth. When a child was going about the village with
several gaps in his front teeth, his companions jeered at him if he still
slept in his grandmother's hut, and his father took the view that it was
time he stopped playing like a child and took up seriously the job of
herding goats and calves. There was often some hesitation, especially
among boys who were not so well grown for their age, at taking the
plunge and going to live in the *laweni*, since once made the step could
not be retraced. It was primarily an individual decision. It meant leaving
the protective affectionate care of the grandmother in the evenings, and
the care-free play all day round the mother's hut with meals provided by
her, for a different sort of existence altogether. *Laweni* life was rigorous
and was dominated by the senior boys living in the hut. The younger
ones were at their mercy, and were made to 'fag' for their elders, clean
up the hut, sometimes steal food from their mothers' stores, and were
beaten if they were slow or careless, or if they threatened to tell the
elders in the village what went on in the *laweni*. The main weapon to
get boys into the *laweni* was the ridicule of their fellows. Once members
of the *laweni* group they were disciplined into obedience by threats and
beating. The age range within a *laweni* was often considerable, from
seven to seventeen years.

All the boys in a *laweni* who were members of houses possessing
cattle—and this as a rule included all sons of Ngoni families of trans-
Zambesi clans—had to take part in herding. Cattle-herding was a
responsible task and could be an arduous one. The boys got up before
dawn, opened the gate of the kraal, and took the cattle to water. They
milked the cattle on an open space near the village and carried the milk
in wooden jars, gourds or petrol tins to the owner of the cattle, keeping

some for themselves as their perquisite. They then drove the cattle to
pasture, and this might be some distance away when grass was scarce in
the dry season. They sometimes drove the cattle back near the village to
rest at noon under the shade trees, but if the pasture was far away the
cattle rested there and went on feeding later. They were brought back
to the kraal in the late afternoon and counted by one of the senior men.

The herd-boys taught each other to fight with sticks, to wrestle, to
catch rats and small birds, to use the knobkerry, catapults, and bows and
arrows. Sometimes in the afternoon they went to other villages and
challenged another herd to a fight between bulls.[1] During the long day's
herding, the boys used to drink milk, make *amasi* (milk curds) in a
gourd and eat it, bake birds in clay and roast ears of maize taken from
their mothers' grain stores. Precedence among the herd-boys depended
first on age and only secondly on the rank and position of the families
they belonged to. There was an easily recognizable air of authority and
almost of arrogance among the older boys responsible for their fathers'
and uncles' cattle. They superintended the process of letting out the
cattle, milking them, driving them to pasture and the return to the
kraal in the evening. Mounted on donkeys, wearing large straw hats
made by themselves, the senior boys acted like ranch owners bossing up
inefficient work hands.

This period of living in the *laweni* was, as we have seen, shared by boys
of a wide age group. In a large village where there were two or three or
four *laweni*, there was often one in each section, which generally meant
that the boys belonging to one *banja* or section shared one *laweni*. This
had the effect of dividing them up to some extent on a basis of family and
rank, but in a *laweni* serving a whole village all the boys went in together
whatever families they came from. There was no respecting of clan
status in the *laweni* and young boys of high-ranking families had to wait
on and obey older boys of lower rank. *Laweni* life was therefore a
democratizing influence among the boys of the village, and no boys were
excused from herding cattle because they belonged to a house which
owned cattle. Even if some went to school and others did not, the school-
boys had to take their share of herding in the holidays. Ngoni chiefs and
leading men laid great emphasis on keeping the boys busy and making
them carry out the work allotted to them. The older boys began to listen
in at court cases and to discuss them among themselves. During the wet
season from time to time they formed hoeing parties for clearing new
ground and for the periodical weeding of gardens. They seldom did any
continuous cultivation, as the women and the older men did, and a boy
who liked to go off and hoe by himself was pointed out as one with
rather peculiar tastes.

During this period of *laweni* life, when in addition to herding the

---

[1] For the relation between the training of herd-boys and preparation for war, see
Part II, Chap. I, p. 30.

boys took more interest and more part in adult occupations and affairs, the emergence of leadership among Ngoni boys of high-ranking families was watched by their elders and recognized by their age mates. This was the formative period when a boy's capacity to succeed his father in a position of authority was carefully observed and judged. The Ngoni had ways of passing over a man who was a physical weakling, a coward in face of danger, a sadistic bully to weaker men, a pursuer of women and a breaker-up of marriages. The *madoda* in a Ngoni village, who appeared to let the boys in the *laweni* manage their own affairs without interfering, had nevertheless a shrewd idea of who was making good and who was proving disappointing. Their comments, showing continued observation over a long period, were often expressed when two or three friends and age mates from the *laweni* decided to go off to the south to work together. The *madoda* would then say: 'We hope they will come back soon and not be "lost". So and so is like his father and he will help us here in the village'; or they might comment: 'Good riddance, they were always hanging round the girls—worthless ones, indeed' (*wa chabe ndithu*).

It has already been pointed out that there was no circumcision school nor public initiation rite among the Ngoni. At puberty the ritual observed was a private and personal affair. On a boy's first nocturnal emission his age mates informed an older boy in the *laweni*, who told him to go at once before it was light and bathe in the river, and to do so each morning after an emission. This use of cold water was believed to give a boy strength and virility. The boy was also instructed by the older boys in the *laweni* on how to behave to his equals and his elders and to women. This stage was called *ukuchayiwa nga' manzi*, 'to be beaten with water', and was not reported to the older people. When the older people noticed that the boy's voice was breaking, his father inquired whether he had passed puberty and, on being assured of this, he found a man who knew the *uludengele* medicine. The father killed a goat, and the medicine man took some of the unchewed cud from the goat's stomach, mixed it with the bitter *uludengele* root and put it on a pan over a fire. This took place near the gate of the kraal or near the parents' hut, with the father and the father's male relatives standing by. When the mixture boiled, the boy was told to dip the tips of his fingers in the pan one after the other and lick each one quickly. At the same time he kept jumping over the fire and striking his elbows against his sides. The Ngoni believed that this medicine gave boys physical strength and stamina and they administered it to their servants' sons as well. It was still practised in the 1930's among Ngoni who were educated and partly westernized.

While the organization of the *laweni* catered for all boys from their second teeth till their marriage, including boys from the age sets called *abantwana* and *amajaha*, the organization of girls' life followed a different pattern. They also went to sleep with a grandmother or some other older member of the family when they were old enough to be excluded from their mother's hut at night, and they shared with their small brothers the grandmother's care and her story-telling round the fire in the evenings. During the day the girls continued as part of their mother's household group, eating with her and the younger children. As little girls they were taught to sit down carefully and to smooth down the cloth which they wore round their waists. They were trained to speak correctly and to know the right forms of address, to greet strangers politely, to avoid touching their father's mats or bed, to eat tidily and with restraint. The emphasis was on exclusiveness for these high-born Ngoni girls, lest, as a result of mixing too freely with everyone, they should forget the teaching given and the behaviour which was expected of them. In contrast to their brothers' rigorous training in the *laweni*, Ngoni girls, as they showed signs of approaching puberty, were guarded and looked after and instructed further in correct behaviour.

When a girl found that she was menstruating for the first time, she told one of her age mates and sent her to tell her *gogo*.[1] The *gogo* told her to stay in the hut during the period and showed her how to wear a cloth between her legs, which she had henceforth to wear always whether menstruating or not. She was told to sleep from now on in a different part of the hut from the smaller children and never to bathe with younger girls. At the end of her first period the girl was escorted to the women's bathing-place by her father's sisters and other female members of her father's family. She was made to wash in the stream and squat in the cold water while doing so. I saw more than one child trying to control her shivering while her relatives watched to see if she would be strong and brave, or weak and cowardly. When she was in the water she was made to face south-east—the quarter which the Ngoni called *kwathu* (our home). After this ceremony the girl's father and mother were informed, and her father informed the head of his *banja* and the head of the village. The news was greeted with rejoicing and made generally public.

From about the age of ten or eleven, the Ngoni girl belonged to an age set distinguished by a separate name. She was no longer included in the group of children, as were her brothers of the same age, but was marked out by belonging to the age set called *inkakazana* or *mabuthu*. After her first menstruation she belonged to the age set called *izintombi* or *anamwali*. From this stage, Ngoni girls were under the close supervision of the older women. The association of a *gogo* or older woman with each house in a Ngoni village meant that the girls of the house were under her special care, particularly after they had passed puberty. There

---

[1] *gogo* in this context is used for grandmother or for the elderly woman to whose care the girl was assigned.

were clearly defined aims in this care of girls after puberty, including instruction in personal hygiene and in pre-marital sexual relations. A girl's father's sisters and her own mother wanted to be able to say, when marriage negotiations began: *Ngombe zake zidzala*, 'her cattle are full', which was the comment made when girls were examined periodically to see if they were still virgin. To achieve this they constantly said to her: '*Mudzisunge, mudziletse*', 'take care of yourself, control yourself'; and the *gogo* explained to the girl how she could protect herself. In one area where I lived, the chief's daughter was examined every week, with her *izidandani* or companions, and the girls who helped in the big house were examined every month. The strict behaviour required of Ngoni girls of good family was expected also of those of the same age who were members of the same household, either appointed to be with them as companions or as servants in the big house.

Looking forward to marriage involved not only preservation of her virginity. An Ngoni girl going to a strange village had to know how to perform women's work in the home, how to do it herself as well as how to direct others, and she had to be carefully trained in that meticulous and exclusive social behaviour required of Ngoni women of good family. She might be going to marry a man who intended to 'marry up', in which case she might be thought in one sense to be 'marrying below her station'. Yet her personal position as a member of her father's clan and family could not be altered by her marriage, and she was well aware that she was conferring something on the man and on the family she married into.

While the boys were learning their roles in later life in the democratic atmosphere of the *laweni* and of the boys' pursuits in the village, the girls in the later stage of their training after puberty were treated more individually, and were not left to find their level in a group of their age mates. The adult women took an active part in telling them how to behave, how to dress and how to cook. The girls of high-ranking families sometimes pounded maize with their age mates, singing as they did so, but more for fun than because their food depended on it. They learned to dress their hair and put on clothes, and to walk and dance in company with other girls, but always with the critical eye of their *gogo* upon them. Their lower-ranking companions could make mistakes and be careless, and walk and dance in an exaggerated fashion. Ngoni girls might never pass certain bounds of decorum, and the standard expected of them was high and exacting. I have heard *manina* of leading clans scold young girls many times for careless behaviour and badly done work.

In this training, as throughout that of the boys, there was a deliberate preparation for leadership. A girl's character and ability were being watched and, while an awareness of her personal dignity and position was being fostered, it was accompanied by requirements of obedience and docility, especially to older women. This last was intended to stand her in good stead when she went to be married in a strange village and would be expected to show subservience to her mother-in-law. At the same time, since the girl belonged to a high-ranking clan, she knew, and so did those who were training her, that she would eventually have to exercise authority and teach others what to do and show them how to do it. She would also be expected to have a mind of her own and to speak out on occasions to her husband and, when she grew older, to rebuke women in her house or in her service if they did anything amiss.

In pre-European days, between the private puberty ritual and her marriage, the Ngoni girl went through another ceremony, the *umsindo*. This was a pre-marriage rite, and was in many instances followed almost immediately by marriage. It was held for girls of high-ranking families, though their companions from their own and other villages shared in the ritual. The ceremony was abandoned after the missionaries came, but many of the songs and the dances were well-known to the leading Ngoni women. I saw many *umsindo* dances in the northern and central kingdoms and collected a number of the songs which were still in use, some sung to solo instruments, such as the *igubu*, and others sung at funerals or at tribal gatherings. Those *umsindo* songs which referred to sexual intercourse and used expressions which were considered obscene, had been sung only at the ceremony itself. The Ngoni made a practice of referring to genital organs and to sexual intercourse in veiled language. As soon as the meaning of the terms became obvious, they were disguised by other allusive terms. The degree of obscenity in the actual words of songs was therefore very difficult to establish, but Ngoni informants were always clear about which could be sung in public and which only on occasions of licence or strictly in private.

The *umsindo* ceremony as a preliminary to marriage fulfilled certain functions. It was a public declaration that the girl for whom it was held had been examined and found to be a virgin, for it was not held for anyone who had been deflowered in earlier love affairs. It emphasized the social rank and the wealth of the girl's father, for only rich and important men could afford to hold *umsindo* for their daughters. It had a strong element of a *rite de passage* in it, for the girls were secluded in a hut during most of the ceremony, they fasted, they were given instruction by older women, and they were finally 'brought out' of the hut and adorned with parts of the beasts slaughtered, and with beads given as presents by friends and relatives. Perhaps the chief significance of the *umsindo* was the fact that it was a ceremony held for the girl in her father's village. It was an assertion of her membership in her own family and village circle, and of her father's status and of his regard for her. There is no doubt that the Ngoni women of high rank had a keen sense of their own importance and position; the *umsindo* ceremony emphasized this, and was a reminder of their careful bringing up in their father's village surrounded by their attendant girls and older women.

Many of the *umsindo* songs referred to well-known events in Ngoni history. Others were warnings against jealousy when living in a poly-gynous household. One of these, said to be a lament of the women about the difficulties of polygynous households, was very popular in the northern kingdom and was used by Ngoni ministers in the churches when speaking against polygamy, even though the actual words of the song seemed to be referring to a historical event.

The boys and girls went through one common ceremony about the age of seven, when their second teeth were coming. The local tribes practised various forms of scarification, including facial tribal markings. The Ngoni never did this in the past and said that they despised it. Their distinctive marking was the piercing of the ear lobes in order to insert a small piece of reed, or a stud, or some beads. Formerly, when captives were taken in war, or when a village was conquered and annexed, the local people, especially the younger men, were forced to have their ears pierced as a condition of service in the regiments. After the Europeans came, the forcible ear-piercing was resisted by the local tribes, but among the Ngoni, especially those of trans-Zambesi clans, it continued to be practised, and I saw it being carried out in several vil-lages. It was done in the dry cold-weather months, usually by one of the senior women of the children's family or house, and included all the children of about the same age who wanted to have their ears pierced. The woman pierced the lobe with a thorn, or a needle if she had one, and threaded some cotton through the hole. A day or so later they put in tiny bits of grass and replaced these with larger and larger bits until the hole was considered the right size.

After this ear-piercing ceremony, the boys' and girls' groups developed on their separate lines until their members became interested in each other as members of the opposite sex. Then, as I said at the beginning of the chapter, the groups of youths and girls were the two most prominent age groups in a village. They paid great attention to their clothes, washed with sweet-smelling leaves, used fats to anoint their hair, and the girls wore bead ornaments in their hair and on neck and wrists. Thus adorned, they spent their leisure time, especially in the cold weather after harvest, visiting other villages, usually in separate groups of youths and girls, except when they went as a team to dance *ngoma* in a neighbouring village.

In the social life of young people in Ngoni villages, the *ngoma* dance played an important part, especially in the northern kingdom. It took place after the harvest and was organized on a 'village team' basis. The boys practised their dance outside the cattle kraal in the evenings, and the girls did their dancing by themselves as a rule. But on the occasion of an *ngoma* 'competition' the team was made up of lads and girls of about fourteen to eighteen years old. They went off to another village, having announced their arrival previously, and challenged the 'home team' to dance *ngoma*. The dancing was in the kraal with the adults looking on and acting as judges. It was all very decorous and orderly and the competing teams were in dead earnest. As we have noticed already, the Ngoni danced without drums. The steady beat of the feet of the young men made the rhythm for the dance, but the co-ordination in the long lines of boys in front and girls behind needed assiduous practice to produce harmonious results. In both northern and central Ngoniland the Paramounts had forbidden all dances except Ngoni dances, and in the north the *ngoma* was encouraged by the chiefs because it was considered a 'good dance' for young people.

After marriage, the young women were absorbed in the care of their huts and young children and only appeared as an age set when they took part in a communal hoeing; on such occasions they were inclined to keep apart from the older women, sometimes on the grounds that they did not drink the full-strength beer, and therefore clustered round a pot of 'sweet' beer when they knocked off work. In most Ngoni villages the young men after marriage went off to find work and, as a group of friends within an age set, they would get together to talk things over, make their preparations and travel to the south.

In day-to-day village affairs, as well as on ceremonial occasions, the age sets of the *manina* and *madoda* were very much in evidence. The *madoda* met at meal-times by the gate of the kraal, and they went there to count the cattle when they came back in the evening. The same group could be seen either at the kraal gate or on a verandah talking about village affairs or drinking together, or at a court listening to cases. The *manina* usually gathered in the verandah of the *indlunkulu* to talk over women's affairs or to receive guests. As an age set they met less frequently than the men because the larger part of their tasks lay in their own huts or in the group of women associated with a house. On all occasions when the formal reception of strangers took place, or when ritual feasting or shaving or washing occurred, or when important decisions had to be made, the *manina* and the *madoda* in their separate sets were in evidence.

Although the age sets in village life were social units carrying definite responsibilities and performing recognized activities, their chief importance in Ngoni social life was in regulating behavioural patterns and prescribing mutual relationships. Here we have to take note of a selective principle at work among the *manina* and *madoda*. Although in one sense all women and men of forty to forty-five and upwards belonged to these age sets, the individuals who carried out the characteristic activities of these groups did not include all the men and women of that age. The very old people did not continue to exercise any influence in village affairs unless they were exceptionally vigorous mentally and physically, or the kind of dominating personality who could not be overlooked. It was evident also that individuals of weak character or evil disposition were not included in the group. I saw one or two such persons who bore a bad reputation in village society turned away from a senior group which was talking over a difficult village affair, with the caustic comment: 'Who is that worthless one? We cannot know him.' On the other hand, on social occasions when food or beer was being dispensed, all the old ones and the less reputable ones would be given their share, though sometimes with a cutting remark about the people who never missed a party but never did any work.

Selection in the senior age sets was intended to show that only persons who could be trusted, that is who were of known good character, were qualified to supervise the growing up of boys and girls, for whom the village elders as a group felt responsible. The maintenance of Ngoni standards of behaviour in young people was in the hands of this older group, who could and did exercise authority over and above that of the family and house. There were no more ardent supporters of Ngoni behaviour patterns than some of the older men and women of Ntumba clans in the central kingdom who had been brought up in the houses of Swazi or trans-Zambesi clans, and were recognized as *manina* and *madoda* in their villages.

Among the younger people below the group of elders, it was common to hear them address each other as *ntanga yami*, or *mnzanga*, 'my age mate'. Boys shouted it at each other on the cattle ground, young women called to each other in those terms when pounding maize, and when on a visit as an *ngoma* dance team it was a frequent form of address among the youths and girls. There was inherent in that form of address an ease of relationship, an absence of seniority or inferiority, and an acknowledgement of a tie which went beyond that of the family or house or clan. It was most commonly used within a village, but it was sometimes used between young people of different villages.

Within these groups of youths and girls and among young married men and women, there was a recognized friendship relation, *cibwenzi*, which existed as a rule between pairs of individuals of the same sex and age. It was sometimes a continuation of a playmate companionship; sometimes an expression of the need of a young boy in a *laweni* or a young married woman for a confidante or sympathizer. Most often it was a spontaneous specialized liking for another person, expressed invariably through an exchange of small gifts and generally of confidences, and often by going off together to bathe or cut firewood or catapult small birds. Such friendships were said as a rule to be permanent, though girls and women sometimes referred contemptuously to someone as 'She was my friend. Now she hates me and does not give me anything.' The decision to go off in search of work was often taken by two youths who were friends and who announced their intention, and then were joined by other pairs.

These forms of an age-set system which the Ngoni brought with them from the south were still in the 1930's a significant element in village life. The greatest change had occurred in the cessation of warfare and, with the enforcement of peace, the recognized stages mentioned in the beginning of this chapter had to a large extent disappeared. Though the boys and men were no longer divided into pre-warriors, warriors, and post-warriors, the institution of the *laweni* and the important role played by the *madoda* were two distinctive elements in Ngoni village life. So also was the form and content of the training given to Ngoni girls of Swazi clans, which largely determined the role played by the *manina* in village affairs.

PART IV

THE ANCESTOR CULT OF THE NGONI

CHAPTER I

THE ANCESTRAL SPIRITS AND THE ARISTOCRATIC TRADITION

THIS section is not an account of Ngoni religion. It would require a study in itself to examine their beliefs about supernatural beings, their ideas on cosmogony, their concepts of the causes of disaster and sickness, their approach to and practice of forms of magic, and their attitude to witchcraft. Living in Ngoni villages, listening to individuals of different ages discussing prosperity and disaster, the seen and the unseen, the known and the feared, it was clear that it would be difficult to isolate a comprehensive system of beliefs and say that these were distinctively Ngoni beliefs concerning religion and magic and witchcraft. The observer was always aware of the intermingling of ideas and practices from the many Nyasaland tribal peoples who lived side by side and were in constant contact with one another in all those spheres of thought and action which demanded explanation and some remedial or therapeutic treatment. Among the Nyasaland tribes in the 1930's the influence of sixty years of Christian teaching by the missions played an important part, since the missions had introduced western medicine and education as well as a new religion and ethic, and so had influenced both thinking and action among their converts and their families.

In this complex situation it was virtually impossible to say: this is the Cewa religion, this is the Tumbuka cosmogony, this is Ntumba magic. It was nevertheless clear that there was an Ngoni cult of their ancestral spirits, which was not shared, in the form in which they practised it, by any of the neighbouring peoples, and the Ngoni had their own selective methods of relating it to Christian beliefs and practices. One reason why the Ngoni ancestor cult could be singled out as peculiar to them was its foundation in their aristocratic tradition. As long as the Ngoni political and social structure and organization survived, including the reciprocal roles of leading men and important women, the concept of houses with their ownership of cattle, and the role of the *gogo* house in maintaining tradition and carrying out ritual, the performance of the cult of ancestral spirits was assured. The eminent ancestors whose spirits were guarded in a village and who were known and remembered were addressed in times of trouble, and meat was offered to them as a form of sacrifice from the herd of cattle associated with the house to which they had belonged. This section will deal with the cult of ancestral spirits of the Swazi and trans-Zambesi clans who formed the political and social aristocracy. Thus, in the form described here, the cult is exclusively related to the aristocratic tradition, and no account will be given or analysis made of ancestor cults practised by those groups in the two Ngoni kingdoms who were not of the leading clans. In the ancestor cult, as it will be described here, the emphasis was always on known and named spirits of the dead, associated with the village where the ritual was performed. In the approach to these known and named spirits—an approach which I have called a cult—there were three essential components: the diviner, the ritual address and the cattle. The diviner's role we shall discuss in Chapter III and the ritual forms of addressing the ancestors in Chapter IV. The Ngoni believed they could not approach their ancestral spirits except through their cattle, which had first to show that the spirits agreed to prayers being made, and the sign was that the beast urinated. The sacrifice of a beast was an integral part of the rite, which was concluded by the suppliants eating the meat together. At no point in their common life did the Ngoni more clearly demonstrate their dependence on their cattle than in the ritual of addressing their ancestral spirits. For this reason, in Chapter II we shall review the place of cattle in Ngoni life and relate it to their role in the ancestor cult.

Ancestral spirits of the Ngoni Paramounts.

The reigning Paramount and his predecessors in that office held an unchallenged supremacy in the hierarchy of the Ngoni kingdoms. The Ngoni believed that the line of dead Paramounts similarly led the hierarchy of the ancestral spirits, and that the dead Paramounts had power to help the Ngoni nation in time of need. It was taken for granted that when Paramounts died they would continue to be powerful and held in great respect, and that their position in the spirit world would enable them to influence UMkulumqango, the Great Spirit. This Great Spirit was believed to be the creator of all things and the ultimate source of power, particularly of sending rain, success in war, and deliverance from pestilence; and he was in general regarded as the giver of health and strength to mankind. The Ngoni held that those ancestors who were nearest to the living in time, whose names they knew, possessed less power than the remote ancestors whose names had been forgotten. On the same principle UMkulumqango, the Great Spirit, the originator of all creation, possessed more power than any other being, but, since he was so far removed in time from the living, no one could know his praise-names or his genealogy, and therefore he could not be addressed directly. In the same way the remotest ancestors of the Paramount could not be addressed directly because their praise-names were unknown to living men. Only those direct ancestors of the Paramount, whose names and genealogy and praise-names were known, could be addressed correctly and they could be counted on to use their influence with remoter and more powerful ancestral spirits and with the Great Spirit himself.

As one of the Ngoni said: 'The spirits of the dead Paramounts were the guardians of the whole nation. These *amadlozi* stood between UMku-lumqango and the people. They were never worshipped at times of plenty and prosperity, but at the time of crisis and danger.'

In pre-European days there had been two special occasions when the spirits of former Paramounts were addressed on behalf on the whole nation. One was at the time of the *incwala* or first-fruits ceremony, which as we have seen was given up before the final settlement in Nyasaland. This was an occasion uniting all the people with songs and dances at the village of the Paramount. The second occasion was in time of war before the army went out on a raid. This could take place more than once during the fighting season, and always at the Paramount's village.

The remaining occasions for addressing the spirits of former Para-mounts on behalf of the nation were when epidemics threatened, when there was a drought, or in the serious illness of the Paramount or of a leading member of his family. In prayer for rain or for the recovery from illness of someone of the royal clan, the diviner had to be consulted about which of the ancestors of the Paramount should be addressed. The ancestor indicated by the diviner had to be named in the ritual, his genealogy given and, as a rule, his particular attributes and his praise-names mentioned. The following account was given to me by Mlonyeni Jere, who prayed for rain in Elangeni in 1935:

❛ When the rain stopped, the *amadoda* spoke among themselves 'What shall be done?' If they could not find out who had made the rain to stop, they said 'We must ask the *isanusi* (diviner). Perhaps it is one of the *amadlozi* (spirits) who are stopping the rain.'

If the *isanusi* finds it is the spirit of Hlacwayo, then all the big people are called to come to the kraal at Elangeni. Then they say 'We should choose a black ox with no white spot and bring it to the kraal.' They appointed a speaker who knows how to speak well all the names of the chiefs who have died. This man says to the spirit 'This cow is yours. You must eat it all. Then you must tell UMkulumqango our troubles.' If it urinates or makes dung, the spirits agree. This praying to the spirits is in the kraal in the evening. At early dawn next day someone is sent to kill the ox. While it was being flayed, the huts of the chief wives were smeared with cow dung on the floors and on the place outside the door. The meat was cooked in the kraal by the *amadoda*. Some of it was taken into the *indlunkulu* and kept there for one night so that the spirit might lick it.

The Paramount had already eaten in the kraal and the meat was divided for the *amadoda* according to their age regiments. After they have eaten, a big man rises up to thank the spirit with his titles and praise-names, and all the people answer *Bayete* and there is a war-dance in the kraal. Then they look up and see clouds coming. Then the rain comes.

This particularizing of the appeal to an individual dead Paramount in the ancestor cult was an essential element in the ritual, and there seemed

to be no occasion and no form of ritual in which a generalized appeal
was made to the spirits of all former Paramounts.

The reasons for this were related to the place of the sacrifice and the
herd of cattle used. The place was determined by the village where the
spirit of the dead Paramount was guarded by a particular house, and
where some at least of the cattle belonging to that house were kraaled.
Thus, in the northern kingdom, the spirit of Zwangendaba Jere was
addressed in Ekwendeni; of Hlacwayo his father in Elangeni; and of
Magangata his grandfather in Hoho. In the central kingdom the spirit
of Mputa was addressed in Mcakhatha and also in Lizulu; and of his
father, Ngwana, in a village in Portuguese territory. I heard no reference
to the spirits of more recent Paramounts being addressed, and when I
asked the reason several informants suggested that it was important to
address the Ngoni Paramount who had been with his people in the
south, and who therefore knew the names of the spirits of former Paramounts who had died in the south, names which the Ngoni in Nyasaland
had forgotten. On the other hand, provision was made for the guardianship of the spirit of each successive Paramount, and in central Ngoniland
there was provision for guarding the spirit of a Queen Mother, NaMlangeni, the big wife of Mputa who survived him, and of her daughter, the
Royal Sister Bambo Manga. The reason given for the guardianship of
the spirits of these two royal women in Mcakhatha illustrates the close
link between the village where the spirit was guarded and the herd of
cattle kept there and was explained by informants in the following terms.
While the central Ngoni were still in Songea Paramount Mputa wanted
cattle to give as *lobola* for his marriage to NaMlangeni. He went to
Golozela, the head of the Nzunga clan, and asked him for cattle, which
were handed over to the father of NaMlangeni. Golozela Nzunga then
became the *induna* of the house of NaMlangeni in the royal village and
her daughter Bambo Manga lived in his section. The cattle given for her
lobola when she was married were put in the kraal of Golozela Nzunga to
repay him for his previous gift. After her husband's death, Bambo Manga
returned to the Nzunga head village where her cattle were, and assumed
the guardianship of the spirits of her mother and of her father Mputa.

Ancestral spirits of Swazi and trans-Zambesi clans

Ngoni informants often made statements such as the following by
Cibambo:

❡ The Ngoni believed that each family had its own line of spirits
(*amadlozi*) dating far back to the origin of that family, and that these in
succession carried the messages until they reached the unknown ancestors,
who in turn had the right to carry the message to UMkulumqango.

When such a statement was checked in several areas it was clear that
the families of the Swazi and trans-Zambesi clans focussed their

ancestor cult in the head village of their clan. If they were asked 'How do you address the spirit (*teta idlozi*)?' they gave the names and genealogy of the former heads of the clan and their attributes if they were known. If they were asked 'Where do you address the spirits?' the reply was always in terms of a particular village where a certain spirit was guarded.

The occasions on which the Swazi clan ancestors were addressed and sacrifices made were in cases of sickness of an important member of the clan. It was sometimes suggested that there might be trouble in the clan villages for which prayer should be made to the clan spirits, but when pressed the only specific instance informants could give was when the cattle did not thrive. They repudiated immediately any idea of prayer to the clan spirits in cases of drought or epidemics in the clan villages since those troubles, wherever they occurred, could only be helped by the spirits of the Paramounts who were concerned with all the land and all its people.

The procedure followed in the clan head village was the same as that for addressing the spirits of the Paramounts. In that village a diviner was consulted, he named the spirit who should be addressed, a beast was sacrificed and prayers were made. This was the Ngoni pattern of the ancestor cult, and it was limited to the Swazi and some of the trans-Zambesi clans. Its correct observance required that combination of cattle, houses, and known genealogies which only the leading clans possessed.

The living and the dead

At times such as funerals, and when talking about the ancestor cult, the Ngoni often used the phrase: 'Death cannot cut life.' They believed that human spirits had a continued existence after death, and that this existence was related to the place where they had dwelt, the people who were of their family and clan, and the cattle which belonged to their house and village. This continued association was not an automatic process. It had to be assured by the correct performance of the burial rites, the observance of stages of mourning and the deliberate 'bringing back' of the spirit to the village where it would be guarded and honoured after the final mourning ceremony was over.

In the Ngoni funeral rites there were distinctive elements in the burial of those belonging to Swazi and trans-Zambesi clans. In handling the corpse the legs were bent and drawn up to the body and the arms folded and crossed each side of the neck, so that the corpse seemed to be sitting and holding its head in its hands. It was wrapped in the skin of a newly killed beast. In the central kingdom men and women of Swazi clans were wrapped first in a sheep-skin, with a cow-skin put over it. The grave was a circular pit, with a small side chamber or shelf where the body was placed in a sitting position, propped up with large stones and facing south-east to the ancestral homeland. Personal possessions, such as skins and shields and baskets, were either put in the grave or taken to be burned immediately after the burial on the banks of the stream where the living performed their ritual washing. Small children who were related to the dead took charcoal in their hands, and walked up to the grave backwards and threw the charcoal in without looking. Some leaders of the Swazi clans were buried on the edge of the kraal of the house to which they belonged, and the fence was enlarged to include the grave. The Ngoni comment on this place of burial was: 'If we make a grave, we make it outside the kraal, and afterwards build the kraal round that place so that cattle may walk over it and lie on it. Thus it may become flat as if it were nothing, for Ngoni people do not want a grave to be seen from the outside.' The women who were near relatives of the dead were allowed to mourn in the hut where the person had died, or they could if they chose take part in the war-songs and dances which were the only form of mourning allowed to the male relatives and to the men and women of the village who were not closely related to the dead person. The usual procedure was for a group of older women to wail and sob in the hut, but for all the rest, men and women, to mourn in the Ngoni way by taking part in war-dances and songs.

Much of this ritual appears to have had as its purpose to remove the fear of death from the living. That was the explanation of why the children threw charcoal in the grave—that they should not remember with fear the dead person being put in the earth. The obliteration of the grave site on the edge of the kraal had a dual purpose. One has been already referred to—that the grave should not be seen. The other was to identify the grave of a leading man or woman with the kraal site and the cattle herded there. If the village moved and a new kraal was set up, people would still say 'X was buried here', adding 'He was buried here when we were on Domwe—or in Songea', referring to an earlier site of the village. Placing the corpse facing south-east, and singing Ngoni war-songs which had come from the south, linked the newly dead with the ancestral dead, and emphasized the chain of communication between the living and the dead, which a new ancestral spirit could help to forge. It was establishing this means of communication which was the dominant note in the ritual of the funeral and in the post-burial rites.

When a death took place, the first action taken after the corpse had been prepared and wrapped in a skin was to send out a summons to come and mourn. We saw in the chapter on the Paramount that at his death the summons was in the formula 'The skies have fallen.' For others the announcement was: 'So and so has died. Come and mourn.' The obligation to mourn was binding. If relatives and fellow clansmen could not come at the time of the burial, or were away in the south, one of their first duties on returning to their home village was to go and mourn by the kraal where the dead person was buried. This was intended partly to show sympathy for the bereaved, but also to acknowledge and salute a new ancestral spirit, and to demonstrate the re-integration of the group of those living relatives who had performed or were about to perform certain rites for the newly dead.

These rites were the stages of mourning laid down in the Ngoni funeral ritual. They were stages in which all adults took part, and they fulfilled the need to build up the future links with the spirit who had joined the ancestors and to bring together in common acts those from whom death had removed one of their number. The following text by one of the leaders of a Swazi clan in the central kingdom puts together briefly the successive stages of shaving, drinking beer, eating meat, singing war-songs, ritual cleansing and widow inheritance, and bringing back the spirit.

❡ If a man died, the second day they shave; after 5 or 6 months they shave again and cook beer. This means the widows must take off their white *zitambo* (head bands). After 12 months they take off their black *zitambo* and kill a beast to praise the spirit so that he may return to his house. This is also the time for inheriting the widows.

When they take off the white *zitambo*, the brother of the one who died takes sheep dung and sprinkles it in the houses where the widows are sleeping. At the same time the men wash their hands with cattle dung. The meaning of this is to tell the widows to cook food for the brothers of the dead man to send to them when they sit by the kraal. This they do before they can see them.

From the ritual witnessed at many funeral ceremonies, which never altered in its main elements, and from discussions with Ngoni informants, it was possible to gain some idea of Ngoni beliefs about the relation between the living and the dead. It was clear that the attitude of the living towards the dead was one of respect and honour, but not predominantly one of avoidance and fear as among some of the neighbouring tribes. The post-burial ritual culminated in 'bringing back the spirit' to the village, and we shall examine this further in the last chapter of this section. An observer was always conscious of a sense that people were waiting for the return of the spirit, which had to be planned for and carried out by the living. During the interval between the death and bringing back the spirit, it was said to be 'in the bush'. When asked where in fact the spirit was, the answer was always 'We do not know. How can we know?' They admitted that the life of the spirits was unknown to them, and there was evidence of a slightly uneasy relationship during this interval of waiting. When the spirit had been brought back and was being guarded by some woman appointed for that purpose, then it was once more near to the living and their cattle, and it could be addressed correctly. In the absence of any clear concepts about life in a spirit world, the Ngoni clung to the ritual by which they believed they could establish and maintain contact of a safe and respectful nature between the living and the dead.

In the central kingdom there were two instances of a modern adaptation of the ancestor cult, both of which were evidence of its close links with the aristocratic tradition; one related to a *mulumuzana* of a Swazi clan, the other to the royal clan. One of the first things which caught the eye of a visitor to the village of Mcakhatha was a large circular brick and cement tomb with a wooden cross on the top, in the middle of the village by the main kraal and within sight of the ruling chief's hut. It was the tomb of Njolomole Nzunga I, son of Golozela Nzunga who gave the cattle for NaMlangeni's *lobola*, and father of the ruling Chief Njolomole Nzunga II. The idea of this memorial originated with Lopati Nzunga, younger brother of Njolomole I and head of the *gogo* section of the village, and he had organized its erection. The bricks and cement were given by Europeans in the neighbourhood, and three beasts were killed for meat for those who carried the materials. The money to pay for the bricklayers' wages was raised by the sale of another beast. The name on the wooden cross was cut by the Chief's brother-in-law who was a carpenter, and Lopati said that the cross was for writing the name on and had no Christian significance. The tomb was declared 'open' to the public in the presence of a large number of people. A beast was presented to the Paramount Chief, and another beast was killed and cooked for a feast in the village. Beer was brewed in the huts of the two leading widows who had been in the big house and second house of Njolomole I.

This tomb was a memorial and not a grave, for Njolomole I had been buried in Ngoni fashion on the edge of the kraal, the fence of which was enlarged to take in the grave. It was regarded as a central point in the village. Ngoni visitors saluted it as they went by with the right arm upraised in Ngoni fashion, and war-dances and *ngoma* dances took place beside it. The idea of a brick tomb with a cross on top was of course a modern concept taken from European cemeteries in Nyasaland which Lopati had seen. It cost six cattle to put it up and 'open' it, and these cattle were taken from the herds of the big house of Njolomole I.

In the chapter on the Paramount (Part II, Chapter II) it was pointed out that in the central kingdom the Paramount Gomani I was shot as a result of the 'war with the English' when he refused to walk to Zomba for his trial. On the Zomba road near the turning to the mission station of Dombole was a track leading into some woods. In an open clearing was a brick and cement tomb to Gomani I, subscribed to by the central Ngoni (including those living in the towns of Blantyre and Zomba). A memorial fund called 'The late Gomani Memorial Fund' was opened in 1926, and three years later those who had organized the fund formed the Angoni Highlands Association, mainly of Ngoni working in Blantyre and Zomba and wishing to maintain their links with their home villages. In discussing the origin of this fund for the memorial informants pointed out that they were aware that Gomani I, unlike his father and grandfather, had been a fierce ruler, and had gathered round him bands of young men who were not easily restrained. Though they could judge his character in this objective way, they respected his office, and hence his death and the confiscation of cattle which followed were a deep injury to Ngoni pride. So thirty years after his death they collected money and put up the memorial, and the appeal was supported for three main reasons. One was to commemorate this Paramount who had not had the traditional cremation by a river; another was to remove the shame of his death; the last was to draw together all his people in a common act. Every year numbers of Ngoni gathered at this memorial and held a Christian service which was followed by a general meeting. This memorial service and meeting had a definite link with the ancestor cult, and illustrated in a particular form Ngoni beliefs in the relation of the living and the dead.

In the 1930's, as we saw in Chapter III of Part I, the form of Ngoni funerals and the ritual of mourning were closely related to the ancestor cult and were practised by the Ngoni aristocracy. These forms of ritual and their beliefs they brought with them from the south, and they were an important part of Ngoni culture. We shall see in a later chapter how some of these cultural elements were combined with Christian ritual, both for leading individuals of Swazi clans and for lesser members of those clans.

CHAPTER II

CATTLE AND THE ANCESTOR CULT

THERE are many references throughout this study to the importance of cattle among the Ngoni. In this chapter the place of cattle in Ngoni life will be examined with reference to the ancestor cult, and hence certain limitations have been imposed in the selection of material and its interpretation. There will, for example, be no analysis of the role of cattle in the economic life of Ngoni families and villages. Much of the material discussed has an economic significance which is immediately apparent, but the limitations set will not allow the economic implications of certain practices to be pursued further here. It is important for the main purpose of this chapter to make a brief analysis of some factors in the ownership, care, and use of cattle, and to follow that with references to some of the values and attitudes inherent in the Ngoni ownership and use of cattle. I made a preliminary analysis of these factors in a memorandum on standards of living in the central kingdom, published in 1938.[1] The sociological and ritual significance of these factors will be the chief emphasis here, with reference to earlier chapters in this book on Ngoni culture and on the structure of Ngoni society.

In the sociological significance of cattle-ownership there are certain outstanding points to be emphasized, which will be indicated here and developed further in the analysis which follows. One is the connexion between cattle-ownership and status, illustrated by the dominance of the Swazi and trans-Zambesi clans in village life, since their possession of cattle was related to the kraal and to the siting of huts and to their house organization. The cattle horns on the roof of the *indlunkulu* were no trivial ornament. They were a proud assertion of cattle-ownership attached to the residences of the leading women, with all the implications of 'house herds' of cattle and of *lobola* given and received. Closely related to cattle-ownership and status was the power conferred by the possession of herds. The status of leading families was enhanced by the ability to give feasts, to give *lobola* for their sons' wives, to make sacrifices to the ancestors and, as we saw at the end of the last chapter, to realize cash by the sale of beasts belonging to the herd. Cattle-owners did at times have to decide whether to maintain and augment their herds and thereby be known as wealthy cattle-owning families; or to sell cattle in order to command labour to build a modern brick house, or to buy fine clothes for their wives and display their wealth in another form.

In the organization of Ngoni society, cattle were an important factor in uniting groups of persons. We have seen how the house, as a group of men and women, and its variant, the central Ngoni form of *banja*, had common possession of a herd of cattle which formed a source of wealth for all members of the house. Within the house the senior men were bound together by the responsibilities attached to the ownership and care of a herd. Within the village the senior men of a house or *banja* united in the upkeep of the kraal, the supervision of the herd-boys, the tending of sick cattle, and in meeting or resisting the Government's demands for culling or dipping stock. Where cattle were boarded out in another village, ties of association in the care of the beasts and in accountability for them bound together the cattle-owners or cattle-keepers of more than one village. A stage in the adjustment of a young wife to a strange village was reached when she added to the herd of the house she had married into the gift cattle given her by her father and so partly compensated for those which had been given to him by her husband's family. A new wife's standing in a village was thus advanced through any cattle which flowed in the opposite direction from those of the *lobola* cattle. Finally, and this is the main theme of this chapter, cattle were an essential link between the living and the dead.

[1] Read, M. *Native Standards of Living and African Culture Change.* Memorandum XVI of International African Institute, 1938.

The relation of cattle-ownership to social integration, which was so marked a feature of Ngoni society, was limited to the Swazi and trans-Zambesi clans. There was evidence that the acquisition of herds by former captives and by the local Cewa and other tribes created conflicts within the society. The following statement was made by an Ntumba village headman, commenting on several court cases relating to cattle-ownership. The reference in the last sentence is to the Ngoni practice in the ownership of cattle.

℃ Sometimes people say 'If your father was caught and was the slave of a certain person, and also if your mother was caught and was a slave of another man, then if you buy cattle and put them in the kraal of your father, those who caught your father say "These cattle are mine (or ours)." And those who caught your mother say "These cattle are ours." ' They all say so because it was they who caught your ancestors. So those cattle do not recognize their real owner. And sometimes those cattle do not bear well, and sometimes they just die.

Then perhaps you die and leave your cattle, and those people are quarrelling to find out who is the owner of those cattle, since there are three people who want those same cattle: your father, the one who caught your father, and the one who caught your mother.

And it is really best if there are many masters that you, a child, should not buy cattle, but just leave off because they are a source of trouble. But one who is a free man without any masters, he ought to buy cattle because there will be no trouble for him.

Among the local Cewa tribes, when a man wanted to start a herd and had money to buy cattle, he was expected to give the money to his *malume* (mother's brother) who then bought the cattle and took charge of them and regarded them as his.[1] This assertion of ownership of cattle bought with another man's money was part of the services to which the mother's brother was entitled from his sister's children, in return for services which he had performed or would perform for them. If those relationships between a man and his *malume* were not working smoothly and the *malume* was not helping his nephew, there was a tendency for the man to turn to his own father and give him the money, and vest the ownership of the cattle in him, often because the father had paid the school fees or a court fine for his son. When the *malume* realized that his position had been usurped and that his chance of owning cattle had gone, his dislike of the man's father and his family showed itself in jealousy and quarrels between the two individuals and friction between the families. The Cewa matrilineal *mbumba* as a cattle-owning group under a senior man had not the continuity of the Ngoni house, for an *mbumba* was said to be 'finished' when a woman and all

[1] The Cewa believed that if cattle were to survive and increase, they had to be owned and cared for by senior men. On the highlands round Dedza the Cewa had had cattle before the Ngoni came.

her daughters had died, and the herd of cattle was either inherited by the senior daughter's eldest son or divided among the sons of different daughters. Cewa informants said that quarrels constantly arose over the ownership of cattle, and two modern developments—the spread of *utengwa*[1] marriage and of a patrilineal form of *mbumba* with its repercussions on cattle acquisition and disposal—caused further tensions in Cewa society.

The role which cattle played in Ngoni social life partly depended on the structure and inter-relationships of the Ngoni social groups. The house and the family within the larger village unit were so organized that group ownership and group disposal of cattle caused no permanent friction. There were arguments about the disposal of cattle, but they were temporary and relatively trivial. The strength of tradition in the concept of ownership, and in the values and attitudes inherent in cattle-owning and keeping, was firmly established and was related to modern needs by the ingenuity of the Ngoni in manipulating traditional practices to suit new situations. Cattle therefore strengthened the integration of existing social units, and helped to preserve that unity and cohesion in Ngoni society which the ancestors were said to commend and to wish for. On this plane of conformity to a required pattern, cattle influenced the living and their behaviour. They also, through the structure and function of the houses, belonged to the spirit who was guarded in a particular house. As we shall see in Chapter IV, the ritual formula of address to the ancestor at the sacrifice of a beast was always 'Here is your beast . . . Here is your meat.' The living and the dead were joined therefore in the common ownership of a herd or part of a herd. The actual practices in social and ritual life where cattle were concerned, and the ideas and concepts from which the practices arose, will take up most of this chapter and form the necessary prelude to the further analysis of the ancestor cult.

Ownership of cattle and care of herds

'The war of the cattle-tax' was the name given in the central kingdom to the installation of dipping tanks in the 1930's and the levying of a tax of a shilling per head of cattle on all cattle-owners. The attempt by the Government to focus responsibility for dipping and to collect the taxes due brought out clearly the difficulties of applying English conceptions of ownership to the Ngoni. In the English meaning of the word ownership, a man can claim as his possession cattle which he has bought or inherited, and their offspring. This individual ownership means that he alone has the right to sell the animals or their milk, to regard the profits from such sale as his, and at any time to kill an animal for meat. He can will them to his descendants or to anyone he chooses after his

[1] Marriages in which the man took his wife to live in his village, but did not give *lobola* for her.

death, or he can give them to anyone he likes during his lifetime. Hence individual acquisition in the English sense involves the legal right of individual disposal; the individual possession of profits from such disposal; and the individual responsibility for complying with any regulations concerning cattle, such as inoculation, slaughter for foot-and-mouth disease, and testing of milk.

In Ngoni usage the concept of ownership involved the acquisition and disposal of, and the responsibility for, cattle, but behind this apparent similarity of terms lay a wide difference in interpretation. Cattle could be acquired by inheritance, by natural increase, by *lobola*, as payment in a court case, as a gift, or by purchase. Formerly cattle could be acquired in warfare and raiding, but never by purchase. With this exception of buying cattle for cash, the methods of acquiring cattle had not altered since the Ngoni settled in Nyasaland. In pre-European days in the Ngoni kingdoms only the Paramount, the subordinate chiefs, the *alumuzana* and the big *izinduna* possessed cattle. Having a herd marked the owner as a leading member of a leading clan, or as a famous warrior of a lesser clan whose distinguished war service had been rewarded by the Paramount giving him cattle, or allowing him to keep some of those he had taken from the enemy. New herds were formed when a Paramount or a chief moved out of his father's village and set up his own *lusungulu* village, taking with him one or more of his mothers who, together with his big wife, set up houses in the new village, and these houses were allotted cattle from the former undivided herd. Another way in which a herd was divided was when a big *induna* in charge of the house of a leading wife of a Paramount or a chief built a kraal for the cattle of that house near his own huts, and added to that herd any cattle which he acquired. Large Ngoni villages in pre-European days usually had one or more kraals on the edge of the village, as well as the big central one. When the large villages broke up and the *induna* moved off to found his own village, he still took care of the cattle of that house. If the house was one where an ancestral spirit was guarded, a successor was always appointed to live in the hut and guard the spirit. Hence the relationship of the house, its spirit guardian, its cattle and the *induna* in charge continued, though the personalities changed through death and for other reasons. This explained how in the 1930's cattle were found in one kraal which were said to belong to a house or a woman guardian of a spirit miles away in another village. Sometimes they were described as the cattle of a man long dead.

It is clear, therefore, that the Ngoni methods of acquiring cattle and building up herds did not result in a concept of individual ownership. Cattle were not willed from father to son, but the son of a Paramount or a chief, when he made his new *lusungulu* village, had the right to receive and to take with him the cattle of his mother's house; and the head of the *gogo* village who stayed behind also received and looked after the cattle of *his* mother's house and those of other widows of his father, even though the widows remarried and went to live elsewhere. The ownership of a herd, in the sense of authority to acquire and to dispose of the cattle, was in fact vested in the senior male members belonging to each house in whose name cattle were held. This senior male leadership of a house had, in the central kingdom, a parallel in the senior male members of a *banja*. The implication in both was the same—that there was a group of senior men linked by membership of a house or a *banja*, who took responsibility for all the cattle in the herd of that house or *banja* and for all additions to the herd. Any new beasts acquired through natural increase, *lobola*, court payments, gifts, or purchase, by any member of that house went into the herd belonging to it. Thus it was easy for young men working in the south to send back money to their fathers or fathers' brothers to buy cattle. They knew the choice would be well made and that the cattle would be well cared for until their return.

The right of disposal of cattle in a herd belonging to a house or *banja* was based on the same concept of ownership. The senior male group had to decide which beasts to send for the *lobola* when a young man of their house married. They undertook, as owners of the cattle, to pay fines in court cases when a member of the house was fined. If money was needed, either by the group as a whole or by an individual member, a beast was chosen and sold by the senior men; part of the proceeds was given to the individual who needed help, and part either buried under the floor of the hut of the woman who was head of the house, or converted into cloth and stored in the hut. Gifts of cattle were sometimes given to important visitors, or as an expression of sympathy when mourning at a funeral, or for a sacrifice to the ancestors. On all such occasions the decision to dispose of one or more beasts and the selection of them were in the hands of the senior male group. Though prolonged discussion might go on before a decision to sell or make a gift was made, once there was agreement the selection was often made very quickly. The leading men would go to the kraal, point out the beasts to the herd-boys, and tell them to drive them to the appointed place.

The care of the herds was primarily the responsibility of the senior men, though the actual herding was delegated to the herd-boys. Informants said that in pre-European days great care was taken of the animals in the rainy season; the ant-hills in the kraal were preserved so that the animals might get out of the mud, and calf-houses with roofs were always provided for shelter for the calves. I saw some calf-houses of this kind, and some kraals with ant-hills left in them, but neither was common practice, and the reason given was that the kraals and herds were much smaller than in pre-European days.

There were two chief objectives in the care of herds: that the cattle should keep well and avoid disease, and that they should multiply. The

cattle never came back to the kraal in the evening without one or more
of the senior men standing by the gate and watching them and counting
them as they went in. Sick cattle were noted and the herd-boys questioned about them. Mating was observed and noted, but not regulated,
though poorly developed male beasts were sometimes castrated by one
of the men who had acquired skill as a cattle doctor. Such a man would
also administer drenches and other medicines, but the responsibility
for calling a *sing'anga*, the specialist in medicines, to perform a ritual
for a sick beast was taken by the whole group. They also made the
decision to call a *sing'anga* to protect the kraal against lions. On several
occasions I was in a village where lions attempted to get into the kraal
at night, and the next morning the senior men who were responsible
for the herd discussed the efficacy of this or that man's 'lion medicine'
and decided who should be sent for to make the kraal safe again.

Important decisions were taken from time to time about placing the
cattle belonging to the herd of a house in other kraals. This custom of
kuikilila (lit. to entrust) was common in the central kingdom and had
been adapted to modern needs as one means of evading the cattle-tax
by appearing to have few cattle, whereas a number were boarded out
in other areas. This boarding out was a long-established custom of
the Ngoni and was practised for various reasons. One reason, and
probably the most important formerly, was to build up good relations
with leading men in the outlying villages by entrusting cattle to their
care. The reward if the cattle throve was often the gift of a beast, and
this was one means by which men of local tribes could build up a herd.
It was also a signal honour to have cattle entrusted in this way and it
was acknowledged by sending to such a 'keeper' the head of any beast
killed from this herd. Another reason for boarding out was to prevent
diseases spreading among a whole herd all kept in one kraal, and yet
another was a belief that certain men had latent power with cattle, and
that beasts put in their care throve and multiplied. This emphasis on
enlarging the herds by natural increase was the main motive for letting
the calves have all the milk they needed in order that they might thrive.

The uses of cattle and cattle products

Many of the uses to which cattle were put and for which they were
greatly valued have been referred to in this chapter and in earlier sections of this book. We shall now examine the consumption of meat, milk
and blood as food, and the forms of exchange in which cattle were
directly exchanged or converted into cash. The ritual use of cattle will
be discussed at the end of this chapter.

The testimony of early Europeans in Nyasaland and the accounts by
the Ngoni of their life in the pre-European period agree in giving the
consumption of meat, milk, and blood a high place in the diet of the
cattle-owning families. It was a widespread European criticism in the

1930's that the Ngoni did not live as well as they might and had, in fact, an impoverished diet, because they did not make full use, and sometimes very little use, of the milk and meat which they had available. In pre-European days, when the possession of cattle was confined to the Paramount, the chiefs and leading *alumuzana*, there was a continuous slaughter of animals to provide a regular diet of meat and *ulubende*, the cooked blood which the Ngoni liked very much. The heads of the big houses saw that there was always on hand *amasi*, the milk curds which was the form in which adults took their milk, fresh milk being reserved for young children and herd-boys. This provision of meat, *ulubende* and *amasi* was only possible for those who had plenty of cattle, and in both kingdoms wars and raids were carried out partly to obtain fresh supplies of cattle from neighbouring and unconquered tribes. As we saw in the chapter on the Paramount, in pre-European days the *alumuzana* who lived near enough to the royal village made a practice of calling frequently, if not daily, and such calls were rewarded by their being asked to eat with the Paramount, and 'food' in those days was predominantly meat. Between fighting seasons, that is during the rains, the young men (*amajaha*) who were newly recruited to the regiments were kept busy in and around the Paramount's village and the head villages of the *alumuzana*, mending fences, making shields, and clearing new land. When they were thus employed they also were fed by the Paramount or *mulumuzana*, who regarded these periodic feasts for the *amajaha* as one of the first calls on the consumption of his cattle. The Ngoni later rationalized this earlier procedure of restricting meat and milk consumption to certain groups of people by arguing that it made the young warriors strong and able to fight and endure hardships, and they declared that the senior men and women who also shared the Paramount's supplies lived long and had great wisdom and strength of character. This rationalization was not only looking back to a past Utopia. It was also based on the argument that Europeans ate meat regularly and that they were strong, both physically and politically.

The European criticism in the 1930's that the Ngoni did not make full dietary use of their cattle and their products was justified, but there are two factors to note in this connexion. One was that the number of those who lived well on meat and milk in the old days was relatively small—confined in fact to cattle-owners, women owners of big houses, and warriors. The situation changed after the Europeans came, and a large number of people owned a few cattle and many of the new owners had no tradition about using their products. Among the cattle-owners of the Swazi clans the tradition of cooking blood and making curds continued and both were valued as food, but some of those who had only recently become owners of cattle did not know these practices, and I came across many cattle-owners of local tribes who did not know how to milk a cow. The failure to use milk in the Ngoni diet was due partly to the method of rearing calves by letting them take all the milk they wanted, and partly to the practice of letting the herd-boys have the rest. In villages under a *mulumuzana* of a Swazi clan, who had a wife in his big house also of a Swazi clan, the consumption of milk was to some extent organized. These senior women saw that the herd-boys brought them a certain amount of milk each day, and they gave it to young children or invalids, and made some into *amasi*.

Another practice which restricted the use of meat and milk as regular items of diet was that the building up of the herds was regarded as a primary responsibility of the owners and guardians of cattle. Hence calves were given milk, which in western countries would be drawn off for human use, and the killing of beasts, unless they were sick, was restricted to selling the meat for cash or using it in ritual. One of the embarrassments suffered by an anthropologist was being presented with a beast by people who hardly ever killed one for their own use. It was true that a general share-out took place when the beast was killed, but it was none the less one beast fewer in the herd, and it was the maintenance and increase of the herds which was the cattle-owners' chief concern.

This emphasis on numbers rather than quality, which caused so much misunderstanding between government departments and cattle-owners, was closely related to the forms of exchange in cattle. Formerly cattle were handed over either as *lobola* or as penalties for the infringement of laws. Both these forms of transfer continued, but there were additional demands which cattle-owners or potential owners had to be aware of in watching the increase or diminution of their herds. One characteristic of these modern forms of exchange was the ready convertibility of cattle into cash and of cash into cattle. We have seen how young men away at work sent money back to their fathers or fathers' brothers to buy cattle. We have seen too how the possession of cattle made it possible to sell a beast and obtain cash for various purposes, and the proximity of markets where there were butchers' stalls encouraged this sale of cattle.

One of the most frequent reasons for the conversion of cattle into cash was for the purpose of hiring labour. We saw in Chapter I of this section how Lopati Nzunga killed cattle to feed the men who carried bricks and cement for his brother's tomb and sold another beast to pay wages to the bricklayers. The traditional way of paying labourers had been by feeding them with meat, and the modern method was to pay them cash wages and to find the money for it by the sale of cattle. Such labour could be for cultivating, house-building, fence-building, road-making and other local work. The possession of cattle which were easily convertible into cash made possible this payment of labour, and this relationship between the role of cattle-owner and the role of employer of labour was common.

The pressure on the Ngoni to possess ready cash was directly related to their prestige in the villages and kingdoms, and to the status of the Swazi and trans-Zambesi clans. Money was needed for good buildings and good clothing, two of the modern signs of status which the Ngoni could not ignore. Faced with this situation, and unwilling, except among the urban Ngoni, to invest savings in banks,[1] they manipulated their cattle tradition to suit the new situation in several ways. In place of the frequent slaughter for food, there were occasional sales for cash. Money earned in wages was invested in cattle. The drive therefore was all the time to increase the herds, in order to be able to convert them into cash when the need arose.

Values and attitudes in cattle-ownership

Any attempt to probe below the surface of current practices in acquiring, caring for and using cattle should be preceded by an extensive survey of cattle-keeping, including the full implications of their place in the economy of Ngoni village and family life. Since a complete survey is not possible here, the assessment of the values inherent in the ownership of cattle and the resultant attitudes towards their acquisition and use is related in this chapter to the relationships between the living Ngoni and their ancestors. These values were primarily those of the senior men and women of Swazi and trans-Zambesi clans, and hence those of the aristocracy. They were reflected in the attitudes of groups who owned cattle in the villages. Further analysis would show variations in the attitudes of individual members of those groups who possessed cattle, and would also show an approximation to the Ngoni attitudes by members of other groups, for example, village headmen of Ntumba clans whose fathers had journeyed and fought with the Ngoni in the past. The spread of cattle-keeping beyond the former exclusive monopoly of the leading clans and of leading men in them resulted in a number of different attitudes towards the acquisition and use of cattle. Some of these variations were suggested earlier in this chapter in the brief comparisons of Cewa and Ngoni ownership of cattle.

The primary value of cattle to the Ngoni was the security they represented. This security lay in assurance of social position, in being able to meet penalties imposed by the courts, in the potential command of labour, in the enjoyment of much prized food, in the performance of ritual for the dead and in sacrifices to the ancestors. The converse of this security was the fear of losing cattle, and this was primarily a group attitude rather than an individual one. A man living in a town who had sent money to his father to buy cattle, and who heard that they had died, very often shrugged his shoulders when he heard of the loss and

[1] The Ngoni in Blantyre put about half of their savings into banks and sent the rest to their home villages to buy cattle.

considered it his individual bad luck. On the other hand the house which depended on its herd for mutual help among its members and for the performance of ritual in sickness was deeply concerned at the loss of cattle and at any diminution of its herd.

After security, pleasure and emotional satisfaction were important Ngoni values in relation to cattle. This outlet for interest and enjoyment was very marked among Ngoni men. It began with the young herd-boys and continued until old age. Cattle were an endless topic for discussion, and in remote areas, where few strangers came and local affairs played a predominant part in village life, the fortunes of individual beasts and the progress of herds were talked about continuously. The advent of a letter from a son in the south sending money to his father to buy a beast gave a fillip to village life which little else provided. When the young men themselves came home, they went during their first evening to the kraal where the cattle they had paid for were kept, and showed interest and pleasure in the herd which was shared by all. The older men who had carried the responsibility were there, and on the fringes of the group the herd-boys hung around, listening to their elders, proud of having done their bit for the cattle which were the common concern of all three age-groups.

The Ngoni were aware that security in their cattle and the pleasure they got from them had to be won, and there was a price to pay. Hence they attached great value to knowledge and experience and to the ability to organize. Among the senior men responsible for a herd in a house or *banja*, some would be known for their knowledge and skill in handling cattle and for their experience in dealing with sick beasts, in castrating bullocks, and in choosing well when buying new beasts. The Ngoni recognized an innate quality of skill, which they called *mphumi wabwino*, 'the good forehead', a term used as an equivalent for the 'green thumb' when talking about crops. They also recognized the knowledge which came from experience and which might or might not be associated with *mphumi wabwino*. In any village where there were cattle, men were pointed out who possessed knowledge about cattle-tending, and the choice of a neighbouring village kraal for boarding out purposes was generally decided on the reputation of the owner of the kraal as a good cattle man. Not all the people who had this specialized knowledge had ability to organize the care of cattle, a characteristic Ngoni quality on which they set a high value. Foresight and planning were necessary in the choice of kraals for boarding out, in the selection of animals for *lobola*, fines, gifts or slaughter, and above all in buying and selling cattle. This kind of organizing ability required the possession of information about local markets and about potential sellers or buyers of cattle. It also demanded some nice calculations when sending cattle for *lobola* or giving a beast as a gift. Men were often torn between wishing to appear generous to the point of lavishness, and not wanting to give away the prize animals in the herd. Their formula in presenting a beast was 'Here is a small sheep.' This belittling of a gift was the social counterpart of their inner desire for a reputation for generosity.

It has been clear from many previous references that mutual assistance among members of a house was inherent in the social pattern of cattle-ownership. The Ngoni attached great value to this reciprocity of service, and it was deeply embedded in their social ethic. Young men in Ngoni villages thought twice before they deliberately took action which would bring them into the courts, because the fine would have to be paid by their elders from the common herd of cattle. The implications of this service proved no ultimate deterrent to hot-headed youth, but the lesson was constantly being rubbed in. After a court case for adultery, when a young man's father and his father's brothers had handed over a beast for a fine, they would grumble in the evening by the kraal at this waste of good cattle, and suggest it was time the young man went off to the south and sent money home to buy more cattle. This was the cycle of mutual help—the elders provided cattle from the herd for *lobola* and fines for the young men, who in turn went off to work and sent back money to buy more cattle. Reference has been made to 'the cloth of the spirits', when cattle were sold to provide cash for a young man who needed it, and the balance was used to buy cloth which was kept in the hut where the ancestral spirit was guarded. This cloth was the common property of all who belonged to the house owning the herd, and was returnable to the hut after it had been worn for some festive occasion. The forms which this mutual help could take were numerous and varied, and they all illustrated the fact that the correct and continuous observance of this reciprocity was considered by the Ngoni as one of the basic values underlying the ownership and use of cattle.

Among the group bound together by cattle-ownership this emphasis on mutual help as a desirable behaviour pattern had its counterpart in the social concept of integration. As we have seen, the Ngoni put a high value on 'staying together', on being united when challenged by a situation which made for disintegration. Within the social units of the house and family, the ownership of cattle and their care and use demanded some degree of co-operation through responsibility for the herd which was held in common. Integration between the living and their ancestors was also provided by the cattle. Common possession of a herd did more than just hold people together. The pattern of family and house organization which was characteristically Ngoni was given some stability through the ownership of cattle, allowing for the sub-division of herds when the new village 'went out', the exchanges at marriage, and the sacrifices at death.

Cattle in the ancestor cult

The Ngoni, unlike the Swazi as described by Dr. Kuper,[1] had no clear ideas about the life after death as lived by their immediate ancestors with whom they had associated in their lifetime. They did not, as the Swazi did, picture them living somewhere surrounded with cattle and other familiar creatures and objects. The importance of bringing the spirit back (*ukubuyisa idlozi*) to the house where it would be cared for signified two main things for them. The first was the continuous association of the spirit of the dead with the living persons in the community to which he had belonged, through the individuals belonging to the house, the actual hut where the sacrificial vessels were kept, and the cattle which belonged to the house. The other significant point was that contact with the returned spirit, and through him with the spirits of more remote ancestors, could only be established in the village containing the cattle of the house to which the dead man had belonged.

We shall be examining some aspects of the ritual of addressing the ancestral spirits in a later chapter of this section. Here we shall establish three constituent parts of the ancestor cult in which cattle were essential links between those taking part in the cult and the spirits whom they addressed.

The first part was the group of ceremonies which took place at death, at the burial, at the first ritual shaving and at bringing back the spirit. A text by Lopati Nzunga (see Chapter IV, p. 200) illustrates how three parts of a beast—the skin, the kidney fat (*nseso*) and the gall bladder (*nyongo*)—were considered essential for Ngoni burial. It was interesting to find in Blantyre among educated Ngoni who were Christians and occupied clerical and commercial posts, that they had given up the cow-skin for wrapping the corpse and substituted a coffin. But they admitted confidentially that in most Ngoni funerals the use of the *nseso* and the *nyongo* was customary. After the burial the ritual shaving, shared in by all who attended the funeral, was accompanied by the killing of a beast and the consumption of its meat, though with no ritual significance beyond its association with the purification of the mourners and their integration as a group. From six to twelve months later the second shaving and the bringing back of the spirit was also accompanied by killing a beast and eating its meat. These ceremonies expressed the sense of loss felt for the human person who had died, the sorrow of the mourners, their successive acts of purification which served to bring them together, and the final bringing of the spirit to live among them again. As we have seen, each stage of the death and mourning rites was accompanied by the eating of a beast or the use of certain parts of a beast. The cattle of the house to which the dead person belonged were used to bury him or her, to strengthen the mourners, and to reintegrate the spirit with the living community.

[1] Kuper, H. *An African Aristocracy*, p. 186.

In another part of the cult cattle played a still more direct part. When a diviner advised that prayer should be made to the spirit of a leading man on behalf of someone of his clan who was sick, the man who was in charge of the *gogo* section of the village informed the head of the clan or *banja* and they agreed to address the spirits, and to offer a sacrifice if the spirits were willing. The sign of willingness on the part of the spirits was for the selected beast, when it had been driven out of the kraal, to urinate or make dung. If either happened they said the spirit was willing, and arranged a time for the prayer and sacrifice. If neither happened, if the beast just stood still or lay down, the spirits had 'refused' and the sacrifice could not go forward. This sign or lack of sign by the beast could not be ignored, and was a further illustration that the Ngoni considered cattle to be essential as a medium of approach to the spirits of their ancestors.

When the beast 'refused', those responsible called the diviner again and asked for an explanation. He produced a reason and advised them to try again, and the process was repeated until the sign of agreement was given. There was always anxiety when the beast 'refused', partly because of the delay in sacrificing and partly owing to an uneasy feeling that they had left something undone and the ancestral spirit was not pleased with them.

The main part of the ritual of sacrifice to an ancestral spirit was killing the beast, offering the meat to the spirits and the eating of the meat by the principal persons concerned. This we shall examine more closely in Chapter IV.

CHAPTER III

THE ROLE OF THE DIVINER IN THE ANCESTOR CULT

IT has been apparent in the chapters on the Paramount and on warfare in Part II, and in the two previous chapters of Part IV, that divining by an accredited person was a necessary preliminary for sacrificing to and addressing the ancestors.[1] I never heard or received any account of the ancestor cult in which divining was not specifically mentioned as the first step in the performance of the ritual. Moreover, all the diviners of good standing were themselves operating because they had contact with and were possessed by the spirit of an ancestor. By virtue of this direct contact with the spirit world the diviners claimed their special powers.

---

[1] The one possible exception was the first-fruits ceremony, but this had been given up before the Ngoni settled in Nyasaland, and the old men had no clear memories of the ritual followed.

Dr. Kuper called the diviners among the Swazi 'the most powerful and respected specialists operating in both individual and national situations'.[1] I found that among the Ngoni also they were greatly respected once they had established their reputation for prophecy and diagnosis. Except on the occasions when they were called upon to carry out their functions the majority of diviners whom I saw in the 1930's lived in relative seclusion, and had no outward signs of power in any political or economic sense, though in the past some of the 'prophets' had also been warriors and leaders. Socially they were always shown great honour when they came in response to a call, or when they went visiting on non-professional occasions. They were addressed in a respectful tone of voice, given a mat to sit on, and village noises around them were hushed. They were, however, essentially recluses, withdrawn from public life except when they were called on to help in time of crisis, and they did not show any ostentation of wealth or position.

Dr. Kuper used the term 'specialist' to describe the diviners among the Swazi. In the Ngoni kingdoms there were many kinds of specialists owing to the existence of several tribal groups each with its traditional system of religion and magic, and each with varying methods of treating sickness, diagnosing the causes of misfortune, and interpreting omens and dreams. The diviners in the Ngoni kingdoms who were best known and on whom the greatest responsibility lay were those who were called by the Paramount in times of national crisis. Such responsibility and such fame had in pre-European days corresponding risks. The following story, which was told me in Hoho by Timoti Jere and which I heard quoted in several areas in the northern kingdom, puts in a traditional setting and with much circumstantial detail the kind of demands formerly made on diviners and the kind of treatment meted out to them:

❪ Zwangendaba in his coming out of South Africa arrived in the country of the Maculu at Mabiri. It is there now. When the *impi* was summoned it went out to contend for the country of the Sukuma. That *impi* wanted very much to be victorious, because it went to fight in two countries, in that of the Sukuma, where they took the long-horned cattle, and in that of the Ngonde, where they took the cattle without horns and with big humps. While the *impi* was away, the Paramount called all the *izinduna* and said 'Why has the *impi* delayed so long? Call the *izanusi* that they may divine. Perhaps the *impi* has run away and turned back.' Then the *izinduna* called the *izanusi*. In their divining they said 'The *impi* has run away and turned back.' There was one *isanusi*, his name was UMakhende Nkosi, who divined and said 'All the *impi* is there and it will return in this month. The long delay of the *impi* is because they have raided two countries, the country of the Sukuma with long-horned cattle and the country of the Ngonde with unhorned cattle.' It was so, and that month the *impi* returned and arrived at Mabiri with many herds of cattle as UMakhende Nkosi had said.

[1] Kuper, H. op. cit., p. 163.

After one year Zwangendaba called again all the *izinduna* and said 'Let us test all those *izanusi* in their divining.' So they spoke together secretly and said 'Let us take a goat and kill it, and take its blood, and let us sprinkle it on the doorways of the huts and on the posts of the door-ways.' The *izinduna* agreed and no man knew of it. So they took a goat and stabbed its throat and when the blood came out they received it in the *ngcwembe*, and then sprinkled it on the doorways and the posts of the huts in the enclosure of the Paramount. They did this at night and returned to their huts and slept.

When it was dawn, all the people were astonished at seeing blood on the doorways of the Paramount's huts. The people told the *izinduna* and the *izinduna* told the Paramount. He said 'Call the *izanusi* that they may divine.' They called all the *izanusi* and they divined together and they said, 'That blood is of man. There are flesh eaters here. They are striving that you O Paramount may die.' There was one *isanusi* UMakhende Nkosi who divined alone, and he said 'O Paramount the blood is of a goat. You, together with the *izinduna*, are proving us as *izanusi*. It is you O Paramount and the *izinduna* who have done this thing.' So the Para-mount agreed. He commanded the *izinduna* and said 'Kill all the *izanusi* except UMakhende only.' All the *izanusi* were killed in this way by Paramount Zwangendaba at Mabiri.

The moral of this traditional story, as the Ngoni always pointed out when relating it, was that diviners could be wrong. The specialized skill which they claimed to possess carried with it a recognized responsi-bility for using it correctly and not deceiving the people who consulted them. There was also a suggestion in the story of the contempt for this kind of skill shown by leaders who possessed great political and military power. Hard-headed chiefs and army leaders in the past expected efficiency in their diviners, and punished them severely for ineptness and what appeared as deceit. This veiled contempt, associated as it was with the tacit admission that the diviner as a specialist could not be dis-pensed with in Ngoni life, appeared often in the 1930's when Ngoni leaders were talking about divining and were planning to have recourse to it. As in this story, they were ready to recognize authentic diagnosis when they heard it, but not to regard the diviners as a class as infallible. One of the reasons for this view about divining was the wide range of social background and the diversity of functions among the diviners. The following account by Cibambo suggests that two categories of diviners were recognized by the Ngoni and indicates certain Ngoni attitudes towards their range of operations and the way in which they carried them out. The account refers to pre-European days, and there was in the 1930's little evidence of these distinctions between types of diviners.

❡ There were men who acted as go-betweens between the spirits and the people called *izanusi*. Just as in the days of the Jews there were true and false prophets, so it was among the Ngoni. It is going too far, indeed it is untrue, to say that all the prophets were false. Some were true go-betweens between the land of the spirits and the land of men. They received in dreams, sometimes in visions, things that related to the people of their time. God himself agreed to make them his workers and messengers even though these men sought for him in twisty ways.

The real go-betweens or prophets were called *izanusi*, 'those who smell something', and *abantu benhloko*, 'people of the head, people of dreams'. These men were considered to meet with the spirits in dreams or by their medicines which lifted them up to see the things of the spirit land. The people thought that these men received news from the spirits which they were to give to the earth people.

These men who had the gift of seeing in dreams were not allowed to live in big villages where there were often noises, but the chiefs sent them out to build for themselves a little distance from the chief's village along with their family. They were afraid that people would be disturbing them and making a noise when they met with the spirits. They were also afraid that in the big villages there would be many people who did not walk in an orderly way, and so these men, meeting those people, would spoil their own good sense.

These men did not talk with the spirits all the time. Often they did not receive any messages, but on other days their heads were stirred up and they spoke.

In the central kingdom there had been in the past the same distinction mentioned by Cibambo between diviners who dreamed, and those who used medicines to smell before giving their message. Informants said that there was also a distinction between those who took the initiative in announcing that they had something to say, and those who waited to be called for consultation. In pre-European days, in the hierarchy of diviners, the highest esteem was given to those who dreamed only (*abantu benhloko*) and who announced as a result of their dreams that they had something of importance to tell the Paramount. The Maseko line of Paramounts had, in the days of Mputa, a famous woman diviner called NaNdumbu who was of a Swazi clan. She went north to Tanganyika with the Paramount Mputa and was regarded as the *isanusi* for the whole country who foretold events as a result of her dreams. An informant who had seen her described her after she had had a dream or a vision coming into the *bwalo*, the open space in front of the Paramount's hut, and dancing with the little stick which the women carry in the *umsindo* dance. When the Paramount saw her dancing thus he came out to her and she spoke with him alone, telling him of her dream. Then, when the people around were silent, she lifted up her stick high with an outstretched arm, and the Paramount told the people what she had told him, and when they heard it they knocked their sticks on the ground and said '*e e e e*'. After she died her brother took her place as *isanusi*, and his daughter was living in Mcakhatha when I was there. This woman said of her father 'When I was young they told me "Your father has become an *isanusi* today". When he entered the place of his sister, NaNdumbu, he was dreaming. If there was a war he could say "You must not go to that war because all the people will be killed." He was just dreaming and dancing his *isanusi* dance. When he danced that dance on the chief's *bwalo* the people praised him with special praises.'

Two informants remembered fragments of the songs sung by NaNdumbu and her brother, and these songs were also sung by the old *izanusi* in the northern kingdom. I give here the Ngoni versions with an English translation, omitting the repetition of lines and the 'sounds' which accompanied the singing:

Uyezwa mihlolo	Do you see the omens?
Inkanyezo ipuma	The star comes out,
Ipuma yanga	It comes out in the East.
. . . .	. . . .
Ubaba uyangibiza	My father is calling me.
Hamba ekaya	Go home.
Indaba zikuyandela	Things have turned against you,
Hamba ekaya	Go home.

Although these diviners acted at times on their own initiative, this did not prevent their being called on in time of crisis to diagnose the reason for disaster or sickness. *Izanusi* who used their own medicines to smell could prophesy and speak on their own initiative as well as waiting to be called on. These medicines were said to induce the dreams on which the prophecy was based, and they were generally contained in the tail of a gnu or in a sheep's horn, or some other horn.

Below this category of the prophets, whether *abantu benhloko* or *izanusi*, came those who used lots when called on to diagnose a particular situation. These were often men who dreamed, or who used their own medicines to receive messages from their ancestral spirits, but instead of announcing their message directly, they brought with them some form of lots which they used when they were consulted, and gave their diagnosis as a result of observing the lots. Sometimes they sang their own songs, accompanied by dancing, which led to an almost trance-like condition; sometimes they used their lots without any previous working up of an emotional state through song or dance. I never met any of the dreamer type of prophet who used no medicines and no lots. There was general agreement among the Ngoni that they had died out, that their main service had been in times of war, and that the number of men or women who possessed such powers had, even in the past, been very small indeed. I did, however, see one diviner at work who used the song and dance technique with the lots, and two who used the lots without song or dance.

The *isanusi* whom I saw in the northern kingdom was divining for sickness at the request of a party of people who had come to consult him about a sick relative. He asked for a preliminary payment in cash from me before he would say anything in front of me, having already received the customary present of fowls from the sick man's relatives. There was an atmosphere of part pantomime, part reluctant performance in front of a stranger whose presence seemed to trouble him more than it did his clients. He wore a python-skin cap with beads dangling from it, and carried the tail of a black cow bound with lead and a small skin bag with the lots in it. At first he sat holding the tail in his hands and sniffing it occasionally. Then he suddenly shook the lots out of the bag—six large beans called *kulumo* and about twenty small round nuts called *mapi*. He put snuff on the top of each bean, sprinkled snuff on the nuts, picked the nuts up in both hands, shook his hands together and threw the nuts on the ground. Some fell near the big beans, others rolled between them. He looked intently at them, then at the group waiting to consult him. 'There is someone who is sick,' he said to them and the group replied '*Siyavuma*' (we agree). They continued to chant *siyavuma* in a low tone over and over again, with an almost mesmeric effect. He meantime went on to describe the sickness, that it was a pain inside the man (the chant-ing was loud), that it had been on the right side (less response), in the stomach (less response), on the left side (loud response). At intervals he waved the tail in the air and knocked the leaded end on the ground to emphasize the louder response. He did not specify the complaint but advised the people consulting him to go home and kill a goat as a sacrifice to their ancestors, and give the sick man some medicines which he would sell them.

It may have been the mixture of a real consultation with my visit which produced his slightly mountebank performance, and it may also have been his combination of the role of diviner with peddling medi-cines which the people present for the consultation evidently expected to obtain from him. This aspect of his performance impressed itself on the Ngoni informant who was with me. He was slightly contemptuous throughout, even when the songs were being sung and taken down. He kept on muttering 'This is Nsenga,' and said afterwards as we were going away that this diviner worked only for ordinary people and their sickness, as witnessed by his telling them to sacrifice a goat, and that he would not have been acknowledged by the real Ngoni. He was making comparisons all the time between the 'people of the head' and the diviners of this type, illustrating the Ngoni esteem for the real dreamers, and the slight, sometimes great, contempt for those who combined divining with recommending medicines as remedies.

The contrast between the performance of this diviner and that of the two *izanusi* whom I saw at work in the central kingdom was consider-able. My long residence in Mcakhatha and the entrée I had to all that was taking place in connexion with the sickness of Bambo Manga no doubt helped to give confidence to the diviners. The chief and his brother arranged for first one *isanusi* and then, when he became ill, for another to come and see me. In each case they concluded that I was consulting them and foretold what would happen and gave me advice, warning and assurance. There was great seriousness of purpose and no mountebank atmosphere, even though they came to the courtyard of my hut and saw round them all the paraphernalia of a European's camping equipment.

The first diviner, who was of a Venda clan, was a very old man and greatly respected and trusted by the Nzunga clan, who were looking after Bambo Manga in Mcakhatha and who had called him several times to divine for them during her illness. His story was that he was the son of an *isanusi* and when the signs of his initiation began to appear before he reached puberty, his father recognized the fainting and the pain and refusal to eat, and said 'This child will be a diviner also.' The spirit who came to him in dreams was his father's father who had died south of the Zambesi, where his father had been born.

This man was very definite about the kind of situations for which he could and would divine and the type of advice he would give. Questioned further on this point, he gave in this order: sickness, journeys, auspicious days for holding an *ngoma* dance or a hunt, 'absent treatment' of relatives in trouble in the south asked for by letter, sickness of cattle, moving a village to a new site. He refused contemptuously any divining about stealing or death, or agricultural practices such as choosing new gardens or beginning cultivation. Neither he nor the people with him made any specific reference to the different roles of an *isanusi* among the Ngoni and the local Cewa and other tribes, but since they used the same terms for divining, *kuombeza maula* (to throw the lots), they were careful to point out what the Ngoni diviners did *not* do. In the case of sickness due to 'spirits troubling', of auspicious days for journeys and other events, of cattle sickness, of moving villages, his invariable advice was to sacrifice a beast to the spirits. Most of the inquiries addressed to him were about sickness. When such an inquiry came to him in his village, he smelled his medicines and asked of *his* ancestral spirit 'Is the man likely to live or not? Who is troubling him? What shall he do?'

The first occasion on which I saw him divine was in the hut of a widow of the former chief, Njolomole I, which had been newly swept and a new fire made. The chief and his uncle sat on either side of the fire, the diviner on the right-hand side of the door and I on the left on the woman's side. The diviner was told to begin. He pulled out his *ntibo*, the stem of a gourd, which was wrapped in bark and cloth and had inside it the medicine, and which was waxed at each end. He scraped bits of the *nsika* root into a pot with a little water in it. He put the *ntibo* in the water for a moment and then took it out and rubbed it in his hands. He put it under a flat food basket and swept his hand over the top of the basket once or twice before putting the pot on top. He gazed into the pot, which he kept turning with his right hand, and he murmured in a low voice from time to time, and shook his head. The only words which were audible were '*Inu tamverani*', 'You, please listen.' After three minutes he tried to lift the pot, but it seemed to stick to the basket. All this time he was very calm and unexcited, though the pot appeared to stick every time. Finally he said the spirits of the Maseko chiefs were not willing for a sacrifice to be made. The reason, he said, was that I was there and they were afraid of a white face, because the Europeans had killed Gomani I and the spirits 'were ashamed' before white people. The following day the lots were tried again when I was not present and the spirits gave the diviner the sign that they agreed to the sacrifice.

About three weeks later, at the suggestion of the head of the *gogo* house in the village, he came to see me, having been asked to tell me about his initiation. He treated the call as a genuine summons to a consultation, however, and performed for me the ritual I had seen him carry out in the hut. This time he consulted the spirits of his father and grandfather. I had made no specific inquiry of him, but he asked his spirits for advice about my movements, whether I should go or stay, addressing them with '*Tamverani*', 'Please listen.' The pot came off the basket after the second effort and he looked at the bits of *nsika* root as they floated inside. Then he looked up at me and said 'You must not leave here. Perhaps you were thinking of returning to the Paramount's village. You should not do this because my spirits tell me that the spirits here want you to stay.'

When this old diviner became ill, another one of an Ntumba clan was called to Mcakhatha to divine about the illness of one of the leading women. His father had also been a diviner, a dreamer who did not dance or throw lots for sickness, but told of things to come, especially about war. His father had been in the Tengo country in Songea with Mputa and had spoken Ngoni there, and the spirit of his father's father was the one who came to him at his initiation as a young man. His equipment and technique were slightly different from those of the former diviner. He had a small duiker horn which had medicine inside it of the *ciswambalame* tree roots and, like the *ntibo*, was waxed at the end and rounded so that it could swivel on its base. At first he smelled the horn and made deep belching noises, almost like retching. He put the horn in an empty gourd cup, waxed end down, and left it by his left thigh. Out of a skin bag he took ten small half-shells of nuts, four large and six small, which he said he got from the Venda people. They were called *zihlobo*. He arranged them face down in front of him, the larger ones in the middle. He gathered them up again, smelled them, belched and threw them down. Five fell face down and five face up. He picked them up and threw them five times until they fell in the position he wanted, muttering as he did so '*ai, ai*' (no, no), and finally '*akondwera*' (they are happy).

N.N.—N

He left the shells, picked up a small rattle, a little gourd with stones in it, and knocked it on his knees. Meantime he picked up the gourd with the horn in it, and held it on the palm of his left hand with the base resting on his extended fingers. The horn rocked on its base inside the gourd and came to rest, touching one edge of the gourd or another and sometimes standing erect without touching the rim of the gourd. During this part he was much disturbed and sweat ran down his face while he murmured to his spirits '*Nanga inu*' (What are you doing?), '*Mubodza ndithu*' (You are surely lying), '*Ai ai ndithudi*' (No, no truly). Finally the horn came to rest against the rim of the gourd towards him, and he put it down, and wiped his forehead. Then he said to me 'You will be ill, but you will recover. You will not die in this country. So do not fear. You will not die'.[1]

During the rocking of the horn in the gourd the diviner was listening to and speaking to his spirits. His obvious distress at first, and his subsequent relief were genuine and onlookers said that with this man such swaying of fortunes, through appeal to his spirits, often took place. He was considered a very powerful diviner, in that he could argue with the spirits and did not depend only on what the lots said or take them as the final word. His combination of the use of the medicated horn with the throwing of lots was considered a sign of power. He said himself that he always knew the day before when a man was coming to consult him about someone who was ill and that night he dreamed and his spirits told him what to say.

Several references have been made to the initiation of a diviner, which was an essential preparation for his role, and an experience which marked him out as different from other men. Both the diviners whom I saw at work in the central kingdom gave short accounts of what happened before they became diviners. In the first (*a*) that of the very old man, most emphasis was laid on the finding and preparing of the medicines. In the second (*b*) the emphasis was on the re-birth element of the initiation, denoted by the expression *ukutwasa* which was used for the reappearance of the new moon after the period of darkness.

❡ (*a*) When I began to divine I slept, and in the night I dreamed dreams, and they said go and fetch a tree, its name is *nsika*, and when you have done so take the handle of a gourd and put some of the *nsika* inside, and shut each end of the handle with wax and on the wax put beads. Find a pot and pour water in it and put in pieces of *nsika* bark. Take that handle and put it on the ground and cover it with an *nsengwa* and put the pot on top and what you say will be true.

They told me just to go anywhere to find that tree. These dreams came to me when I was a young man. After these dreams I was very ill, near to death, and another thing I had pains in my heart; and my mother and my father thought I was dead.

---

[1] This prophecy was remembered by the people and often quoted when two weeks later I was attacked by a swarm of wild bees and nearly died.

(*b*) At first I died and when I rose up again I felt the wind of the spirits. My dying was my initiation. This *ukutwasa* was like that of the moon when it is new. I began to speak and speak and I danced with the python skin on my head. Then the people tested me whether I had bad or good spirits and after that I began to divine. The spirit of my grandfather, he has told me about this work. I am talking with his spirit when the horn is going round.

The fact of my being in Mcakhatha during the illness and death of Bambo Manga, and witnessing all the attendant ritual, gave me many opportunities of discussing the role of diviners in the ancestor cult, as well as of observing two of them at work. No such opportunity presented itself in the northern kingdom, but the role of the diviner was very fully discussed with leading Ngoni in Ekwendeni, Ezondweni and Hoho, and the account given by Cibambo at the beginning of this chapter was partly the result of these talks.

I have made several references to the graded hierarchy among the diviners, though I have not made any connexion between those diviners who either prophesied or made a diagnosis and those others, whether they were called *izanusi* or *izing'anga*, who made a diagnosis and also gave treatment through medicines. I have limited the analysis here to the diviners who operated through their own ancestral spirits and who, by virtue of this contact of theirs, claimed to be able to interpret the will of the ancestral spirits of the Ngoni clans. It was a notable fact that very few of the famous diviners, and none of the less well-known, were of Swazi clans, though the one true prophet in the story of the slaughter at Mabiri was of a Swazi clan. Two great *izinduna* and *alumuzana*, who were also dreamers and prophets, Gwaza Jere in the north and Golozela Nzunga in the central kingdom, were of Swazi clans. So also was the famous woman diviner NaNdumbu. It appeared that the capacity to become a diviner and the successful practice of the art was very unusual among the leading Ngoni. They depended therefore on men of lesser trans-Zambesi and cis-Zambesi clans to perform these duties for them. The attitude shown by leading Ngoni towards the diviners, already referred to, may have been partly a rationalization of their dependence on this kind of skill as well as on force of arms. It may also have been due to the necessity, admitted somewhat reluctantly, of using men of lower social status, that is of cis-Zambesi clans, for such vital services to the nation and to their own families. The Ngoni had a strong pragmatic streak which led them to suspect knowledge and skill which could not be reduced to concrete terms, and hence they were always ready to accuse the less well accredited diviners of lying and deceit.

In spite of Ngoni doubts and suspicions about the class of diviners as a whole, within their kingdoms these persons were recognized as specialists for certain reasons. They had all been through the experience described as *ukutwasa*. It began with physical symptoms, such as fainting, lack of appetite, forgetfulness, sweating. These manifestations could take place in childhood, around puberty, or when the man was fully grown, though the most usual age was in the late teens. The symptoms culminated in sharp pains and a prolonged collapse, and after that a deep sleep. It was then that the dreams came giving the man the assurance that he was henceforth a medium, and that through the spirit of his grandfather, or whoever was now appearing to him, he could communicate with the spirit world. At this time also he was told in dreams where to find medicines and what to do with them. A constant feature in the initiation of well known and accredited diviners was that they knew the name and identity of the spirit with whom they were in contact, and it appeared to be always someone related to them and most often their father's father.

As they returned to normality from an experience which was frightening in its intensity, it dawned on them that they now had to practise as a diviner, to make use of the powers which had come to them. There was evidence that they accepted this role with reluctance. Their relatives, when they saw them going through the earlier stages, were aware that there was an inevitable sequel, that of practising as a diviner, and they too shared the reluctance of the man himself. Sometimes a diviner began to practise by associating as a junior partner with a successful practitioner; sometimes he began hesitantly by himself. The criterion of the validity of their calling was their success. No one seemed to know what became of diviners who were unsuccessful and never became accredited. They apparently disappeared from the field because no one employed them.

The diviners whom I met and talked with, as well as those few whom I saw practising their calling, were considered by the Ngoni to possess a distinctive temperament. It was evident that they wished to live somewhat apart, and that they were withdrawn in a social as well as in a spatial sense. They married, but usually only one wife, and had children, but played little part in extended family or village affairs. Their huts were always on the outskirts of villages and were neither large and prosperous nor very poor looking. They had a reputation for being unpunctual and forgetful, but they were far from being unobservant. Part of their skill lay in watching people and learning about their concerns from observation and storing events in a good memory. Though they could work themselves up into emotionally excited states during a consultation, at other times they gave the impression of being controlled, rather quiet, detached, and uninfluenced by the currents of talk and opinion around them.

The rewards for their services were in kind as a rule, and could be articles of household equipment, food, cloth, and sometimes European clothes or goods from the stores, such as lanterns, soap, matches and cigarettes. There appeared to be no bargaining over payment. The goods were handed over, the diviner thanked the giver in the customary manner, and his wife or child carried the gifts away. Informants said that leading Ngoni would never be mean in their payments to diviners, and that diviners of the upper grades would never bargain over their rewards. It was openly said that a leading diviner cared most for his reputation as a successful specialist, and that the kind of life he led and the sort of man he was did not induce a desire to be wealthy.

One aspect of the diviner's role among the Ngoni was that he, an individualist, was always summoned at the request of a group. In a case of sickness of one of its members, it was the family or the senior men of a house who summoned the diviner, and they gave him his reward and carried out his advice. When a family heard from the diviner that a sick member might recover if a sacrifice were made to their ancestors, they regarded the diviner, in Cibambo's phrase, as a go-between linking the living group and their dead ancestors. The diviner therefore, like the cattle, was an essential link in the relationship between the living and the dead.

CHAPTER IV

THE RITUAL OF ADDRESSING THE ANCESTRAL SPIRITS

In the course of the first three chapters of this section, and in earlier sections, many beliefs and practices have been discussed which bear on the ritual of the ancestor cult. In spite of the risk of some repetition it will be useful to bring together here in one chapter the main elements in the ritual, and in so doing to raise certain theoretical issues.

Dr. Kuper said[1] that among the Swazi, ancestor spirits were not worshipped, and she gave as the reasons for this statement that the spirits were addressed as living persons would be, being sometimes scolded and seldom thanked, and that indignation rather than humility was the attitude of the living when disasters befell them which might have been due to malice or carelessness on the part of the ancestors. Without entering into an argument on the nature of worship and its essential accompaniments, I would state that certain aspects of the Ngoni ancestor cult showed those features which are usually considered to be part of a people's worship. These were sacrifice, prayer, and purification, which, not necessarily in that order, were the main elements in the cult. There was, moreover, a connexion between the ancestor cult and ethical behaviour in Ngoni thinking. The guardianship of an ancestral spirit, involving much respect for the house to

[1] Kuper, H. op. cit., p. 192.

which it belonged, was always given to a woman whose good character was vouched for.[1] The man who inherited the *gogo* village with its particular charge to look after the spirits of the dead, as well as the welfare of the living, also had to be someone of good repute. The responsibility for maintaining social cohesion in a village and among the members of a house with which the cattle, and therefore the spirits, were closely bound up, was one which the senior male members of that house regarded as a solemn duty. If people did not behave well the cattle would not flourish and multiply, and that would upset the spirits and be a sign of their disapproval.

Cibambo wrote the following account of the ancestor cult as a part of the presentation of Ngoni customs to his own people. As a Christian minister he was concerned with making a case to his own people for putting the Ngoni ancestor cult higher in the religious scale than the cults which used images in their worship. He was using his Christian beliefs to rationalize the ancestor cult, particularly in relating it to the concept of a High God. The Ngoni undoubtedly had the idea of a creator, remote and unapproachable by man, as his title implied, but nevertheless referred to as the sender of rain, sickness and other benefits and disasters for the country as a whole. Prayers and sermons by Ngoni ministers in Ngoniland used many of the old Ngoni terms for the creator to express their Christian concept of God.

❡ We think that the worship of the Ngoni was better than the worship of other tribes who were near them, for in their worship there were no images made of wood or stones or other things, but they worshipped spirits who were unseen. Nearly all Central African tribes believe that there is a God who created heaven and earth, and who is unseen by eyes. In worship they could not reach him himself with the things of their hearts, so they did not worship him himself. They followed the custom well known among the black people when they wished to talk to their chiefs or their fathers when there was something of importance. A black man thinks it is a great impertinence and dishonour to speak for himself in front of his chief or his father, so he sends someone of standing as his messenger who carries his words and returns with a reply. This custom took effect also in the worshipping of black peoples. In worshipping the creator they made use of a go-between, who stood between God and men. He knew how to speak for them and pray for them before God. They thought that certain created things ought to accomplish this work.

The Ngoni believed that there was God who was chief of all created things and the source of all. Some of the names they gave him were:

UMkulumqango	The Great Deviser
Uluhlanga	The Original Source
UMkulu Kakulu	The Greatest of All
UMnikazi we Zinto Zonke	The Owner of All Things.

---

[1] On other grounds, such as kinship, such guardianship might have gone to a woman who was not acceptable on moral grounds and was therefore passed over.

In these names it is clear that God was known as the Beginning of All Things, the Owner, the One Above All. They knew him as the nourisher of the earth, sending rain and all good things, but they thought that he had little knowledge of his people. Nor could his people know much of him, so they did not worship him himself or speak with him. His character they did not know and so they were not able to praise or glorify him as they were the spirits of their ancestors, whom they knew thoroughly. They knew him from afar and so they could not pray and speak to him.

Since the Ngoni were not able to be at home with UMkulumqango so in worship they sought others known to them that they should tell them the things of their hearts, and these were the spirits of those who had died. At once when one of themselves died, they thought that now he is a spirit with living power greater than he had when a man on the earth, and that he is a spirit who can watch over and protect his relatives on earth, but they also realized that he had power to rebuke and punish. So this spirit was added to the spirits of the tribe who were worshipped. They thought that each clan had its own spirits, stretching back to the beginning of the clan. They believed that the recent spirits received the news from their friends on earth, and handed it on until it arrived at the spirits of very long ago and now forgotten. These then delivered the message to the Creator of all.

Cibambo's main intention in this account of Ngoni worship was to put the ancestor cult in its setting as a means of approach to the creator. He used the Ngoni concept of an intermediary, who was essential in the approach to a Paramount, to argue that the ancestor cult was not necessarily wrong but was an earlier stage towards Christianity. This was a theme constantly expressed in sermons and prayers in Ngoni churches. In the rest of this account he emphasized 'becoming an ancestral spirit', which we shall examine later in its ritual context; allocation of authority among the ancestral spirits; and the fact that prayer and sacrifice, which he called worship, were made chiefly in times of trouble, and not in times of prosperity.

It is legitimate, in view of Dr. Kuper's statement, to ask whether there was a fundamental difference between addressing an ancestral spirit as a go-between and worshipping him. The Ngoni were not trained theologians, except for Christian ministers like Cibambo, but they had a range of philosophical concepts to which it is impossible to do justice in this context. In the prayers which I heard their thoughts were focused on the ancestors whose names they knew and recited. Questioned afterwards, they said that there were other ancestors whose names they did not know, but the ones they named could not fail to be aware of the living, their descendants, since their spirits were guarded in a house and their cattle were sacrificed in the ritual. They therefore directed their worship, or address, to those who were known to them, believing that they would influence the remoter but possibly more powerful spirits whose names were unknown. Spontaneous references to

UMkulumqango or other names for the High God were rare. When questioned they said that such a High God existed and the spirits knew him, but they, the living, did not. The Ngoni phrase, *asiyazi*, 'we do not know', and its Nyanja version, *sitingadziwa*, 'we cannot know', were constantly on their lips in discussions on this topic. Among Christians like Cibambo as well as non-Christians like Nzunga, their interest in the ancestor cult was part of maintaining their identity as Ngoni. The neighbouring tribes had other forms of ancestor cults but the Ngoni form brought from the south was distinctive, and many of the concepts and practices were known to the South-eastern Bantu peoples.

The ritual for a new ancestral spirit

The Ngoni believed that at the moment of death the spirit left the body. If a sick person fell into a coma and was unconscious for a long time they said that the person had died when the coma began even though they knew he went on breathing. This happened at the death of Bambo Manga when she had periods of unconsciousness before she died. They said that her spirit had left her at the beginning of the last long coma, even though they knew from her pulse and breathing that she was not dead. At the parting of the spirit from the body they had to care for both, in order that the new ancestral spirit might be happy and in the right relationship with the living. Equal importance was attached to caring for the spirit and to caring for the corpse, since the correct performance of ritual had deep significance for the dead and for the living.

When the spirit left the body it was believed to go to the bush at the outskirts of the village where the person had been accustomed to go to relieve himself. Between the death of Bambo Manga and the burial, each morning before it was light, the men marched with a dancing step up the path to the bush where she was wont to go, singing a war song dating from trans-Zambesi days which was sung at the sending out of the *impi*. Marching to the bush and singing the war song was one step in bringing the spirit back or, more correctly perhaps, keeping in touch with it so that it should not go too far away. This approach to the spirit between the death and burial was the first of three ritual acts, each called 'bringing back the spirit'. The other two occurred after the first and second ritual shaving.

The preparation of the corpse for burial has been described in the first chapter of this section. Those features of Ngoni burial were considered essential for the welfare of the spirit, and were carried out in the majority of funerals which I witnessed, whether the dead person was a Christian or not. An account of the burial of a leading *mulumuzana* in the northern kingdom who was a Christian, given to me by another Christian Ngoni and confirmed by some of the missionaries present at the funeral, emphasized all the distinctive Ngoni elements: the round grave with the little shelf at one side, the corpse wrapped in a cow-skin, the *nseso* and *nyongo* on the neck and forehead, the bent legs and upright sitting position facing south-east, and washing the face of the corpse at the grave side with a bunch of grass. On this occasion the Ngoni form of burial was followed by the Christian burial service after the grave had been filled in. During the digging of the grave hymns set to the tunes of Ngoni war songs were sung by the onlookers until the body was brought out of the house. After that there was complete silence while the corpse was lowered into the grave and the grave was filled up, until the service began. This combination of Christian and Ngoni ritual I witnessed many times. One of the missions set its face against the use of the cow-skin and declared that no Christian could be buried except in a coffin, but even this was sometimes disregarded and the full Ngoni ritual was carried out, followed by a Christian service.

After the body had been put in the grave and when the first calling back of the spirit from the bush had reminded the living that they had to care for this new spirit, a series of further duties faced them. These have been referred to as the first and second shaving. The first shaving we shall consider later as a necessary purification before eating the meat of the funeral rites which brought back the spirit right into the village. The second shaving, which took place from six to twelve months after the funeral, was the prelude to the time when the new ancestral spirit came, or was brought back, to its final lodging. The importance of this last rite was emphasized by Lopati Nzunga in his account of the ritual which took place at the tomb put up to the memory of Gomani I (see p. 165) When the building of the tomb under the supervision of Ngoni in the area was finished, many leading Ngoni from all parts, including those from the towns, gathered there for two days. Every morning before dawn they went up the forest paths singing war songs, as they did later at the time of the death of Bambo Manga, to call back the spirit from the bush where it had spent some thirty years. After a Christian service held by the tomb, the Ngoni *alumuzana* 'brought back' the spirit to Lizulu, Gomani I's village, to the house of NaMagagula his big wife. She was a Christian, so could not take the care of the spirit in her hut, but another of the widows of Gomani I, NaNsambi, who was in the house of NaMagagula, was chosen as guardian. Earlier in the proceedings, when they had decided that the tomb was going to be built, a diviner was consulted, the spirits were addressed in the kraal, the cattle showed that they agreed, and a beast from the herd of the house of NaMagagula was sacrificed and the meat offered to the ancestral spirits of the Maseko Paramounts. Then they built a new hut for NaNsambi and put in it new sacrificial vessels. When the spirit of Gomani I was finally brought home it was to this hut and guardianship that it came. They were uncertain about what had happened to the spirit in the thirty years interval and it did not seem advisable to probe

too closely because of the still bitter feeling against Europeans for having
caused the Paramount's death. It was quite clear, however, that since
this essential step in the recognition of an ancestral spirit had been
omitted at the time of his death, it was considered important to make
good the omission, and the 'opening' of the grave appeared as the
logical occasion.

In Mcakhatha village I witnessed a ritual second shaving for a man
of the Nzunga clan, a son of the former chief, Njolomole I. This man
had been absent from the village for many years, having left as a young
man still living in the *laweni*, and his death in the south was reported
by letter from a fellow villager to his relatives in the village. When the
letter was received, a diviner was consulted and he advised a sacrifice
to the spirits. The first ritual shaving of all members of the Nzunga
clan and their affines took place as it would have done on the day after
burial if he had died in the village, and a beast was killed and the meat
offered to the spirits and ritually eaten. The women of the Nzunga clan
and the wives and widows of Nzunga men put on *zitambo* or mourning
caps. Six months later the diviner was consulted again, and a day was
fixed for the second shaving 'to bring back the spirit'. The spirits of the
Nzunga clan were addressed, the beast selected for the sacrifice urinated,
the spirits 'agreed', and the shaving of the Nzunga clan members and
their affines took place; this time the whole head was shaved whereas
the first shaving was only a small patch on the temple. The men were
shaved by the kraal, the women near the hut of the dead man's mother
which was uninhabited. The women who were relatives or affines of
the deceased took off their *zitambo* and unravelled the threads of which
the caps were made, collecting in front of each a little heap of hair and
thread. Then one of the leading women got up and said '*Tiyeni* (Let us
go)', and the women went in procession to the stream, each carrying her
little handful of hair and thread. As they passed they pulled a handful
of dry grass from the roof of the hut by which they had been sitting to
start their fires. By the stream each of the former mourners, eleven in
all, made a fire of grass and dried leaves lit from a bunch of smouldering
grass carried by one of them, put on it the threads and hair and tended
the fire until only ashes were left. All these eleven women stood erect
behind their fires facing the stream, except when bending down to fan
the flames. When the fires died down each woman swept the ashes into
the stream with her hand and splashed water on the site of the fire until
no trace was left, lifting overhanging branches to leave a free passage
for the ashes on to the water. The leading widow, a descendant of
NaNdumbu, the famous woman diviner of Mputa's day, took a look
round to see if all traces of the fires had gone, said 'We have finished',
and led the way to the washing pool where all the women washed their
clothes and their bodies. Meantime the men had been to wash in the
stream on the other side of the village and had also burned their hair

by the stream and swept the ashes into the water. The beast for the sacrifice had been killed early in the morning before the shaving, and the ritual eating of the meat took place. This second shaving and sacrifice were to end the mourning period and to bring back the spirit to the village. A widow of Chief Njolomole I was appointed to guard the spirit and she kept in her hut the baskets which had been used for the sacrifice.

When asked whether this ritual of bringing back the spirit was followed for everyone who died away from home, the answer was 'No. It was done for this man because he was a big one and he was the son of a chief.' Only for members of leading Swazi clans and some others of trans-Zambesi origin was the ritual invariably followed of recalling the spirit to the village where he had lived and where the clan sacrifices were performed with the cattle of the man's house. The ritual ensured that a new ancestor spirit was recognized, that provision could be made for its guardianship, and that the spirit had been brought back to the village even though the man had died and been buried elsewhere. The ritual was based, not on the assumption that the spirit would be angry if not so treated and might injure his living descendants, but on the belief that absence had weakened the bonds between members of the clan and the house, and that the ritual associated with the making of an ancestor spirit gave an opportunity for strengthening these bonds. This was achieved by bringing together the living to commemorate the dead; by repeating once again the traditional pattern of speaking to the ancestors through the cattle; by giving the spirits their meat which the living shared; and by making sure that the spirit of the dead man would henceforth be taken care of by an appointed guardian.

In the case of important people of the royal clan and chiefs, the second shaving was a preliminary to bringing back the spirit to be taken care of permanently and there were two stages to this last ritual in the making of an ancestral spirit. Three months after the death of Bambo Manga there was an elaborate ceremony of the second shaving which was accompanied by brewing vast amounts of beer. On this occasion there was an offering of beer, not meat, to the ancestral spirits. The ritual began with consulting the diviner first about whether the beer would be good. The diviner reported that two quarrelling women were spoiling it, and the quarrel would have to be resolved before the brewing would be successful. The diviner was also asked which spirit should be offered beer on this occasion, and answered that NaQwana, the mother of Mputa and grandmother of Bambo Manga, was the one to be addressed. The next act was making the ritual fire, since all the beer had to be cooked on newly made fires. Lopati Nzunga took the ritual fire-stick from Bambo Manga's hut, two young men kindled a fire outside and the women took grass from Bambo Manga's fence to build a fire. The women picked up bits of this fire to kindle their own new fires before brewing the beer.

When the beer was ready, Lopati took from Bambo Manga's hut the gourd cup (another of the ritual objects kept there), filled it with beer and offered it to the spirit of NaQwana, and left it at the right side of the hut where the corpse had been set upright before the burial. Cups of beer from the other houses who were brewing were also put in the hut and drunk during the night by the old women who had slept there continuously since the death of Bambo Manga in order to guard her spirit. The next morning the *ligubo* (war-dance) was danced by the grave at the edge of the kraal. When the time came for shaving, the men were shaved, first a small lock as at the first shaving, and then the whole head. The women were shaved over the whole head and cut the strings of their *zitambo* and unravelled the threads. Ritual washing at the stream and burning of the hair and threads took place as described earlier, but in this case the *nseso* from the beast killed at the death of Bambo Manga was burned on the same fires. Part of the *nseso* had been put round her neck for the burial, but part had been hung at the back of the hut, and this was now taken down and divided up to be burned.

In the final part of the ceremony the men danced *ligubo* in the court-yard of Bambo Manga's hut, while the old women danced *umsindo* at her grave. All this went on for four days as long as the beer lasted, and the way was then clear for bringing back the spirit. The spirit had been 'guarded' in the hut where the old women slept, lest if it were empty the spirit might depart. The spirit was there, but not quite there, and could not be addressed as an ancestral spirit until the final 'bringing back'.

After the second shaving the leading men of the village had a new hut built in which Ciabwe Maseko, the daughter of Cikusi and older sister of Paramount Gomani I, was installed as guardian of the spirit of Bambo Manga. They bought new baskets, cups and a fire-stick, and destroyed the old ones. After the diviner had been consulted and had appointed a day for the sacrifice, a beast was killed and the meat offered to the spirit of Bambo Manga in the new hut in the new baskets. A sheep was killed at the same time and the meat of both was eaten by the men and boys.

We have now seen the process by which the living descendants and kin of a dead person recognized the spirit of that person as an ancestral spirit. This, as we saw, was no automatic process following on death. Ceremonies had to be undertaken and rituals performed which, through successive stages, brought the spirit of the dead into such relationship with the living that they could offer sacrifices and call on its name in the naming of the ancestors in the cult. These were acts performed by the living for the dead to cause the spirit to be settled in a place it knew and guarded by someone held in respect, and the living community hoped the spirit was therefore content and happy and ready to be approached and addressed as an ancestral spirit.

The ritual of the purification of the living

The living had certain rites to carry out on their own behalf which, if omitted, would bring the displeasure of the ancestors upon them. These were essentially purification rites for they removed the defilement of death from each individual who was closely related to, or had performed some office for, the dead; and through the rites the houses and utensils were cleansed, and the living community was re-integrated after the loss of one of its members. Shaving, burning the hair and mourning bands, and washing in a stream, were the prescribed acts for all who were connected by kinship or marriage with the deceased, or who had taken part in preparing the body or digging the grave. These were a succession of rites as we have seen, and emphasized the need for ritual cleansing over a long period, and for renewed integration between the living.

In addition to this generally practised ritual, there were some acts of ritual purification of houses and utensils found only among the Swazi clans. One informant told of the ritual washing of hoes used to dig the grave in the blood of a newly killed sheep. Several others spoke of the cleansing with sheep dung of the huts of the widows of a dead man at the time of the second shaving. On each occasion when meat was offered to the ancestors after a death, the living who ate the meat had to be made ceremonially clean through the act of shaving, followed by ritual washing at the river.

The ritual of addressing the spirits

There was no set formula for addressing the ancestral spirits but there were three parts in all the prayers which I heard and which were recited to me. The first was the naming of the ancestors. The leading clans in the two kingdoms demonstrated the way in which they prayed to their ancestors by repeating the names of successive heads of the clan. They began with the name of the ancestor who had died in Swaziland and those of his father and grandfather and other forbears if known. The Nhlane clan, for example, told me 'We pray: *UNdina ka UNchaba ka UMulawu ka UMazongolo*' and then added: 'UNdina died in our village of Hoho before we left Swaziland and he was buried in the kraal in Hoho.' The Mhlambi clan in central Ngoniland named their ancestor UNgekwazi who died in Swaziland, but they did not know any names before him. Other clans in the central kingdom used the name of their ancestor who crossed the Zambesi with Mputa. The most important element in the prayer, therefore, was the naming of the 'big spirit', sometimes coupled with more remote ancestors.

The second element in addressing the spirits was to call their attention to the beast which was to be offered to them if they 'agreed'. 'Here is your beast' was the formula. Although three or four beasts or even more were driven out of the kraal before the invocation of the spirits, one had been selected for the sacrifice, and the spirits' attention was drawn to this animal. They were reminded that it was their beast because it belonged to the herd of the house which guarded their spirits, and it was also their beast because it was to be killed and its meat offered to them if they showed agreement.

The third part of the prayer was mentioning the needs of the person on whose behalf the spirits were being addressed. The following words were used by Lopati Nzunga when he spoke this prayer to the spirits when Bambo Manga was ill:

> O thou Gumede!
> O thou Mputa!
> O thou great chief!
> Here is your beast.
> That your child may be healed,
> Look on what is yours.
> May you remain well
> And your child recover.
> We do not know,
> We do not know.
> If you say that she will die,
> She is yours, this child of yours.
> It is your affair.
> As for us, we long that your child may recover.
> If she dies, this child of yours,
> We can only speak your names.
> We cry to you for her.

Bambo Manga was there and her daughter and Chief Njolomole, and while Lopati Nzunga addressed the spirits, the rest murmured the names 'Wena Gumede', 'Wena Mputa', and added 'Mntwanayako' (your child), 'Inkomoyako' (your beast). The form of the prayer varied, and might be a sequence of address and petition as in this one, or a series of ejaculations with little consecutive thought. It depended on the eloquence and skill of the speaker of the prayer, and that form of eloquence was a well-recognized characteristic among the Ngoni. In the central kingdom before the Europeans came, the head of the Phungwako clan had addressed the spirits of the Maseko Paramounts. Since the Phungwako chiefs had separated from Gomani's kingdom, the Nzunga clan performed this ritual for Bambo Manga in their head village. In addition to speaking the prayer, the same man had to see that all was done in order, the cattle driven out, the chief people assembled, and the subsequent action taken in accordance with the sign given by the spirits, either to kill a beast for sacrifice, or to find out from the diviners why the spirits had failed to agree. When the spirits 'refused' the first time Lopati Nzunga addressed them, he concluded the proceedings by gently reminding the spirits that all depended on them. There was no tone of scolding in the words but a respectful plea for attention and help.

> Alas O Paramount,
> Alas O Father,
> Why do you refuse us?
> What do you say about your child?
> We say we are your people,
> Alas O Paramount.

In prayers for rain the same form of address was used with the three parts of the prayer. The ancestral spirits addressed were those of the line of the Paramounts, since the needs of the whole country were involved. The beast chosen for the offering to the spirits was a black one with no white markings, and in place of the sick person's name, the need for rain was mentioned. In the account given by Mlonyeni Jere (quoted in the first chapter of Part IV) he used this formula, mentioning the names, presenting the cow, and then asking the ancestral spirits to tell UMkulumqango how greatly they were troubled through lack of rain.

The ritual of sacrificing to the spirits

The essential equipment in the ritual of sacrificing was the spear with which the beast was killed; baskets, both the wide winnowing basket (*lichero*) and the food basket (*nsengwa*); the wooden dish (*ngcwembe*) on which the meat was placed; and the gourd cups for beer. These have been mentioned already in several contexts as the sacrificial vessels or ritual objects connected with the ancestor cult and kept in the hut of the woman who was guardian of a particular ancestral spirit. In the northern kingdom one of the Nhlane clan who carried out the ritual for sacrifices to UNdina Nhlane at Hoho said that in the hut of UNtani Nzima who died in Swaziland, but whose house had continued, was a spear, a black cloth for rain-making and a wooden meat dish. These were kept on the right-hand side at the back of the hut, and no one passing by could stand erect; he had to bend his back and head 'as men do when passing the *inkosi*'. Since the coming of the missions these had been thrown away.

In the central kingdom I saw in several houses this collection of ritual vessels. There was always a spear, a food basket, one or more gourds for beer, and one or more of the wide, flat, winnowing baskets on which uncooked flour was carried and which was used for meat if there was no wooden dish. These were kept at the back of the hut hanging on the wall, above the place where sacrificial meat was laid.

The first stage of the ritual sacrifice was killing and flaying the beast. It was killed either in the kraal or just outside the fence, with a thrust from the spear, or more than one if necessary, by some member of the leading clan. At the time of the sacrifice when Bambo Manga was ill the killing and the flaying were done just outside the kraal by young men of the Nzunga clan, younger brothers of the chief. The cow ran backward as she was stabbed and a second blow killed her, and she was dragged round when she fell to lie with her head to the south-east. Some of the blood from the wound was collected immediately by Lopati and taken by him and put in Bambo Manga's hut in 'the place of the spirits'. The cow was skinned with a few neat strokes of the knife, and a thin strip of meat about six inches wide was cut from the back. This Lopati put in the sacrificial food basket and he and the chief went with it to Bambo Manga's house. The three firestones were removed and the meat was spread on the glowing logs till it was cooked through and quite white. Bambo Manga, who was lying on her mat, washed her hands and face with water brought by her daughter and rinsed out her mouth. Two small pieces of the meat were given to her to eat, and the rest was cut up in small pieces and eaten by Lopati, the chief, his sister and Bambo Manga's daughter. This meat could only be eaten by that inner group.

The men who had skinned the beast cut it up and, following an Ngoni practice, laid all the meat on the gate of the reed fence surrounding the *bwalo*, and carried it to the hut and laid it outside the door. Holding the sacrificial winnowing basket Lopati directed the men to put in it three right ribs, a piece of liver, both stomachs, the heart and lungs, the fat from round the kidneys, a bit of the intestine and the spleen. The head of the beast was arranged facing towards Kabwazi's village, since he had always kraaled some of the Nzunga cattle.

Lopati took the basket into the hut and was followed by the head herd-boy holding the tip of the tail and the gall bladder. The basket with the meat in it was put on the floor at the back of the hut in 'the place of the spirits'. Lopati and the chief squatted on their haunches nearby, and Bambo Manga knelt on her mat while her daughter wiped the soles of her feet, and she went forward on her knees to the place of the spirits. Lopati intervened and said 'Please walk upright', but she refused and said 'I will do as my ancestors did'. Her daughter knelt behind her.

Then Lopati began to praise the spirits, calling on Mputa by name, saying 'Here is your meat. Please eat. We praise you. We are your children.' The rest ejaculated '*Wena Nkosi*', '*Wena, Gumede*' as if supporting him, keeping quite still and facing the place of the spirits. After the invocation Bambo Manga went back to her mat, and Lopati took the gall bladder and sprinkled the juice round her, and then round the meat basket and round the hearth-stones. The gall bladder was then put in a small pot with water in it and laid on the floor, and the tip of the tail was tied above the place of the spirits. The skin of the beast, which had been washed but not scraped, was brought in and laid on the ground between the firestones and the wall and the gate with the meat on was placed on it. The meat in the basket and on the gate stayed there all night.

Following the ritual of offering meat to the spirits came the ritual of cooking and eating the meat, both that offered to the spirits and the rest. After the basket of meat had been left all night in the place of the spirits, the large quantity on the gate was carried away and cooked by an old woman outside the hut of Bambo Manga's granddaughter. The meat in the basket which had been offered to the spirits was put in a pot and cooked on the fire in Bambo Manga's hut. It stayed cooking all day and all night till the following morning. Dzinthenga Phungwako, an old and highly respected *lidoda*, came to the hut and divided the sacrificial meat among all who were in the house, that is Bambo Manga, her daughter and granddaughter and several senior women. When they had finished the leading women stood up and thanked '*Zikhomo Maseko*', '*Zikhomo Magwagwa*'. Then they washed their hands and went to their own houses.

The large quantity of meat which had been laid on the gate and cooked on another fire in another *bwalo* was carried in a big pot and put down outside Bambo Manga's hut in the late afternoon. Her daughter came outside and divided the meat into three piles: a small one from the breast-bones for the women, a leg for the chief, the head for Kabwazi the headman of a neighbouring village, and the rest in a big pot for the men. A boy came to tell Lopati that all was ready and he and the chief went out to the place where the beast was killed, near the gate of the kraal. There were four groups already sitting there and the chief and Lopati made a fifth: the *madoda*, the senior men; the *majaha*, the young men; the *mabusa*, the herd-boys; and the little boys. Before Lopati divided the meat he and the chief washed elaborately with water brought in a gourd, and then he washed the knife before cutting the meat. He called the *madoda* to send someone for their portion in a basket, then the young men and the herd-boys were given their portions—a basket for each group, and the small boys had bits put in their hands. The eating was very sedate, there was no snatching of choice bits, and in each group the one who fetched the meat distributed it. There was the general atmosphere of a ritual meal rather than a feast, though the small boys smacked their lips appreciatively. From time to time Lopati called up someone from a group and gave him a bit more to divide up. When it was all eaten, a boy was sent to fetch water and the soapy leaves which the Ngoni used for washing, and the chief and Lopati and the *madoda* all washed the grease off their fingers. Then Lopati stood up and called out '*Siyadumisa baba, zihomo mntwana wenkosi*', 'We are praising you, father, thank you child of the Paramount', and the others all agreed and said '*Zikhomo baba.*' Then they all went together to Bambo Manga's hut and stood opposite her door and called out the same thanks. The women who had eaten their meat in three age groups on the verandah also came forward and, led by NaNkoloma, a widow of Njolomole I, thanked in the women's language, '*Zimata, zaithwa mntwana wenkosi.*'

I did not witness any ritual sacrifices in the northern kingdom but the accounts given me by informants corresponded closely with the ritual in Mcakhatha just described. When sacrificing for rain to the spirits of the Paramount, a black ox with no white spot was driven into the kraal in the late afternoon and the chosen spokesman addressed the ancestral spirits of the Jere clan telling them that this was their beast, they must eat the meat and tell UMkulumqango that the people needed rain. While this man prayed to the spirits he stood facing the beast, and everyone else sat looking in front of them and keeping very quiet. The women stayed at home in their huts and the Paramount stayed in his hut 'as if mourning'. When the beast urinated and showed that the spirits had heard, a messenger came and informed the Paramount. The beast was killed early the next morning in the kraal. While the flaying took place, all the huts of the chief wives were smeared with dried cow-dung on the floors and on the smooth place outside the doors. The meat, in two parts, was taken into the *indlunkulu* and left there all night at the back, so that the spirits might lick it. The next morning the meat was cooked in the kraal by the *madoda* and when it was ready they reported to the big *induna*. He called all the people into the kraal and divided them into companies according to their sections and head villages. The meat was given to the head of each head village who divided it among his group. When everyone had finished, one of the leading men stood up and began to praise the spirit using his titles and praise-names (*izitokozo*). The rest stood up and shouted *Bayete*. They then began to dance a war-dance but, the informants added, that was soon stopped by torrents of rain.

These chapters on the Ngoni ancestor cult bring to an end this study of the two Ngoni kingdoms in Nyasaland in the 1930's. We have seen how their distinctiveness as a people depended on the culture which they brought with them from the south and how this culture was found among the families of the Swazi and trans-Zambesi clans. In the topics included in the three sections of this book: the political system, the social organization, and the ancestor cult, the main features of Ngoni culture are most clearly seen. In much of their economic and agricultural life there was little to distinguish them from their neighbours among the other Nyasaland peoples. The changes brought about by the missions, the schools, new forms of local government, and new types of occupation, were all tending to make the Ngoni less distinctive as a people. The conversion of some leading Ngoni to Christianity, as suggested in Chapter V of Part II, and the spread of schools were together the most powerful influences in altering Ngoni traditional culture. The organization of houses built on polygynous marriage, the ancestor cult, and other aspects of Ngoni culture, were profoundly affected by the teaching of Christianity and by the ideas and practices expected of adherents of the churches. Some leading Ngoni Christians like Cibambo attempted to make a synthesis between their past and their present, between traditional culture and modern life. Others said 'All is finished now.'

Two points which clearly emerged from a study of the Ngoni in the 1930's might indicate that the Ngoni as a distinct people were not 'finished'. One was their tenacity in adhering to certain traditional practices; the other was the ability they had shown in adapting their culture and political system to the mixed populations in their kingdoms.

GLOSSARY OF NGONI TERMS

abantu benhloko, prophets, diviners, dreamers of dreams

alezi (sing. *mlezi*), nursemaids

(*m*)*alumuzana* (sing. *mulumuzana*), heads of leading clans

amadlozi (sing. *idlozi*), ancestral spirits

amajaha, young men

amakanda, head villages

amanxusa, messengers

amasi, milk curds

amilaga, outlying villages

azungu, the English

baba, *bambo*, father

banja (Nyanja), family group

Bayete, greeting given only to Paramount

bwalo (Nyanja), open space by chief hut, court

cibale, relationship of brotherhood

cibwenzi, friendship, specially among age mates

cidlodlo, head-ring which senior men were allowed to wear

cigodlo, section of village behind chief hut

cingoni, that which is Ngoni

ciponde, period of lawlessness after death of Paramount

gogo, grandparent, elderly female attendant; also used for house where ancestral spirits are guarded and village left in care of *gogo* house

hlonipa, respect, honour

imihubo (sing. *muhubo*), songs sung by detachments of army

imitulo, tribute

impi, army

incwala, festival of first-fruits

indaba, meeting, affair

indlukulu, chief hut (in village), big house

ingcwembe, wooden dish for meat

inkosi, Paramount Chief

inkosikazi, big wife (of Paramount)

isihlutu, form of hair-dressing, chignon

izanusi (sing. *isanusi*), diviners

izibongo (sing. *cibongo*), praises, names used in thanking, clan names

izidandani (sing. *isidandani*), girl companions, attendants

izigawa, hamlets

izinduna (sing. *induna*), war leaders, officials

izitokozo, honorific epithets, 'thanking' names

izwe, land, country

kwathu, homeland

laweni, boys' dormitory

lichero, winnowing basket

ligiya, hero's dance

ligubo, war-dance

lobola, marriage payment, cattle transferred at marriage

lusungulu, new village (of chief or Paramount)

mabandla (sing. *libandla*), military companies based on districts

mabuto (sing. *libuto*), age sets, regiments

(*a*)*madoda* (sing. *lidoda*), senior men

(*a*)*makosana*, members of royal clan

(*a*)*makosikazi*, royal women

malume, mother's brother

manina, senior women

mbumba (Cewa), group of man, his sisters and sisters' children

mcando, beast given by bride's people to bridegroom's mother's house

mfumu (Nyanja), chief

micetho, domestic slaves, servants, pages

(*u*)*mlobokazi*, woman married with transfer of cattle; bride

mlomo wenkosi, mouthpiece of Paramount

mtimba, marriage ceremony

mtunzi, shadow

mwini, owner

ngoma, Ngoni dance

nhlanzi, substitute or additional wife (usually wife's sister)

nkomo, honorific title

nsengwa (Nyanja), food-basket

nseso, fat of kidneys (of cattle or sheep)

nsima (Nyanja), porridge of maize flour

nyongo, gall bladder (of cattle)

pasangweni, at the gateway of kraal; men's meeting-place

sing'anga, specialist in medicines

(*in*)*tonga*, royal medicines, war medicines

ukuteta, to address the spirits

ukutwasa, reappearance of new moon; rebirth

ulubende, cooked blood

umbongi, official praiser

umsindo, pre-marriage rite for girls

utengwa (Cewa), virilocal marriage without *lobola*

zitambo, head-bands, mourning caps

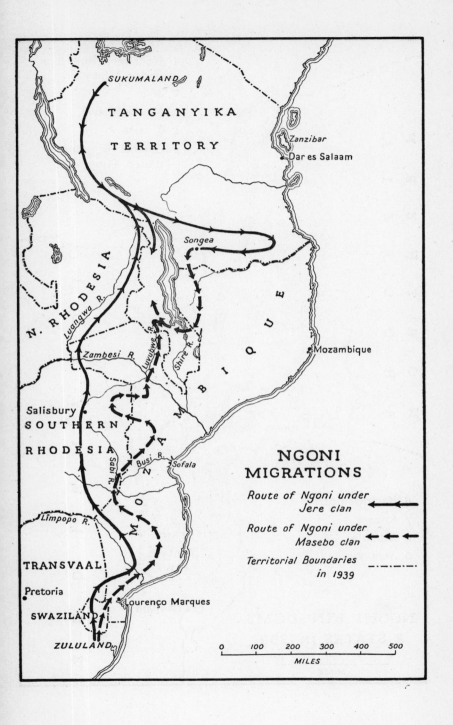

SUKUMALAND

TANGANYIKA

TERRITORY

Zanzibar
Dar es Salaam

Songea

N. RHODESIA

Luangwa R.

Zambesi R.

MOZAMBIQUE

Mozambique

Luvuvye R.

Shire R.

Salisbury

SOUTHERN

RHODESIA

Sabi R.

Busi R.

Sofala

Limpopo R.

TRANSVAAL

Pretoria

SWAZILAND

ZULULAND

Lourenço Marques

NGONI
MIGRATIONS

*Route of Ngoni under
Jere clan*

*Route of Ngoni under
Masebo clan*

*Territorial Boundaries
in 1939*

0   100   200   300   400   500

MILES

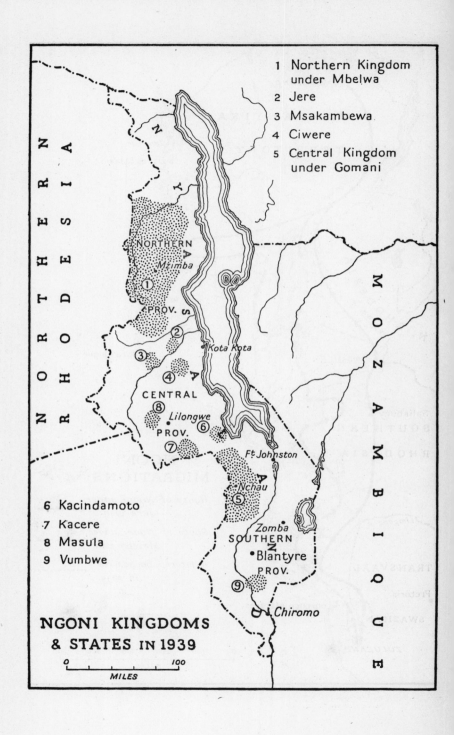

1 Northern Kingdom
   under Mbelwa
2 Jere
3 Msakambewa
4 Ciwere
5 Central Kingdom
   under Gomani

6 Kacindamoto
7 Kacere
8 Masula
9 Vumbwe

NGONI KINGDOMS
& STATES IN 1939

0   100
MILES

INDEX

209